Advance praise for
TRICKY GROUNDS

"Brunette-Debassige illustrates the competing and conflicting tensions and expectations of Indigenous women in university administrative positions, where the mandate to 'Indigenize' their university runs up against the reality of colonial institutions' reluctance to change non-inclusive, inequitable structures and systems."
—**JACQUELINE OTTMANN**, First Nations University of Canada

"...a must read book...revealing senior Indigenous women leaders' in universities struggle for greater accountabilities, responsibilities, and ethical care from Eurocentric post-secondary institutions in the pursuit of decolonization, reconciliation, and Indigenization."
—**DR. MARIE BATTISTE**, Special Advisor to VP Academic, Cape Breton University

"In her must-read book, Candace Brunette-Debassige gives light to the complexities of the embodied experience of Indigenous women leaders in higher education as they navigate the precarious terrain of Canadian universities. This book casts light on Indigenous leadership positions largely held by Indigenous women that are too often stymied by tokenization. Within a university culture that explicitly and complicitly reproduces racial and gender marginalization, this engaging work meets the moment as Canadian universities reckon with what it means to share senior administration leadership power in decolonizing higher education. Animated through story and written with compassion and confidence, this book is a call for change."
—**MARGARET KOVACH**, author of *Indigenous Methodologies*

"As an Indigenous woman in university administration, I am inspired by this book. Brunette-Debassige helps me to see that I am not alone in challenges that I face and encourages me to lead from my unapologetic Two-Spirit lens, as an act of resistance necessary to advance the transformation in Canadian universities."

—**LORI CAMPBELL**, Associate Vice-President, Indigenous Engagement, University of Regina

TRICKY GROUNDS

INDIGENOUS WOMEN'S EXPERIENCES IN CANADIAN UNIVERSITY ADMINISTRATION

CANDACE BRUNETTE-DEBASSIGE

© 2023 Candace Brunette-Debassige

All rights reserved. No part of this work covered by the copyrights hereon may be reproduced or used in any form or by any means—graphic, electronic, or mechanical—without the prior written permission of the publisher. Any request for photocopying, recording, taping, or placement in information storage and retrieval systems of any sort shall be directed in writing to Access Copyright.

Printed and bound in Canada. The text of this book is printed on 100% post-consumer recycled paper with earth-friendly vegetable-based inks.

Cover art: Hawlii Pichette, Urban Iskwew
Cover design: Duncan Campbell, University of Regina Press
Interior layout design: John van der Woude, JVDW Designs
Copyeditor: Ryan Perks
Proofreader: Rachel Taylor

Library and Archives Canada Cataloguing in Publication

Title: Tricky grounds : Indigenous women's experiences in Canadian university administration / Candace Brunette-Debassige.
Names: Brunette-Debassige, Candace, author.
Description: Includes bibliographical references and index.
Identifiers: Canadiana (print) 20230552196 | Canadiana (ebook) 20230552218 | ISBN 9780889779808 (hardcover) | ISBN 9780889779778 (softcover) | ISBN 9780889779785 (PDF) | ISBN 9780889779792 (EPUB)
Subjects: LCSH: Minority women college administrators—Canada. | LCSH: Educational leadership—Canada. | LCSH: Discrimination in higher education—Canada. | LCSH: Sex discrimination in higher education—Canada. | LCSH: Indigenous women—Canada.
Classification: LCC LB2341.8.C3 B78 2024 | DDC 378.1/110820971—dc23

10 9 8 7 6 5 4 3 2 1

University of Regina Press, University of Regina
Regina, Saskatchewan, Canada, S4S 0A2
TEL: (306) 585-4758 FAX: (306) 585-4699
WEB: www.uofrpress.ca

This book has been published with the help of a grant from the Federation for the Humanities and Social Sciences, through the Awards to Scholarly Publications Program, using funds provided by the Social Sciences and Humanities Research Council of Canada.

We acknowledge the support of the Canada Council for the Arts for our publishing program. We acknowledge the financial support of the Government of Canada. / Nous reconnaissons l'appui financier du gouvernement du Canada. This publication was made possible with support from Creative Saskatchewan's Book Publishing Production Grant Program.

  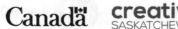 

To my nokum, Daisy Brunette (née Rueben), and all the children of residential schools. When I am tired and defeated from the system, I remember you.

CONTENTS

List of Figures and Tables ix
Acknowledgements xi
Prologue xiii

CHAPTER 1 Finding My Way into the Research 1
CHAPTER 2 The Roots and Life-Support System of the Settler Colonial Academy 15
CHAPTER 3 Navigating the Discursive Terrain 57
CHAPTER 4 Indigenous Women in Educational Leadership 67
CHAPTER 5 An Indigenous Feminist Storied Decolonial Look at Experience 85
CHAPTER 6 My Approach to Research 101
CHAPTER 7 A Play: *Flight: Journeying for Change* 117
CHAPTER 8 Being the Solution and the Problem: Embodied Experiences of Indigenous Women Administrators 149
CHAPTER 9 "It's Not as Easy as It Sounds": The Trickiness of Indigenizing Policy Enactments 183
CHAPTER 10 Refusals as Part of an Indigenous Leadership Praxis 215
CHAPTER 11 Concluding Thoughts 239

Epilogue 257
References 261
Notes 295
Index 301

LIST *of* FIGURES *and* TABLES

FIGURES

Figure 1 Pillars of Higher Education in Canada   16
Figure 2 My Theoretical Lens   86
Figure 3 My Cree Floral Research Design   102
Figure 4 My Mushkego Epistemological Lens Design   104

TABLES

Table 1 Four-Part Timeline for Indigenous Education   27
Table 2 Critical Questions for Veracity   252

ACKNOWLEDGEMENTS

I am grateful to Kitchi Manitou and all my Ancestors, who are always guiding me no matter where I am and what I do. I pay respect to the Indigenous peoples past and present of the lands on which I conducted my research—special thanks to the Great Lakes region of Turtle Island and the Anishnaabek, Haudenosaunee, Lenapewak, and Chonnocton peoples.

I am forever indebted to the eleven Indigenous women who shared their knowledge and participated in this study. Chi Meegwetch for offering your stories and engaging with me throughout the research process. My enduring hope is that you all feel seen and heard in this work.

I express my deepest appreciation to my PhD supervisor, Melody Viczko, who supported me doing this research. I wish to thank Maggie Kovach for being my external examiner and encouraging me to publish my dissertation. I thank everyone at University of Regina Press—Karen Clark, Rachel F. Stapleton, Shannon Parr, Ryan Perks, Duncan Campbell, and Rachel Taylor—for their endless support. Sincere gratitude goes out to the peer reviewers. The time you took to carefully and thoughtfully engage with the manuscript helped me revise and strengthen this work. A heartfelt gratitude goes out to my sister Holly, Urban Iskwew, for sharing her art for the cover. Nokum and dad are surely shining proud of us in the starworld.

I wish to thank my partner, Brent Debassige, for always supporting me. Meegwetch to my children, Brayden and Ashton, who sacrificed countless evenings and weekends with me so that I could complete my research. I can only hope that one day you, my children, will understand "the calling" in your own way. Thank you to my child-care provider, Tiffany, for supporting our family during this time.

Meegwetch to my committee, Erica Neeganagwedgin and Lina Sunseri. I am extremely grateful for your deep engagement and generous feedback. I am grateful as well to my examining committee members, Maggie Kovach, Jerry White, Erica Neeganagwedgin, and Rita Gardiner. Our conversation around my work was generative and enriching. I also cannot begin to express my thanks to my writing teacher and editor at different stages, Margaret McNay.

I am grateful to Leanne Betasamosake Simpson for your ethical advice on Indigenous storytelling, to Holly Pichette for your graphic illustrative artwork on my floral research design, and to Greg Spence for checking my Cree language translations.

I offer special thanks to my mother, Doreen Pichette—the one who first taught me about the righteousness of justice and working for the people. I also wish to thank my mother- and father-in-law, Joyce and Nelson Debassige. Your teachings around the importance of family forever ground me.

Meegwetch to many colleagues and friends at Western who have supported me over time. There are too many of you to name.

Thank you to all my teachers over the years. In particular, I express deep gratitude to my mentors in the area of Indigenous theatre: you have forever shaped my ways of seeing the world and my style of storytelling.

I end by thanking the Mushkegowuk Nation and Council for supporting me at different stages throughout my university journey.

PROLOGUE

There are many different stories among the Original Peoples of Turtle Island. Many of these stories embody Trickster figures such as Nanabozoo, Coyote, Raven, Glooscap, and, most relevant to my research, Weesakechahk. I am Mushkego Cree, so Cree Weesakechahk stories resonate deeply for me. I have searched out these stories from my home Territory, and listened and reflected on them for insights into my own life, and more recently in my research focusing on Indigenous women administrators' experiences working in Canadian universities. The intention of this book is share some of these stories while simultaneously drawing on Trickster Weesakechahk to make meaning.

Among the Omushkegowuk, many good stories are told about Weesakechahk. Yet storytelling traditions have also been shattered by colonialism, which has sought to actively fragment and silence Indigenous voices and knowledge. Colonial educational systems imposed on Indigenous peoples have contributed to the loss of our stories. I have hunted for fragments of Cree stories, listened to pieces of them from Elders, read others in historical anthropological colonial archives. Louis Bird, Omushkego Cree storyteller from Peawanuk, has, thankfully, documented some Cree stories that explain how Weesakechahk offers a map of the Cree world view and the origins of the land, including animal and rock formations; a map created as "Weesakechahk journeyed from the

East to the West, interacting with various peoples and animals along the way" (2005, p. 60).

What I have learned is that Weesakechahk never shows up when you want them to; rather, they appear unexpectedly at different times and in different forms, teaching me lessons about life's many contradictions, teaching me about navigating the unpredictability of foreign places and how to do so drawing on Cree ethics, laws, and spirituality. Coming to an understanding of Weesakechahk stories has been a twenty-year journey for me, one that continues to unfold. As a Mushkego Cree woman with mixed Cree and French lineage, I am an intergenerational survivor of Canada's residential schools. My family was severed from the Cree narrative tradition, and I have spent much of my adult life searching for reconnection and reclamation. During my search, I found a small, vibrant, yet marginalized space in the academy in Indigenous studies, an intellectual and spiritual hub where I first returned to Indigenous stories. Here I was introduced to the idea that Indigenous stories are our theories. Indigenous theatre and Cree and Anishnawbe ceremonial sites of learning deepened my connections and understandings of this Indigenous truth. In my mid-twenties, I became involved in Indigenous community-based theatre, working with an artistic team to travel home to my Territory to engage thirteen Elders (including my nokum) and gather Cree stories to put on the contemporary stage. Weesakechahk never showed up explicitly in the stories the Elders shared with us. Through our artistic research, we uncovered and worked with other historical stories about the river system, and we worked with sacred stories about Ehep and Chacabesh from Louis Bird's oral accounts. As a learner of Mushkego Cree oral teachings, I discovered a Weesakechahk story in this research years later when I looked back at the book entitled *âtalôhkâna nesta tipâcimôwina: Cree Legends and Narratives from the West Coast of James Bay*, published by the University of Manitoba Press in 1995. Unlike previous historical archives dating back to the early 1800s, it was clear to me

PROLOGUE

that the stories embodied in this collection were gathered with care and respect. The researchers worked with Cree translators to make stories accessible in Cree, English, and syllabics, and the Cree storytellers were acknowledged in the text. Xavier Sutherland, the storyteller who told the "Weesakechahk Flies South with the Waveys" story (Ellis, 1995, p. xvi) that I draw on in this book, hailed from Fort Albany (and Peawanuk), the First Nation community with which I am affiliated.

As an off-reserve First Nation woman, I did not grow up in Fort Albany. Yet the discovery of the story was nonetheless a directional moment for me as a scholar, because I had been grappling with how to privilege Cree epistemology and elevate Cree stories as theory in my research. In reflecting on the Weesakechahk story, I felt as if Weesakechahk had found me, and that my late grandmother was somehow guiding me too. Since then, I can only assume that Xavier Sutherland shared these collective stories with researchers to document them publicly, with the hope that one day Cree people such as I would search for them, draw meaning, and make them relevant in our contemporary lives. This book is my attempt to make meaning of today's realities by drawing on Cree stories.

I am not a traditional storyteller; I am an emerging Cree scholar and artist who is picking up the pieces of our Cree stories and positioning them as our teachers and our theories today. Through my journeying, I have come to understand Cree stories as part of my living birthright, part of a collective ancestral knowledge that I have a responsibility to learn and pass on to my children. Accompanying this responsibility is a duty to be transparent about who I am in terms of both connections and disconnections. In respecting this birthright, I accept the responsibility of learning Cree stories and sharing them respectfully with people in this generation. In that process, I also recognize that Weesakechahk stories are often told within the complex ethical and linguistic practices of storytellers and their families. There are many different versions of this Weesakechahk story within Cree and Anishnawbe communities, depending on geographic and linguistic ties and family interrelations. Among many storytellers, it is critical to respect the tradition that the name Weesakechahk (and other sacred stories) be uttered out loud only during the winter storytelling months, when the stars are highest and brightest in the night sky.

The following story is a Weesakechahk story that for me speaks to my own journey of travelling from north to south in search of my place in the world of education and academic administration. This particular story, originally entitled "Weesakechahk Flies South with the Waveys," was first told by Xavier Sutherland but is retold here through my humble and forever growing Mushkego iskwew lens.

There are stories about being in formation, and there are stories about dropping out, into the dark unknown, free-falling past sparkling lights, behind a constellation of stars.

One day, Weesakechahk found themself walking along the muskeg waterline near the sipi (river) in the early ta-kwa-kin (fall), about that time in the Cree cyclical calendar when the niskak (geese) fly south.

Unbeknownst to the niskak, Weesakechahk was watching them working away, visiting and gathering in the bay, getting ready to take their long flight south. And so, like Weesakechahk often did, Weesakechahk thought, "Wouldn't it be great if I went along? Maybe even led the flock this time? Surely it can't be that hard."

So off Weesakechahk went to find the okimaw (leader) of the geese. Weesakechahk came across a couple of niskak feeding along the bay and started asking all sorts of questions:

"What are you doing?"

"Where are you going?"

"Who is the leader?"

PROLOGUE

"What are you eating?"

"Can I come?"

The niskak just ignored Weesakechahk. They didn't say anything; they tolerated all Weesakechahk's bold questions and kept on munching away, just thinking to themselves, "Just watch and listen, will you?"

The niskak kept on eating. Chomp, chomp, chomp. Crunch, crunch, crunch, on all the yummy plants. Mmm, another niska said; cattails, pondweed, and horsetail. Mmm.

No one paid attention to poor Weesakechahk.

Weesakechahk did not like being ignored, not one little bit, and that got Weesakechahk thinking, "How can I get these niskak's attention?"

Then, suddenly, one of the niska chirped up and said, "We're leaving tonight; pepoon (winter) is coming, and it's going to get real cold—freezing temperatures. We've got to fatten up. We need energy for our long flight!"

And so, the niskak continued to eat. Chomp, chomp, chomp. Crunch, crunch, crunch, on all the yummy plants. Cattails, pondweed, and horsetail galore.

Now Weesakechahk had a little bit of information—and a little information can be a dangerous thing. Weesakechahk thought this was the moment to join in. So Weesakechahk inched in, blending in with the others. After all, Weesakechahk always loved a good feast followed by a nice, long nap.

After everyone was done the feast and just before Weesakechahk was starting to doze off into a deep, heavy slumber inside a fluffy, comfy nest, the Okimaw Niska shouted out, "We leave at sundown sharp!" All the niskak started cleaning themselves feverishly. One by one, diving into the water, shaking off beads of water, and plucking all their loose feathers. Feathers flying everywhere.

But Weesakechahk just kept on sleeping. Every once in a while, Weesakechahk opened one eye, to see what was going on. Weesakechahk was so comfortable and kept on dozing in and out of dreamland.

TRICKY GROUNDS

After a good long time of plucking and cleaning, the niskak started gathering in the bay. Stretching their wings and widening their beaks, warming up their throats. Suddenly, Weesakechahk woke up to a loud "Honk!" Startled, Weesakechahk got up quickly and jumped into the frigid bay.

The Okimaw Niska was standing there along the shoreline giving a pep talk. Okimaw reminded everyone about the long journey ahead, and all the responsibilities involved in flying together. The Okimaw reminded everyone, "Stay focused and, whatever you do, don't look down!"

Suddenly a smaller, less-assuming Okimaw iskwew niska came forward and took the head position. Weesakechahk chuckled under their breath as the small, unassuming bird got into position at the front of the line. Little did Weesakechahk realize, the head position is a shared position only taken up temporarily by those with vision, focus, and an enduring stamina.

There was some commotion, and suddenly the flock started to take off, one by one. Honking to support each other until they had all joined in a cacophony of honking that echoed through the evening air. The niskak were soon up in the sky taking formation. Weesakechahk was among them, and it felt good to be in relation in flight.

After a little while, Weesakechahk thought, "Surely I can relax a bit and enjoy the flight?" Weesakechahk started looking around. Noticing niskak in front, and others beside. Looking to the east and west. Even behind to the north. Weesakechahk was getting very distracted and didn't notice that they were slowly drifting farther and farther away from the flock and out of formation.

All of sudden, bang!!! Weesakechahk was shot. Wing injured. Tumbling from the sky, Weesakechahk watched the flock of niskak get smaller and smaller until they were the size of a speck of dust in the sky, and Weesakechahk was on the ground. Bird down.

CHAPTER 1

FINDING MY WAY
into the RESEARCH

Waban Geesis nintishnikaasim. Peetabeck nintonchi. Muskego-ininew-iskwew entow. My Cree name is Morning Star Light. My English name is Candace Brunette-Debassige. I am a woman of the Mushkegowuk Cree Nation in Treaty 9 Territory and member of Peetabeck (Water in the Bay), also known as Fort Albany, located on the northwestern side of James Bay. My mother, Doreen Pichette (née Brunette), is a Mushkego woman registered with Albany with Cree and French lineage. My father, Julien Pichette, was a settler Franco-Ontarian with some distant Indigenous ancestry. My parents met in Cochrane in the late 1970s but did not stay together as my father passed away at thirty-eight, leaving my mom to raise me and my sister, Holly, as a single mother. While I have mixed Cree and French settler lineage, I have always identified more strongly with my Cree background.

My Cree sense of self has been nurtured by my mother and my nokum (grandmother), Daisy Brunette (née Rueben), who was a formative figure in my early life. My mother got pregnant with me at sixteen, and I spent a lot of time with my maternal grandmother. My nokum was born in Albany (Old Post) in 1925. She met my grandfather, Wilfred Brunette, a Frenchman, in Moose Factory, Ontario, in 1942. My grandparents married at St. Thomas Anglican Church in Moose Factory in 1943, at which time my grandmother lost her Indian Status and my grandparents relocated south. After living at Moose River Crossing for a short time, they eventually settled in Clute Township, on the outskirts of Cochrane, where they had seventeen children together. After my grandmother left Albany, divisions in the community resulted in many of her siblings relocating from Old Post to Kashechewan in the 1960s. In 1986, my grandmother, my mother, and all her fifteen living siblings (re)gained their Indian Status under Bill C-31—a law that reinstated Status to Indigenous women and their children who had lost their Indian Status due to patriarchal sexist exclusions in the *Indian Act*. Unfortunately, my sister and I (and many of our cousins) continued to be excluded (due to our matriline) from obtaining our Indian Status until 2011, when Sharon McIvor successfully concluded her long-standing legal battle with the federal government that resulted in changes to the *Indian Act* and the implementation of Bill C-3. As a result of the *Indian Act*, my own sense of Indigeneity and my connections to my First Nation community have been complexly shaped by ongoing patriarchal and colonial forces.

    I did not grow up in Peetabeck; I was born and raised off-reserve in the small town of Cochrane, in northern Ontario, another place I consider home. In this small-town environment, my mother worked at the Ininew Friendship Centre and my father worked as a skilled labourer. Growing up, I struggled to find a safe place to express my complex Cree identity; in the 1980s and '90s in public school and our small town, it was often safer to blend in in order to survive. For a long time, I did not understand the pressures that I faced to assimilate—I just experienced and struggled with them. Despite the social pressures, however, I have always identified as Cree. Although I recognize that I have both Cree and French ancestry, I never developed a French sense of identity. More importantly, I have always been connected to Indigenous communities wherever I have lived. Growing up, I found a sense of community at the Ininew Friendship Centre. I participated in the Li'l Beavers program, I found summer work at the centre, I did co-ops there, and I hung out at the centre after school. And for this, I proudly declare myself a mixed-blood, urban, off-reserve Friendship Centre kid at heart. Like many urban Indigenous people, my sense of Indigeneity and (dis)connections to land and place are complex and intersectional, and have been strengthened through my efforts to decolonize my understandings, connect with communities, and reclaim my Cree identity and culture with the support of teachers and mentors, both inside and outside the academy.

I begin this book by recognizing the complex nature of my self-location; especially my self-location in relation to my research, as self-location is after all a critical starting point in Indigenous research (Absolon & Willett, 2005), one that has been used in the context of academic research for some time (Kovach, 2009; S. Wilson, 2008). By locating myself, I am grounding myself within the Cree Nation and a Cree epistemology (Absolon & Willett, 2005; Kovach, 2009). Furthermore, both my self-location and my professional experiences working in Indigenous education for over twenty years now are deeply implicated in the topic of my research, which focuses on Indigenous women administrators' experiences enacting Indigenizing policies in Canadian universities since the release of the Truth and Reconciliation Commission report (TRC, 2015).

My professional journey in Indigenous higher education began in 2003 while working at the University of Toronto's First Nations House. Over time, I found myself being called by my own inner voice and through the encouragement of others to take on Indigenous student affairs leadership roles in educational contexts. I have worked in Indigenous education in Ontario at the K–12 and post-secondary levels for over twenty years. For five years, I served as the director of the Indigenous student services unit at Western University, in southwestern Ontario, Canada, where I was later appointed special adviser to the provost (Indigenous initiatives), a role in which I advised senior leadership in the creation of an Indigenous office and senior administrative position. The call to create Indigenous senior administrative roles in universities accelerated after the TRC's 94 Calls to Action were released in 2015. I served in the acting vice-provost (Indigenous initiatives) position at Western while completing my PhD for nearly one year before deciding to take on a tenure-track faculty position.

In Canada, the TRC began its process in 2008 by listening to Indigenous survivors of Indian residential schools. Led by Honourable Justice Murray Sinclair as chairperson and Marie Wilson and Chief Wilton Littlechild as commissioners, the commission aimed to tell the truth of the Indian residential school system. Residential schools were a network of boarding schools targeting Indigenous children and families from the late 1800s to 1996 with the purpose of removing children from their families and lands and civilizing them into Euro-Western Christian values. The residential school system was established and funded by the settler colonial government, which granted legislative authority to the Royal Canadian Mounted Police (RCMP) to apprehend Indigenous children from their families. In the hundreds, residential schools ran for over 150 years across Canada and resulted in the capture of over 150,000 children. The schools were operated by churches with the mandate to "remove the Indian from the child" and indoctrinate Indigenous children into settler colonial white Christianity.

The TRC's work centred on unveiling the government's actions by giving Indigenous survivors the opportunity to share truths about their experiences in these schools with the purpose of understanding the harms of the colonial education system and making recommendations for structural and societal change. The TRC, however, did not come about through the Canadian government's willingness to tell or learn from Indigenous truths; the TRC emerged, rather, out of long-standing intergenerational Indigenous resistance efforts stemming back to the 1996 Royal Commission on Aboriginal Peoples (RCAP) and the 2005 Indian Residential Schools Settlement Agreement (IRSSA). The IRSSA was the largest class-action lawsuit in Canadian history, in which 86,000 residential school survivors—one of whom was my nokum—took the Government of Canada to the Supreme Court in a legal challenge whose results compelled the government to undertake the TRC.

The leadership roles that I was called to take on in the university context following the release of the TRC report focused on implementing the TRC's 94 Calls to Action and advancing what many people have termed Indigenization and decolonization efforts in the academy. Because residential schools and the academy are both considered key sites of ongoing colonialism and have both played instrumental roles in the settler nation-state's project of cultural genocide, post-secondary institutions, including universities, are among those institutions called to take action. Of the 94 Calls to Action, thirteen focus on educational institutions specifically, with five calls centring on post-secondary institutions. These include calls to create mandatory courses in health, education, medicine, law, and media, and a focus on revitalizing Indigenous languages.

Like many Indigenous people labouring in the academy, I have been working as part of a larger Indigenous movement to change the education system since long before the TRC Calls to Action were released. I understand Indigenous work occurring in the university as a collective process and an intervention against the hegemonic nature of the Euro-Western settler colonial academy—an interruption that strives to uncover and redirect the aims of the Euro-Western educational system, to make higher education more inclusive of Indigenous peoples and ways of knowing, and, more importantly, to advance "Indigenous educational sovereignty" (Aguilera-Black Bear & Tippeconnic, 2015). Educational sovereignty is about increasing the abilities of Indigenous peoples to exercise greater control over our educational lives and futures. As one of a handful of Indigenous people working in a formal leadership position at my university, I found myself, post-TRC, called to take on administrative work, including Indigenous policy work aimed at driving institutional reform. Through the collective efforts of an Indigenous education council, our university was called to create a broad-based Indigenous strategic plan in 2014. While initially I had high hopes for the potential of this policy document to shift the university, I witnessed and experienced the advantages and the disadvantages of Indigenous policy in practice, what I refer to in this book as policy enactment—the complex processes whereby policy actors develop, interpret, and translate into action certain policies. I also witnessed and endured the insidious ways in which settler colonial power is operationalized in the policy-enactment process, in ways that do not necessarily benefit Indigenous people or contribute to Indigenous educational sovereignty. Thus, my own leadership struggles as an Indigenous woman leader enacting Indigenizing policies post-TRC have greatly shaped and informed my decision to explore the experiences of other Indigenous women administrators who have been involved in similar efforts. Indigenous women make up a large portion of Indigenous peoples studying and working in Canadian universities, and as a result of their presence, Indigenous women responded to the call to take on leadership roles in universities in an era of reconciliation. Yet Indigenous women's leadership stories have been silent in academic research.

When it came to choosing an approach for my research, my deep desire to make my research epistemologically and pedagogically relevant to a Cree viewpoint led me to an Indigenous storying approach, an approach that would be accessible to a diverse Indigenous audience, who tend to have a deep respect for storytelling. From my earliest childhood memories, storytelling has been an integral way of coming to know myself in relation to my family, Nation, Territory, and the world. My mother often reminds me that from a young age she recognized in me a deep desire and passion for storytelling. I believe that I learned this way of knowing and being from spending time with my nokum, who was an animated and gifted orator in our family. My nokum had a contagious way of bringing people into her world through stories; moving them through time and space, laughter and tears, inspiring them to listen with all their being. As a child, I would listen to her tell stories as I played underneath the kitchen table where she would sit, drinking Red Rose tea while visiting with family members. Here, nestled by her feet and soothed by the scent of her smoked-moose hide moccasins with their intricate beadwork patterns, I would listen to her tell stories centred on the dramas of her childhood life in the bush up north. Often, she would share vivid accounts about my grandparents' experiences living on the muskeg trapline, encountering animals; and of familial ties connected to our Cree historic lineage along the James Bay. She would also sometimes share her childhood experiences as a student at Bishop Horton Residential School in Moose Factory, Ontario, which she attended from the ages of seven to sixteen. I can still hear how she would repeat certain words for emphasis. I also remember how the patterns of her breath and inflections in her voice would assume different shades when she told certain stories. I noticed the silences. I felt her pain. *I still hear my nokum's stories; I hear them as an echo.*

For me, choosing an Indigenous storying methodology is undoubtedly tied to my Cree storytelling traditions, including my grandmother's teachings. When I look back at the stories that my grandmother shared with me, I can now see that they were the early seeds of my own research training and development, teaching me to see the world and share knowledge through an Indigenous (Cree) lens. In reflecting on this realization, I have also come to understand that my nokum's stories were not simply stories. They were powerful acts of survivance—"an active sense of presence, the continuance of native stories, not a mere reaction...a spirited resistance, a life force, a force of nature" (Vizenor, 1999, p. vii). *I hear her; I hear her as an echo.*

I also see how my grandmother's stories, along with my Indigenous studies and Indigenous theatre training, have not only shaped my methodological approach to research, but also taught me to look critically at the ways that settler colonial power appears in the stories Indigenous women administrators shared with me in this research. Grounded in my own Indigenous view of the world, I draw on a critical Indigenous lens to understand how settler colonial relations of power map Indigenous women administrators' experiences, often organizing and subjugating us in gendered, colonial, and racialized ways. Most importantly, my grandmother's insistence on telling her stories has inspired me to *refuse* the erasure of my own subjectivity and of Indigenous women's voices in research and in life. My nokum has deeply influenced my life and my research; it is because of her that I focus on the embodied, lived experiences of Indigenous women administrators (including myself) who strive to change the university from within.

Like my grandmother's stories, the opening Weesakechahk story offers another bridge into a Cree epistemological understanding. I draw upon this story as part of my theoretical lens; Weesakechahk also becomes a pedagogical figure in my storytelling approach used specifically in the play *Flight* in chapter 7. While the opening Weesakechahk story is retold from my own point of view, Weesakechahk and other mythological figures in Cree stories reflect Indigenous/Cree consciousness; they situate the storyteller and listeners in a relational ontology. Among the Cree, Weesakechahk is a great transformer, always in the making, creating and often wreaking havoc by making a mess, but at the same time for me Weesakechahk acts as a mirror and a teacher, teaching humans through their mistakes about how to live in relation to family, community, the land, and the cosmos. When I returned to the "Weesakechahk Flies South with the Waveys" story, I immediately saw parallels with some of my own leadership experiences and the stories that some Indigenous women administrators shared with me. I draw on Weesakechahk to help me drive the storytelling process and share some of the experiences of Indigenous women administrators in this research.

Growing up, I never heard Weesakechahk stories or stories like my nokum's in school. Over the years, I have painfully reflected on this marked absence in our educational system and have subsequently come to realize that the disjuncture between what I heard around my family's kitchen table and what was shared in school has shaped my life's work in education and leadership. In turn, I have focused much of my career on actively creating space for Indigenous stories and voices in educational settings. As a member of the first generation in my family to go to university, I struggled to access education and to find culturally safe and relevant spaces in which to learn and thrive in post-secondary settings. In the late 1990s, I found a sense of refuge from the white settler Euro-Western dominance of education in Indigenous student services and Indigenous studies at my university. Here, in this protective pocket of the academy, I became surrounded by a nurturing community invested in recovering and telling Indigenous stories. This sense of community and epistemological rootedness became a lifeline for me as I continued on in my education; it also became a space I yearned to support in my leadership.

INTRODUCING THE RESEARCH

Undeniably, the TRC has been a powerful driving force in mobilizing Indigenous educational voices and priorities, and in moving them to the top of university administrators' minds (Gaudry & Lorenz, 2018b). At the same time, it is clear that the Indigenizing policy movement is accompanied by a number of challenges for Indigenous people, who are often expected to implement the policy movement's promises (Greenwood et al., 2008; Pidgeon, 2016; Sasakamoose & Pete, 2015). Amid increasing debates about the performative nature and rhetoric around Indigenizing policies in universities (Gaudry & Lorenz, 2018b), new Indigenous senior administrative positions have been instituted in many Canadian institutions (Cote-Meek, 2020; Lavallee, 2020; Pidgeon, 2016; Academic Women's Association, 2019). Moreover, many of these new leadership roles are occupied by Indigenous women (Academic Women's Association, 2019), who find themselves working in administrative settings that are largely dominated by white male settlers (Blackmore, 2010; Fitzgerald, 2006; Lavallee, 2020). That being the case, the increasing number of Indigenous women administrators in universities does not speak to the challenges they face, and media reports have begun to shine a light on some of the negative experiences some Indigenous women leaders have experienced when taking on these administrative roles (UofM, 2018; Lavallee, 2019; Prokopchuk, 2018). Research on Indigenous women administrators' experiences in Canadian universities is thus not only timely and relevant, but desperately needed in order to undo the "deafening silence" (Fitzgerald, 2003a, 2006, 2010, 2014) of Indigenous women's voices in educational leadership research and practice.

The purpose of this book is to document the experiences and challenges that Indigenous women administrators face in enacting Indigenizing policies in Canadian universities, and to do so in order to inform more transformative, decolonial approaches to Indigenous leadership and policy practices. In this work, I aim to amplify Indigenous women administrators' voices in higher education—because Indigenous women's perspectives have been chronically silenced, marginalized, and altogether omitted in Western research, leadership, and policy discourses to date, and because their voices can provide critical insights into understanding the limits of the settler colonial academy. I also strive to go beyond quantitative approaches to measuring the success of Indigenization policy implementation through representational data (Academic Women's Association, 2019), and instead to privilege Indigenous women administrators' lived and embodied experiences through a qualitative Indigenous storying approach to research.

There are undeniable gaps in the educational leadership literature relating to Indigenous women leaders in general, and little academic literature that focuses on Indigenous women administrators in universities (Faircloth, 2017; Santamaría, 2013; Warner, 1995), and in Canada specifically (Cote-Meek, 2020; Lavallee, 2020). This research builds on prior work linking Indigenous women educational leaders' experiences of marginalization to the intersections of their Indigeneity and gender (Faircloth, 2017; Fitzgerald, 2003a, 2006, 2010, 2014; V. Johnson, 1997; Lajimodiere, 2013; Tippeconnic-Fox et al., 2015; Warner, 1995). I further corroborate previous research that demonstrates how Indigenous women leaders face "cultural dissonance" (Warner, 1995) because they are expected to occupy intermediary positions in between Euro-Western educational systems and Indigenous communities (Ah Nee-Benham & Cooper, 1998; Faircloth, 2017; Fitzgerald, 2003a, 2003b, 2006, 2010, 2014; V. Johnson, 1997; Johnson et al., 2003; Kenny & Fraser, 2012; Khalifa et al., 2019; Marker, 2015; Minthorn & Chavez, 2015; Ottmann et al., 2010; Santamaría, 2013). I also make new contributions to the field of educational leadership by examining the ways in which Indigenous women experience, talk about, and respond to settler colonialism through their academic leadership and policy work, and how they often negotiate complex intersectional power by enacting Indigenous refusals in order to effect institutional change and assert Indigenous educational sovereignty.

From a policy perspective, Indigenous women leaders are increasingly finding their way into university administrative positions where they are drawing on policies to incite deeper reforms. From a critical policy perspective, however, I argue that Indigenizing policies are not simply developed and implemented; they are complexly enacted (Ball et al., 2012) by various actors with different positionalities, understandings, and competing agendas. To date, there are gaps in the research focusing on critical Indigenizing policy enactments in educational contexts. There is also a lack of research on Indigenizing policies from critical

Indigenous standpoints (Andreotti et al., 2015; Fallon & Paquette, 2014; Gaudry & Lorenz, 2018b; Pete & Sasakamoose, 2015) and using Indigenous methodological frameworks. This study strives to address some of these gaps by exploring, through an Indigenous storying methodological approach, Indigenous women administrators' experiences of enacting Indigenizing policies.

This book is framed around four overarching questions:

- How do Indigenous women administrators experience their leadership work amid increasing pressures to Indigenize and decolonize the academy?
- What challenges do Indigenous women administrators face when enacting Indigenizing policies within Canadian universities?
- How do Indigenous women administrators encounter the settler colonial academy in their leadership and policy work?
- How can Indigenous women administrators contest and resist settler colonialism in their educational leadership work?

ORGANIZATION OF THE BOOK

The book is organized into eleven chapters plus a prologue and epilogue. Following this introductory chapter, I begin chapter 2 by offering a history of the Euro-Western university and its ties to the larger projects of global imperialism and settler colonialism. I also provide a brief outline of Indigenous peoples' participation in Canadian universities. In chapter 3, I introduce some of the scholarly debates around the contentious concepts of Indigenization, decolonization, reconciliation, and resurgence in the growing movement to Indigenize the academy. In chapter 4, I contextualize the field of Indigenous educational leadership and the experiences of Indigenous women in the sphere of leadership specifically. In chapter 5, I offer a way of seeing Indigenous women's experience through an Indigenous narrative conveyed through a feminist and decolonial lens; here I locate my usage of Trickster theory by drawing on a Weesakechahk story. In chapter 6, I share my unique approach to doing qualitative research and outline my Cree floral research framework design. In chapter 7, I share an example of a Cree storied approach to research that draws on performance writing to share a play entitled *Flight: Journeying for Change* that includes ten scenes. In chapter 8, I share some thematic findings around the embodied experiences of Indigenous women leaders. In chapter 9, I focus on the tricky nature of policy enactment while outlining some of the limitations of Indigenizing policies in practice. In chapter 10, I share the emergence of Indigenous refusal as part of an Indigenous decolonial leadership disposition. In chapter 11, I attempt to make sense of the trickiness of leadership and policy practices in this research. I end with an epilogue that looks back at the beginning story through my own Cree lens.

CHAPTER 2

The ROOTS *and* LIFE-SUPPORT SYSTEM *of the* SETTLER COLONIAL ACADEMY

The roots of the "Westernized university" (Grosfoguel, 2016) provides a significant starting point when looking at the topic of Indigenous women leaders' policy experiences in Canadian universities. The Westernized university is a concept that considers the complex historical imperial and colonial interconnections of universities around the world. Puerto Rican Chicano/Latino scholar Ramon Grosfoguel describes the Westernized university as having a geographic, political, and linguistic genesis within European lands, Euro-Western ways of knowing, and the English language. Tracing the lineages of the Westernized university, Grosfoguel et al. (2016) find that the academy was exported from Europe to many places around the world, including Turtle Island (North America), where it was transplanted onto Indigenous lands, contributing to

Figure 1. Pillars of Higher Education in Canada

dispossessing Indigenous peoples from sovereignty over their lives and futures. Moreover, universities were "built not just on Indigenous lands, but with Indigenous lands" (Harvey, 2021); in other words, many early universities used the money generated by the sales of Indigenous lands under settler colonial laws to raise university capital and grow their institutions. More recently, some scholars have exposed this common settler colonial institutional practice among Commonwealth universities around the world (Harvey, forthcoming) and land-grab universities in the United States (Ahtone & Lee, 2021; Nash, 2019; Stein, 2017, 2023). In a Canadian context, Westernized universities are not immune from a connection to these settler colonial projects (Harvey, forthcoming), or from being institutionally implicated in using the civilizing mission of early university education as a key rationale in their early fundraising efforts (Cross & Peace, 2021).

Beyond the Westernized university model forming part of a complex international network of imperial and colonial universities, it has also been tied to the entrenchment of a "Eurocentric fundamentalism" (Grosfoguel, 2016)—especially in the form of the universalizing of knowledge around the world. Modern universalism was the pursuit of European

Enlightenment thinkers who believed in and asserted a common knowledge framework across groups and borders. Decolonial scholars illuminate the interconnections between modernity and coloniality (Mignolo, 2010) as central to the global universalizing movement (Andreotti et al., 2015; Stein, 2023). Modernity is not simply a historical period (the modern era), but an ideological movement that decolonial scholars argue is steeped in European thinking. This type of modernist thinking can be further tied to the Enlightenment (the so-called age of reason)—a movement that worked alongside imperial and colonial academic projects to justify European imperial and colonial expansion and the taking over of Indigenous peoples' lands. Embodied within modernist thinking are assumptions of human progress along with a tendency to organize humans and non-humans, time, and knowledge in relation to European power and Eurocentric notions of time and space (Machado de Oliveira, 2022). These ideologies have become so engrained in Western societies that they are hegemonic and taken for granted. In other words, grand philosophies of progress, linear time, scientific reasoning, the formation of nation-states, democracies, and industrialization are commonly positioned in modernist thinking as universal and superior to non-Western ways of knowing and doing (Andreotti et al., 2015). Mignolo (2007) further illuminates the relationship between modernity and coloniality as two sides of the same coin—here the light side is modernity, while the dark side is coloniality. The light side of modernity involves the promises that education will lead to social mobilization, economic growth, and public good. Whereas the dark side of modernity in education is coloniality, which is inherently violent and often relies on the exploitation of different peoples, lands, and knowledges. Many decolonial scholars are invested in exposing the ways that modernistic and colonial thinking shape institutional and common-sense modes of being and doing in higher education. With the Indigenization movement in Canadian universities in mind, it is critical to expose the modernistic promises made by the Westernized university, and to understand how the education system continues to drive modernist assumptions and thereby conceal the academy's role in exploiting Indigenous peoples and knowledges as part of larger imperial global networks.

From an epistemological standpoint, the university as a Westernized model of education has been positioned as the authority in the production of universal knowledge. Through this position of power, the Westernized university system was brought to Turtle Island, where it contributed to the manufacturing of epistemic superiority along with the advancement of settler social powers and settler colonial projects; the university's key function has been to serve nation building, advance economic development, and train civil servants in modernistic and colonial ideologies. Scholars such as Grosfoguel trace the genealogies of Westernized universities around the world as part of a massive global imperial network responsible for advancing Euro-Western global domination, including epistemic male perspectives, memories, and histories in educational systems worldwide (Grosfoguel, 2016; Cupples & Grosfoguel, 2018).

In Canada, universities emerged at different stages over time, starting as early as 1635 with the establishment of the Collège de Québec by the Jesuits. Other early universities like the Université Laval, University of New Brunswick, and the University of Toronto, among others, emerged in the mid-1800s with religious affiliations (Eastman et al., 2023). As a result, many early universities in Canada had complex relationships with church and state (Cross & Peace, 2021) and have been associated with training clergy as part of the Indian residential school system. By the early twentieth century, there were three predominant university models in Canada: the private, the non-denominational, and the public (Eastman et al., 2023). Regardless of the different types of universities and the different times at which they emerged, all Canadian universities can be traced back to their ties to European fundamentalism, which is structurally embedded into the university system and its Eurocentric disciplinary structures, forms of academic governance, curricula, canons, policies, practices, and academic norms.

Consequently, an empire of epistemologies has been advanced through the Westernized university system in Canada, which has resulted in the undermining of non-European ways of knowing—most relevant to this book, the undervaluing of Indigenous ways of knowing. To highlight Euro-Western academic hegemony and hierarchies of knowledge, Walter Mignolo poignantly describes how the academy often positions Indigenous peoples and knowledges: "the first world has knowledge, the third world has culture; Native Americans have wisdom and Anglo-Americans have science" (2009, p. 160). Marie Battiste (1986, 1998), Mi'kmaq professor and education scholar, has long made similar arguments that Eurocentric dominance within education systems is a form of "cognitive imperialism"—the taken-for-granted way in which universities privilege Euro-Western knowledges, ideologies, norms, and values as not only universal but superior. Battiste further asserts that as a result of Euro-Western domination in education, relatively little is known about or valued in most universities in relation to Indigenous ways of knowing (Battiste & Youngblood, 2009; Smith & Smith, 2018). Other scholars have asserted that Westernized universities, by reducing and overlooking Indigenous ways of knowing, have contributed (alongside settler government laws and policies) to forms of "epistemicide" (Grosfoguel, 2016) and "linguisticide" (Hall, 2018)—the near obliteration of Indigenous ways of knowing and languages in dominant education systems.

Despite the historical marginalization of Indigenous knowledges in the academy, Indigenous peoples have participated in universities and asserted Indigenous paradigms (Battiste & Youngblood, 2009; Battiste & Youngblood, 2000) and Indigenous epistemologies and methodologies in academic research. These academic assertions began to appear in the late 1990s, positioning Indigenous knowledge as unique and distinct from Western paradigms and knowledges (Archibald, 2009b; Battiste, 2000; Castellano, 1999; Kovach, 2009; Wilson, 2009). Sámi scholar Rauna Kuokkanen (2007) uses the term "episteme" to describe these fundamental overarching differences. Kuokkanen argues that an episteme is "the beliefs, assumptions, and ways of relating to the world that have been dominant in certain societies, and thus have influenced the construction of predominant discourses, not individual psyches and behaviors" (2007, p. 314). She further asserts that Indigenous epistemes are dynamic and constantly changing in space and time; however, she argues, like other Indigenous scholars, that Indigenous epistemes uniquely order the world, humans, and non-humans in relation to land and place.

While Indigenous scholars have more recently articulated Indigenous knowledges in the academy, Indigenous peoples have always created knowledge. Yet Indigenous peoples struggled under the subjugation of Western research paradigms, which have long domesticated Indigenous peoples to Western scholarly gazes, thereby silencing Indigenous voices. Linda Tuhiwai Smith's (1999) watershed scholarship uncovered the devastating impacts that Western research has had on Indigenous peoples around the world. As she argues, when Western researchers have taken up Indigenous people in their scholarship, they have historically done so through their Eurocentric white male colonial lenses, thereby contributing to an "Other[ing]" (Said, 1978) and a silencing of Indigenous peoples' authorial voices in processes of knowing. Othering is a long-standing colonial technique that supresses Indigenous people by recourse to colonial and racist lenses that tend to position Indigenous ways of knowing as inferior to Western ways of knowing. The underlying motivation for ignoring and/or Othering Indigenous peoples and ways of knowing in Euro-Westernized universities can be attributed to the colonial project, and the need for early colonists to undermine Indigenous peoples by casting them as subhuman, uncivilized, a problem, and inferior to Europeans in order to legitimize European claims to control Indigenous peoples and take their lands. Othering in the academy has also contributed to an "epistemic violence" (Spivak, 1998) and the silencing and racialization of Indigenous people in academic discourses across disciplines. Othering has further fuelled a number of violent and problematic theories and associated institutional policies in the areas of eugenics, intelligence, and human development (Smith, 1999). More relevant to Indigenous women, Othering has not only been a colonial tactic but a gendered one that has marginalized and silenced Indigenous women's voices in colonial archives and early Western research.

In examining Indigenous peoples in higher education, I argue that it is necessary to trace the colonial lineage of Othering in "Indian policies" in Canada, and to uncover the persistent myth of the "Indian problem" (Dyck, 1991; Episkenew, 2009) in educational policy work (Maxwell et al., 2018). The "Indian problem" has been widely used in colonial contexts as a way to impose the category of "Other" (Said, 1978) on Indigenous peoples so as to position Europeans ("us") as superior and in need of controlling Indigenous peoples, positioning ("them"/"Other") as inferior. "Other" is a common deficit category grounded in the false colonial belief that "Indians" are "backwards," "inferior," "savage," "illiterate," "primitive," "uncivilized," and as such incapable of governing themselves. Settler colonial educational policy narratives have long drawn on deficit approaches (Cherubini, 2012) that are based on and propagate the "Indian problem" (Maxwell et al., 2018) as a justification for educational authorities to control and "fix" Indigenous peoples and assimilate Indigenous populations into dominant Euro-Western educational systems, aims, and even measures of success. The colonial myth of the "Indian problem" is rooted in two colonial falsehoods: (1) that Indigenous peoples are the problem (not the settler colonial government or the Euro-Western education system and its associated myths/ideologies); and (2) that Euro-Western ways of knowing (based in settler colonial governance, education, and even early Christianity) can solve the "Indian problem" (Dyck, 1991).

More disturbingly, these underlying colonial assumptions have fuelled many colonial projects, including the Indian residential school system, the boarding school system, involuntary/voluntary enfranchisement laws, the pass system, the reservation system, the ban on the Potlatch and Sun Dance, the elimination of the buffalo, Métis removal, the overlooking of Treaties, forced sterilization of Indigenous women, and military and police controls over Indigenous lives and lands, to name just a few. Moreover, these interrelated colonial projects are all tethered to the master colonial policy: the *Indian Act*, based on the greatest myth of all, the doctrine of discovery and *terra nullius*, a Latin expression meaning "no man's land," and which has been used in international and settler laws and academic theories to justify colonialization and the erasure of Indigenous sovereignty over Indigenous lands. The doctrine of discovery has served to validate European settler governments' title and control over Indigenous lands, and to legitimate settler governments' paternalistic relationship over Indigenous people. More troublingly, universities have long served to maintain these complex and interrelated colonial systems by reproducing and disseminating colonial ideologies, thereby acting as "arms of the settler state" (Grande, 2015; Tuck, 2018).

THE CONTEMPORARY SETTLER COLONIAL ACADEMY

Despite the well-established imperial and colonial roots of the broader Westernized academic system in Canada, over the past century, universities have shifted and taken on different roles in society (Eastman et al., 2022). Moreover, universities today are not immune to the ongoing nature of settler colonialism and its connection to global capitalism. Settler colonialism is an ordering structure, not an event (Wolfe, 2006), one that continues to shape Indigenous peoples' relationships to the nation-state, its laws, policies, public institutions, and the underlying ideologies that maintain the settler system. Global capitalism is the all-encompassing economic system that naturalizes unequal wealth accumulation around the world, often through the expropriation and exploitation of humans and non-humans and the land (Stein, 2023).

In Canada, there are ninety-six universities operating across ten provinces and three territories, ranging from small teaching-focused universities to large research-intensive institutions that compete for recognition and students at a global level. Universities generally claim to contribute to society through their core missions of teaching, research, and innovation. Most modern universities in Canada hold unique legal status and have their own acts that allow them to operate as both public institutions and corporations. The majority of Canadian universities today are governed according to a bicameral model, which divides the academic and daily operations of the university into two overarching governance structures—the Senate (overseeing academic matters) and the Board of Governors (overseeing financial matters). In this way, contemporary universities are quite complex organizationally and legally; they are influenced and governed by different corporate, academic, collegial, charitable, and other dimensions (Shanahan, 2019). In other words, "Canadian universities are autonomous, non-profit corporations created by provincial Acts or charters" (Jones et al., 2001, p. 136).

The Senate is generally comprised of the majority of internal representatives, with faculty members making up the majority; however, greater student and staff participation has increased over time. On the other hand, the Board of Governors is generally made up of a large number of lay members, with some seats for students, staff, and faculty (Jones et al., 2001). In the era of reconciliation, some universities have begun electing local First Nations people to sit on these boards, but most of these positions are not dedicated seats (Eastman et al., 2023).

When looking more closely at contemporary university governance, we can see that these institutions are complex in that they do almost everything that states do. In this way, contemporary universities are not only focused on higher education and research; "they are also landlords, real estate developers, arts and cultural venues, health care and food service providers, day care operators, waste managers, animal care providers, operators of nuclear reactors, and so on. As such, universities are regulated by the state in almost everything they do" (Eastman et al., 2021, p. 58).

While contemporary universities are undeniably regulated by various federal and provincial laws, they are also shaped by broader ongoing global capitalist forces. For example, contemporary universities operate as business ventures on a global scale by selling their degrees in international markets. In this way, university administrators have been criticized for leaning toward business approaches to education as a way to survive chronic government underfunding and in a competitive global economy (Giroux, 2014; Lincoln, 2018). These corporate approaches to education have arguably shifted power dynamics on university campuses, positioning students as consumers as opposed to learners. Under an increasingly neoliberal approach to education, former liberal notions of education as a public good and democratic purpose have become subordinated to various economic considerations. University administrative decision making has also become increasingly influenced by these neoliberal logics, turning education into a private over public good. The marketization of higher education has been identified as a major concern by many scholars and educators who view this shift as a threat to the foundations of academic freedom. "Academic freedom is fundamental to the mandate of universities to pursue truth, educate students, and disseminate knowledge." (UC, 2023) Academic freedom protects the rights of scholars to teach and research topics without fear of political interference or administrative reprisal. Academic freedom is distinct from the notion of free speech as academic freedom is based in academic integrity and standards of inquiry.

When it comes to increasing the presence of Indigenous peoples and knowledges in universities in a reconciliation era, neoliberal agendas operate alongside neo-colonialism, which can have dire consequences for Indigenous education, Indigenous communities, and Indigenous knowledges. For example, under neo-colonial logics, Indigenous knowledges can easily become captive to "knowledge prospecting, controlling intellectual and cultural property rights, and defining Indigenous research in narrow and standardized (i.e., universalized) ways" (Smith & Smith, 2018, p. 9).

Therefore, contemporary neoliberal and neo-colonial institutional tendencies present some dangerous challenges for the institutional Indigenization work that the Indigenous women profiled in this book strive to lead. For example, institutional Indigenization work that seeks to ethically include Indigenous peoples and knowledges in the university and be accountable to Indigenous communities can become contained within global market economies that undermine Indigenous collective knowledges and rights. In this sense, Indigenous university administrators must be wary and critical of the ways that neoliberalization and neo-colonization can marginalize Indigenous voices, needs, and control in favour of hierarchal decision making and commodification of knowledge (Smith & Smith, 2018). As a result of these complex and fluid systemic factors, some Indigenous scholars have argued that "there are parts of the higher education project that are too invested in settler colonialism [and global capitalism] to be rescued" (Tuck, 2018, p. 149). Among such decolonial critiques, Indigenous scholars like Sandy Grande (2018a, 2018b) and Eve Tuck (2018) warn that the modern Euro-Western academy is so deeply entrenched within the interconnections between settler colonialism, global capitalism, and hetero-patriarchy that, more often than not, it automatically reproduces unequal power relations and further domesticates Indigenous people and ways of knowing. These deeper systemic factors call on many Indigenous peoples to ask some of the following questions: What are the limits of the settler colonial academy? Is it possible for a Westernized university to advance Indigenous educational sovereignty? And to what extent can Indigenous peoples' labour within the academy advance Indigenous decolonial freedom? These critical debates pose unique tensions and challenges for the Indigenous women administrators engaged in my study as they navigate the contemporary settler colonial academy.

INDIGENOUS PEOPLE IN CANADIAN UNIVERSITIES

Despite long-standing critiques concerning the limits of university reform, Indigenous people are entering the academy more than ever before. However, the inclusion of Indigenous people in universities, and their access to post-secondary education more broadly, is still a relatively recent phenomenon; after all, historically, generations of Indigenous people have been denied full participation in the Euro-Westernized university in Canada. In this next section, I organize the history of Indigenous people's participation in Canadian universities into a four-part timeline (table 1). In this timeline, I outline a four-phase process: (1) forced assimilation, from the mid-1800s to 1950; (2) assumed assimilation, from about 1951 to the 1970s; (3) Indigenous equity and inclusion, from the 1970s to present (Brunette & Richmond, 2018b); and (4) "Indigenization-reconciliation" (Gaudry & Lorenz, 2018), from 2015 to present. While I outlined the first three phases in earlier curriculum work, the fourth phase has been added in response to the TRC's work in Canada. In the following section I describe each phase in terms of five general themes relating to Indigenous people's relationship with the academy and to larger settler colonial policies impacting Indigenous people during each time period: Significant Policies, University Institutional Approaches, Indigenous People's Participation, Teaching Agendas, and Research Agendas.

Table 1. Four-Part Timeline for Indigenous Education

SIGNIFICANT POLICIES

Phase 1: Exclusion and forced assimilation, 1800s to 1950
- 1857: *Gradual Civilization Act* is passed.
- Some early universities acquire Indigenous lands directly or indirectly through the imposition of settler laws and policies.
- Many early universities embody religious affiliations with the residential school system, including training clergy.
- 1867: First residential school in Canada opens.
- 1876: *Indian Act* enacted; Section 86(1) says that Indians obtaining university degrees are automatically enfranchised (i.e., relinquish Treaty rights).

Phase 2: Assumed assimilation, 1951–1969
- 1951: Involuntary enfranchisement ends but voluntary enfranchisement continues.
- 1957: Indian Affairs introduces first scholarship for "Indians" to attend university (Stonechild, 2006).
- 1960: "Status Indian" peoples gain the right to vote.
- 1969: Liberal government attempts to put through the White Paper to abolish Indigenous rights.

Phase 3: Indigenization-inclusion, 1970–2015
- 1972: National Indian Brotherhood releases *Indian Control of Indian Education* paper asserting rights to self-determination in education.
- 1977: Post-Secondary Education Assistance Program established.
- 1982: *Canadian Constitution Act* recognizes Indigenous rights.
- 1985: Aboriginal institutes emerge in Ontario and expand greatly after 2000s.
- 1987: Capping of Indian post-secondary funding begins.
- 1996: Report of the Royal Commission on Aboriginal Peoples released.
- 1996: Last residential school in Canada closes in Saskatchewan.
- 1996: Indian and Northern Affairs Canada launches the federal Post-Secondary Student Support Program—recognized as a social policy (not a Treaty right).

SIGNIFICANT POLICIES

Phase 3: Indigenization-inclusion, 1970–2015
- **2007**: United Nations Declaration on Indigenous Peoples' Rights (UNDRIP) is adopted by the UN General Assembly; Canada reserves objector status.
- **2008**: Government of Canada releases a formal apology on residential schools.
- **2008**: TRC process begins.
- **2010**: The Association of Canadian Deans of Education releases *Accord on Indigenous Education*.
- **2014**: Tri-Council Policy Statement on Ethical Conduct for Research Involving Humans is released; of special significance is chapter 9, "Aboriginal Research."

Phase 4: Indigenization-reconciliation, 2015–present
- **2015**: Report of the Truth and Reconciliation Commission of Canada released.
- **2015**: Universities Canada releases thirteen principles on Indigenous education.
- **2016**: Canadian Association for University Teachers (CAUT) releases policy statement *Indigenizing the Academy*.
- **2017**: Indigenous institutes gain accreditation status.
- **2020**: CAUT releases *Bargaining for Indigenization of the Academy*.

UNIVERSITY INSTITUTIONAL APPROACHES

Phase 1: Exclusion and forced assimilation, 1800s to 1950
Indigenous peoples are not directly considered in university policy approaches.

Phase 2: Assumed assimilation, 1951–1969
- **1969**: First Indigenous studies program launches at Trent University.

Phase 3: Indigenization-inclusion, 1970–2015
- Indigenous student centres are established in Western provinces by the 1970s, and in Ontario by the 1990s.
- **1976**: Federation of Saskatchewan Indian Nations enters into a federation agreement with the University of Regina.
- By the 1990s many Ontario universities institute Indigenous advisory councils (consultation mechanism).

UNIVERSITY INSTITUTIONAL APPROACHES

Phase 3: Indigenization-inclusion, 1970–2015
- 2002: Canadian Association of College and University Student Services (CACUSS) establishes its National Aboriginal Student Services Assembly.

Phase 4: Indigenization-reconciliation, 2015–present
- The higher-education sector starts to respond to the TRC's findings through policy initiatives that place increasing public and social pressure on universities to change.
- Indigenous policy movement increases along with the number of university strategic/action/TRC plans after 2015.
- Universities start to consider institution-wide approaches to Indigenous educational change in areas such as curriculum, policy, and leadership.
- Many universities appoint Indigenous senior administrators or leads.
- Land acknowledgements are widely used in policy and performative practice.

INDIGENOUS PEOPLE'S PARTICIPATION

Phase 1: Exclusion and forced assimilation, 1800s to 1950
Indigenous people are legally prohibited and excluded from attending universities unless they accept enfranchisement and assimilate.

Phase 2: Assumed assimilation, 1951–1969
- Indigenous students are permitted to attend universities but are expected to assimilate into dominant disciplinary and institutional norms.
- First wave of Indigenous scholars enters the academy in small numbers.

Phase 3: Indigenization-inclusion, 1970–2015
- Indigenous students continue to enter the academy, with some services offered to help them acculturate (conditional inclusion).
- A small number of Indigenous scholars begin working in universities as faculty members.

INDIGENOUS PARTICIPATION	**Phase 4: Indigenization-reconciliation, 2015–present** • Indigenous student representation rises at all levels. More direct entry from high schools. An increase in graduate students. • Indigenous senior administrators begin working in universities in Indigenous roles. • Indigenous faculty members are chronically under-represented; cluster hires emerge after TRC as an institutional response to deal with shortage.
TEACHING AGENDAS	**Phase 1: Exclusion and forced assimilation, 1800s to 1950** • Academic disciplines are imported from Europe and represented as universal and superior to non-Western knowledges. • When Indigenous peoples are taken up in university teaching, their voices are subjugated and silenced across academic disciplines.
	Phase 2: Assumed assimilation, 1951–1969 Scholarship about Indigenous people often written through Eurocentric, male, colonial, and deficit lenses. The concept of the "prehistoric Indian" is prevalent.
	Phase 3: Indigenization-inclusion, 1970–2015 • Indigenous access pathways emerge, opening doors for some Indigenous students. • Specific Indigenous academic programs emerge in the areas of Indigenous studies, education, law, and social work (but programs are overly reliant on special funding and lack institutional support).
	Phase 4: Indigenization-reconciliation, 2015–present • Indigenous studies asserts itself as a discipline, in some places rising to the status of faculties and departments. • Movements to Indigenize curriculum expand Indigenous voices across disciplines. Some universities start to hire Indigenous curriculum advisers. • Indigenous scholars begin writing from their own standpoints and epistemological perspectives across disciplines.

SETTLER COLONIAL ACADEMY

RESEARCH AGENDAS

Phase 1: Exclusion and forced assimilation, 1800s to 1950
- Indigenous people are subjected to harmful Euro-Western research practices as part of a salvage research movement (Wilson, 2008).
- Research is done unethically on Indigenous people without consent or accountability.
- Research does not benefit Indigenous people.

Phase 2: Assumed assimilation, 1951–1969

While some early Indigenous scholars enter the academy, many are forced to align with Euro-Western disciplines and research practices in order to survive.

Phase 3: Indigenization-inclusion, 1970–2015
- Journals in Indigenous studies and education are established (e.g., the *Canadian Journal of Native Education* in 1980; the *Canadian Journal of Native Studies* in 1981)
- Indigenous paradigms and research methodologies are articulated and used by Indigenous scholars to expand Indigenous research.

Phase 4: Indigenization-reconciliation, 2015–present
- Indigenous paradigms in research are asserted in scholarship.
- Indigenous ethical considerations in research are more widely taken up in institutional policy and practice.
- Indigenous communities begin to assert their own research agendas and ethics.

EXCLUSION AND FORCED ASSIMILATION, MID-1800S–1950

Early approaches to Indigenous people in universities focused on their exclusion and forced assimilation into Euro-Westernized settler societies. Canada's earliest universities were based on European models of education with deep roots in European religious civilizing missions. These universities often focused mainly on training clergy, lawyers, and doctors in Western traditional disciplines and doctrines of religion, law, and medicine. While Canada's Indian residential schools were government-sponsored institutions run by churches, early universities and residential schools are rarely discussed together even though they share some commonalities in terms of using education as a tool to expand settler control of Indigenous lands and eliminate Indigeneity through colonialism and Christianity (Cross & Peace, 2021). Not only did many early universities train clergy as part of the residential school system, they also educated the political leaders, policy-makers, and administrators of the nation-state and its associated institutions by perpetuating Western colonial notions of law and governance, thereby legitimizing settler authority over Indigenous peoples and lands. One of the clearest examples of this settler colonial network's grip is the appointment of Duncan Campbell Scott as president of the Royal Society of Canada in 1921. An infamous and notorious architect of the residential school system in Canada, Scott drew on his network within the Royal Society to mobilize discussions about colonialism, race, and Indigenous peoples in order to advance Indian policies and settler domination in Canada (Backhouse et al., 2021).

More troublingly, early universities often used assimilatory motivations embedded in Indian policies as key motivators in fundraising for and founding their institutions. Settler historian Thomas Peace (2016) has shed light on the formation of Western University. Peace writes,

> The Bishop of Huron [Isaac Hellmuth]...applied for a grant in aid of the fund being raised by him for the foundation of a university at London, to be called the Western University of London, and [for the] training of both Indian and white students for the ministry of the Church of England in Canada. (Peace, 2016)

In turn, residential schools and early universities like Western University have continued to rely heavily on a combination of settler colonial social and financial networks (Cross & Peace, 2021). Yet university founding stories rarely if ever account for the ways universities relied on Indigenous land and colonial dispossession. Settler decolonial scholar Sharon Stein (2023) documents one Canadian university's founding story in her book *Unsettling the University*. Here she shows how the University of British Columbia (UBC) relied on the provincial colonial government's *University Endowment Act, 1907* to acquire and sell Musqueam lands to fund the university. More recently, other settler scholars have mobilized through research to explore how settlers used Indigenous lands to finance the development of universities across Canada (Chua, 2023). Peace has tied the deep-seated colonial roots of Canadian post-secondary institutions to the appropriation of Indigenous names (e.g., Huron College, Nipissing University, Mohawk College). Because of some of these disturbing settler colonial relationships, some Canadian university presidents—those of UBC and the University of Manitoba, for example—have, since the release of the TRC report, apologized for their universities' roles in perpetuating colonial ideologies and assisting in Canada's Indigenous assimilation project.

Given that the deep religious and political roots of many early universities fuelled the larger colonial project and the residential school system, the few Indigenous people who attended these universities were forced to assimilate into academic norms in troubling ways. For example, First Nations people, a group within the larger Indigenous population of Canada, were until 1921 legally barred from attending universities by the *Gradual Civilization Act* of 1857. In 1880, the settler nation-state increased its efforts to assimilate Indigenous people under the *Indian Act, 1876* by imposing involuntary enfranchisement laws for any First Nation male who attended a university. This exclusionary law was amended in 1920 to include First Nations women (Joseph, 2019). Enfranchisement was a settler colonial legal process that forced First Nations people to surrender their Treaty rights and terminate their Indigenous legal status and connections to

Indigenous reserve lands (Stonechild, 2006). While enfranchisement was an assimilation tactic presented by government as an "opportunity" to join the dominant white settler society, it involved eradicating Indigenous rights to land and eliminating the special status accorded to Indigenous peoples, thereby "getting rid of the Indian problem" and obfuscating the government's fiduciary responsibilities enshrined in Treaty agreements.

ASSUMED ASSIMILATION, 1951–1969

By 1951, First Nations people in Canada were permitted to apply and enter universities without losing their Indigenous legal status (Joseph, 2019; Stonechild, 2006). Euro-Western academic structures and colonial ideologies concerning Indigenous people, however, continued to prevail; it was assumed that Indigenous students would simply assimilate according to dominant white settler colonial disciplinary norms. During this period, however, owing to complex access issues, many Indigenous people did not attend universities. At the time, there were no institutions tracking Indigenous student populations at specific universities or across the sector. Yet one report indicated that by 1967 only about 200 of a potential 60,000 First Nations students had enrolled in Canadian universities (McCue, 2011). Moreover, most post-secondary institutions in Canada did not include Indigenous authorial voices in the curriculum or offer any specialized Indigenous student services or academic programs for Indigenous students. Although most enfranchisement laws were abandoned by the 1960s, governments along with most universities continued to woefully neglect Indigenous people's education and systemically exclude them through the maintenance of the Euro-Western university system. During this assumed assimilation period, the small first wave of Indigenous and First Nations women—which included Freda Ahenakew, Marlene Brant Castellano, Olive Dickason, Verna J. Kirkness, and Gail Valaskakis—graduated and began working in faculty positions in Canadian universities (Archibald, 2009, p. 127). While many early Indigenous scholars were courageous trailblazers, they were marginalized and often compelled early on to align their early scholarship within dominant disciplinary discourses in order to earn their degrees and survive in the academy (Steinhauer, 2001). After they entered the academy, however, many first-wave Indigenous scholars began to challenge the dominant Euro-Westernized institutional curriculum and policies and use their agency to influence deeper levels of institutional and disciplinary change. Arguably, these early Indigenous scholars cut a path through the deep colonial bush, thereby laying the trail for the second wave of Indigenous scholars following in their footsteps. Undoubtedly, Indigenous people's presence as both students and faculty members in Canadian universities during the assumed assimilation period was the result of a great struggle; without their presence and refusal to conform and assimilate completely, the changes witnessed and experienced in academia today would likely not have happened. We must never forget that Indigenous peoples today stand on the shoulders of an enduring intergenerational Indigenous collective.

INDIGENIZATION-INCLUSION, 1970–2015

The changes that took place in universities beginning in the 1970s were largely a result of broader political Indigenous resistance movements emerging in Canada and the United States. Movements that coalesced in the 1960s as the National Indian Brotherhood (now the Assembly of First Nations) in Canada, and the American Indian Movement in the United States, fomented political unrest to advance Indigenous rights. In Canada, Indigenous political resistance rapidly increased after the release of the Liberal government's White Paper of 1969, which attempted to terminate the federal government's special responsibility to First Nations peoples. These larger political moves stimulated Indigenous peoples collectively to create the National Indian Brotherhood, thereby compelling the federal government to recognize First Nations post-secondary educational rights. Soon after, the federal government began creating Indigenous educational policies as a social responsibility rather than a Treaty right (Fallon & Paquette, 2011; Stonechild, 2006). Despite disagreements between the Canadian government and Indigenous Nations, which have continuously asserted First Nations education as a lifelong right tied to nation-to-nation agreements (National Indian Brotherhood, 1972), the federal government, starting in the 1970s, began to provide funding to First Nations to create financial, academic, and student access programs (Malatest & Associates Ltd., 2004; Paquette & Fallon, 2010; Stonechild, 2006; Walters et al., 2004). The Post-Secondary Student Support Program (PSSSP) funding was announced in 1977; however, ten years later funding envelopes were capped (Stonechild, 2006), and the program has since failed to keep pace with inflation costs or with growing First Nations populations, creating a chronic backlog in post-secondary funding (Ottmann, 2017). While both K-12 education and post-secondary education are considered provincial mandates in Canada today, First Nations educational policies, including PSSSP, are driven by federal policy mandates and delegated in terms of their distribution to First Nations band and tribal councils. The jurisdictional divide between federal and provincial oversight of Indigenous post-secondary educational matters has arguably helped the federal government in not taking full responsibility and has thereby likely hindered advancements in First Nation people's full participation in higher education.

Between the 1970s and 2015, many federal policies were followed by provincial educational policies and programs aimed at helping post-secondary institutions establish Indigenous student services and Indigenous academic programs. Consequently, post-secondary policy initiatives beginning in the 1970s started to open doors to Indigenous students and some Indigenous faculty members (Pidgeon, 2016; Stonechild, 2006).

By the 1970s, through the advocacy and activism of Indigenous people, Indigenous student services centres have emerged in the provinces of Alberta, Saskatchewan, and British Columbia (Pidgeon, 2001) as a way to help create a welcoming environment for Indigenous students transitioning to university. By the 1990s, Ontario universities had finally caught up with those of the Western provinces, and began developing Indigenous student services units, which often start off (and remained until after the TRC report was released) as small, under-resourced units within the larger student affairs or equity departments of universities. As a result of these valiant first efforts, over 86 percent of Canadian post-secondary institutions offer some form of Indigenous student services on their campuses today (Universities Canada, n.d.). Moreover, a professionalization of Indigenous student affairs has emerged in higher education (Pidgeon, 2001, 2016). The National Aboriginal Student Services Association (NASSA) was founded in 2002 as part of the Canadian Association of College and University Student Services (CACUSS). NASSA aims to "empower institutions of higher learning to become welcoming environments where Aboriginal People can successfully pursue educational goals while maintaining their cultural identities" (NASSA, n.d.).

In the beginning, provincial governments incentivized post-secondary institutions through policy and temporary funding envelopes to support the development of Indigenous student services roles and units, often with the hope that universities would eventually take over fiscal responsibility. Despite advances in the area of provincial Indigenous educational policy, some scholars have critiqued provincial policy discourses for falling prey to a colonial mindset, including deficit and Othering approaches to positioning Indigenous students (Cherubini, 2012). For example, Ontario's Aboriginal post-secondary policies have been critiqued for perpetuating "closing the gap" discourses that tend to uncritically compare Indigenous to non-Indigenous students, often stigmatizing Indigenous students for underperforming while not recognizing the systemically embedded advantages built into post-secondary systems and society that privilege non-Indigenous learners. Furthermore, Indigenous post-secondary policy discourses tend to measure success in neoliberal ways that reinforce individualism and competition, notions entrenched in Western meritocratic assumptions—meritocracy being the dominant value system that rewards individuals (rather than groups) based on individual performance without recognizing systemic barriers that block certain groups from accessing and fully participating in educational contexts. In other words, Indigenous students in many liberal policy frameworks during this period were commonly misrepresented as underachieving, disengaged, or even resistant to learning (Maxwell et al., 2018). In many ways, this period's policy efforts to include Indigenous students in universities have leaned toward assimilating Indigenous students into the dominant university culture rather than toward changing the university system.

Despite the growth in Indigenous student affairs practices, however, research indicates that many Indigenous student services units within the larger university system at this time continued to face fiscal constraints as well as various structural, financial, and under-staffing issues (Pidgeon, 2001, 2016). Other research outlines how mainstream student success, development, and learning approaches have tended to disregard Indigenous, culturally unique approaches to student affairs, thereby marginalizing Indigenous students' needs (Shotton et al., 2013; Waterman et al., 2019).

In 1996, the report of the Royal Commission on Aboriginal Peoples (RCAP) called on the Government of Canada to take long-term, broad-based policy approaches to education and to respond to Canada's residential school legacy. The report made a number of recommendations to public post-secondary institutions, including the following: developing stronger recruitment, transition, and admission support mechanisms for Aboriginal students; offering Aboriginal courses across disciplines; instituting Aboriginal studies programs; creating Aboriginal advisory councils; appointing Aboriginal people to boards of governors; creating Aboriginal admission policies; instituting Aboriginal student unions; recruiting Aboriginal faculty members; and offering cross-cultural training to all employees (RCAP, 1996). In 2016, twenty years after the release of the RCAP report, members of the Indigenous community gathered for a National Forum on Reconciliation to mark the anniversary. The forum's final report reflected back on the RCAP's recommendations, and how they were "largely ignored at the time as they were considered too radical and difficult to implement" (School of Policy Studies & National Centre for Truth and Reconciliation, 2016, p. 1).

In 2007, the Indian Residential Schools Settlement Agreement came into effect after a long and arduous legal battle, establishing funds for the TRC, which began in 2008. The Government of Canada publicly apologized to former residential school survivors in 2008 and endorsed (although only partially) the United Nations Declaration on the Rights of Indigenous Peoples (UNDRIP) in 2010 by reserving objector status. Of the 140 nations that passed the UN declaration, Canada was among a handful of settler nations, including the United States, Australia, and New Zealand, that reserved this objector status.

During the Indigenization-inclusion period (1970–2015), Indigenous scholarship increased dramatically in the academy. In her book *Kaandossiwin: How We Come to Know*, Kathleen E. Absolon (2011) profiles the research stories of several Indigenous scholars emerging in universities during this period. Absolon documents how scholars continued to struggle in negotiating the colonial boundaries of Western research and advancing Indigenous knowledges in their research. Along with this growing Indigenous scholarly community, Indigenous academic pathways in law, education, social work, and Indigenous studies at the undergraduate and professional levels began to be laid down through the establishment of Indigenous scholarship and academic programs.

Some Indigenous academic journals were developed as early as the 1980s. For example, the *Canadian Journal of Native Education* was first published in 1980, followed by the *Canadian Journal of Native Studies* in 1981. Since then, Indigenous journals have been established in a number of interdisciplinary fields, though they continue to be marginalized under the academic publishing system and conventional research impact measurement standards (Smith, 2018).

Starting as early as the 1990s, Indigenous scholarship in Canada mapping Indigenous/Indigenist research paradigms (Wilson, 2008) and Indigenous research methodologies (Absolon, 2011; Archibald, 2009; Kovach, 2009b; S. Wilson, 2008) emerged in the academy. Despite this increased Indigenous scholarly presence, many Indigenous faculty members continued to struggle within the narrow Euro-Western academic confines that characterize these institutions, including tenure and promotion and annual performance-review processes (Henry, 2012; Louie, 2019).

In addition to Indigenous scholars entering the fields of education, law, and social work in large numbers, Indigenous studies emerged at the program level in many Canadian universities during this Indigenization-inclusion period. While the first Indigenous studies programs in Canada were instituted in the late 1960s (beginning at Trent University in Peterborough, Ontario), they, like Indigenous student services, grew out of Indigenous political unrest spurred by Indigenous activist movements in Canada and the United States (Taner, 1999). Since 1969, Indigenous studies programs have multiplied across the university sector in Canada, taking on many different names that accord with geographic and linguistic specificities and the location of their host universities: Native studies, Aboriginal studies, First Nations studies, and, most recently, Indigenous studies (Andersen & O'Brien, 2017). Algoma University, which has campuses in Brampton, Sault Ste. Marie, and Timmins, Ontario, adopted the name "Anishinaabe studies" to reflect its relationship with local First Nations and the surrounding land.

INDIGENIZATION-RECONCILIATION, 2015–PRESENT

In 2015, the TRC concluded its work with a report outlining 94 Calls to Action; these have been a major catalyst for national change ever since. The report led to a movement that has, arguably, contributed to the forging of deeper relationships between Indigenous and settler Canadians, and brought hope to many Indigenous people (including me) who have been fighting for change in the education system since the RCAP report was released in 1996. Among the TRC's 94 Calls to Action, thirteen focus on post-secondary education, specifically calling for mandatory courses in health, law, education, medicine, and media, as well as for a commitment to advancing Indigenous languages. The TRC's Calls to Action 43 and 44 demand the disavowal of the doctrine of discovery and the full implementation of UNDRIP. For the second time, in 2016, the Liberal government responded to the TRC by publicly supporting UNDRIP and removing the objector status previously enforced by the Conservative government; however, this public endorsement has yet to be fully recognized in Canadian law.

Since the release of the TRC's final report, Indigenizing policies in Canadian universities have risen dramatically in number. These include policy statements released by several national higher education organizations: in 2015, Universities Canada released *Principles on Indigenous Education*; in 2016, the Canadian Association of University Teachers (CAUT) released *Indigenizing the Academy*, the Federation for the Humanities and Social Sciences released *Reconciliation and the Academy*, and the Social Sciences and Humanities Research Council of Canada released *Guidelines for the Merit Review of Indigenous Research*; and in 2020, CAUT released *Bargaining for Indigenization of the Academy*.

Along with the rise of new policies in higher education, significant growth has occurred in the number of Indigenizing policy documents within universities themselves. Academic literature to date has documented Indigenous strategic planning processes (Pete, 2016; Pidgeon, 2016), the release of land acknowledgements (CAUT, 2016a; Wilkes et al., 2017), institutional residential school public apologies, and Indigenous faculty cluster hiring processes (Louie, 2019). I expand the scope of this documentation and organize the influx of Indigenizing policies in universities into seven broad categories: (1) academic, (2) operational, (3) employee relations, (4) organizational plans, (5) councils and committees, (6) data and research, and (7) public statements, including land acknowledgements.

In short, Indigenous educational policies in Canadian higher education compelled by the TRC's Calls to Action have pushed post-secondary institutions to move from student-centred approaches to Indigenous education to institution-wide approaches that focus on Indigenous inclusion across curriculum, governance, operations, research, and student affairs (Gaudry & Lorenz, 2018b; Pidgeon, 2016; Rigney, 2017). While broad policy categories are useful as a typology, they do not necessarily capture the challenging ways in which Indigenizing policies get enacted and constrained within ongoing settler colonial academic systems. The lived and embodied experiences of the Indigenous women administrators who participated in this book, however, highlight just how challenging these different types of Indigenizing policies are to put into practice. Centring participants' experiences illuminates the fact that Indigenizing policies are deeply contested and messy political processes that are difficult to implement and are limited by the ongoing nature of patriarchal colonialism.

Over the last ten years, Indigenous student services units have seen their mandates broadened, and Indigenous studies scholarship has proliferated across disciplines, resulting in a large number of Indigenous studies scholars in areas outside of law, education, and social work.

By 2015, nearly half of all Canadian universities offered an Indigenous studies undergraduate program, and at least three Canadian universities have since raised these programs to department or disciplinary status (the University of Alberta, Trent University, and the University of Winnipeg). Arguably, these institutional advances have helped to ensure that Indigenous peoples and ways of knowing are embedded in academic disciplinary discourses in much deeper ways. Despite academic shifts aimed at making room for Indigenous studies as a program, however, much debate still pervades the field of Indigenous studies. Some scholars see the elevation of Indigenous studies from program to department as an indication of a university's commitment to Indigenization (Henry et al., 2017). Some argue that Indigenous studies should aspire to be interdisciplinary—a borderless discourse much like women's or gender studies that links Indigenous perspectives, peoples, and communities across disciplines and fields of study (Weaver, 2007). Other scholars argue against an interdisciplinary approach to Indigenizing the academy, maintaining that such an approach would undermine the possibility of establishing Indigenous intellectual sovereignty (FitzMaurice, 2011). Most Indigenous studies programs and scholars maintain that the field must focus on exposing colonialism and advancing decolonization. As such, many scholars—myself included—assert that privileging local Indigenous languages, Indigenous ways of knowing, and land-based knowledges, and advancing Indigenous nationhood, are critical to the practice of Indigenous studies (Innes, 2010; Kidwell, 2009), while others emphasize the importance of studying global Indigenous matters (Champagne, 2007) or trans-Indigenous educational approaches. Because of ongoing debates about the nature and purposes of Indigenous studies, many scholars maintain that, sadly, the field is not yet widely recognized as an emerging discipline (Andersen & O'Brien, 2017). More troublingly, Indigenous studies undergraduate programs continue to face structural and fiscal constraints in operating within dominant Euro-Western academic, disciplinary, and budgetary structures (Henry et al., 2017), which I argue needs to be addressed as part of deeper institutional Indigenization efforts.

Since the release of the TRC report, universities have taken on broader approaches to Indigenizing the curriculum outside of Indigenous studies programs, approaches that often involve the hiring of Indigenous curriculum advisers (Raffoul et al., 2021) and engaging multiple sites of Indigenous intellectual leadership across the university (Brunette-Debassige et al., 2022). At the same time, new approaches to Indigenizing the university for the masses has generated some debate in recent years (Gaudry & Lorenz, 2018a). Many Indigenous education practitioners worry that Indigenization efforts cater to non-Indigenous students, as opposed to serving the needs and desires of the Indigenous community.

Nonetheless, shifts in higher education have moved universities from an Indigenization-inclusion approach toward one focused on "Indigenization-reconciliation" (Gaudry & Lorenz, 2018b). Gaudry and Lorenz (2018b) offer important scholarly contributions about the prevalence of Indigenization discourses in Canadian university policies. Like Gaudry and Lorenz (2018b), I argue that Indigenization practices on different campuses are not necessarily congruent with one another, even though universities commonly, since the TRC, assert that their policies fall under the same discursive banner. To help distinguish different Indigenizing policy rhetorics, Gaudry and Lorenz divide Indigenization policy approaches in practice into three broad categories: (1) Indigenization-inclusion, (2) Indigenization-reconciliation, and (3) decolonial-Indigenization. Their first category includes approaches that universities use when they recognize the need to change but are only prepared to include Indigenous people at superficial levels. Gaudry and Lorenz argue that this level of Indigenization subscribes to notions of a liberal "politics of recognition" (Coulthard, 2014) that relies on a form of "conditional inclusion" (Stein, 2019) and does not hinge on substantial and systemic change: "Indigenous inclusion policies expect Indigenous peoples to bear the burden of change...and naturalizes the status quo of academic culture" (Gaudry & Lorenz, 2018b, p. 220).

Gaudry and Lorenz's second category of Indigenization approaches, Indigenization-reconciliation, involves universities attempting to change at deeper structural and epistemic levels by hiring Indigenous senior leaders to drive systemic change, and making room for Indigenous epistemologies in curriculum and research. While an increasing number of universities are moving in this direction since the release of the TRC's final report in 2015, Gaudry and Lorenz assert that this level of change is not a norm, nor has it attained a decolonial level of transformation.

Finally, Gaudry and Lorenz propose a third and more radical category of approaches to Indigenization, which they term "decolonial-Indigenization." Approaches in this category involve attempts to move universities away from conventional hierarchies of governance and knowledge production and toward a realization of Indigenous resurgence and educational sovereignty. Gaudry and Lorenz and others—myself included—argue that no universities are currently achieving this level of decolonial change. These scholars assert that this level of change calls, more challengingly, for a new and dramatically different vision of university educational governance that will make it possible for Treaties to be observed and Indigenous resurgence and futurity to be advanced at multiple levels (Elson, 2019).

Focusing on decolonial reform, Andreotti et al. (2015) sketch a social cartographic map for evaluating decolonial reform approaches in higher education, a map that offers deeper analysis of the epistemological limits of existing approaches and policies. Andreotti et al. (2015) focus on the toxic and dependent relationship between modernistic thinking and the Euro-Westernized university. They argue that modernity is an assemblage of Euro-Western norms and ideologies that reproduces assumptions about ideas of progress, industrialization, democracy, linear time, scientific reasoning, and nation-states, ideas that precondition and order universities around universal reasoning and that limit decolonial possibilities. These authors assert that people must disavow their allegiance to the notion of changing the university, and instead take different approaches to decolonization, including witnessing or providing hospice to the dying modern university, or both (Grande, 2018a, 2018b; Machado de Oliveira, 2021; Tuck, 2018), and participate in system walkouts and system hacking (Andreotti et al., 2015). While at first glance, critiques of academic change centred on decolonial abolition may seem hypocritical since many (though not all) come from scholars, and scholars continue to work within and benefit from the academy, it is important to realize that many of these scholars are not simply arguing for the complete abandonment of Euro-Westernized universities. Instead, they are inviting everyone, including themselves, to critically unpack complex positionalities and complicities under current educational frameworks that continue to reproduce dominant Euro-Western systems of power. Moreover, many decolonial scholars argue that refocusing their limited time and energy on learning from the past and unlearning colonial ways of being and doing with the goal of preparing everyone for the transition to a decolonial future is paramount (Machado de Oliveira, 2021). Much of this collective pedagogical work is experimental and experiential, centring on refusing academic conventions (Grande, 2018a, 2018b) and learning in collectively embodied and artistic ways that strive to support the building of more sustainable futures.

INDIGENIZING THE ACADEMY

While the TRC has played an incredibly powerful role in recent years, it is important to note that Indigenous people in academic institutions have been calling on universities to "Indigenize" for well over two decades (Kirkness & Barnhardt, 1991; Battiste & Youngblood Henderson, 2009; Battiste et al., 2002; Heath-Justice, 2004; Kirkness & Barnhart, 2001; Kuokkannen, 2007, 2008; Mihesuah, 2003; Mihesuah & Wilson, 2004). The topic of Indigenizing the academy was the subject of a book coedited by Choctaw scholar Devon Abbott Mihesuah and Dakota professor Angela Cavender Wilson in 2004. These authors presented Indigenization as part of a larger decolonizing movement led by Indigenous people that seeks to reclaim dominant Euro-Westernized educational spaces to ensure that "Indigenous values and knowledge are respected; to create an environment that supports research and methodologies useful to Indigenous nation-building; to support one another as institutional foundations are shaken; and to compel institutional responsiveness to Indigenous issues, concerns and communities" (Mihesuah & Wilson, 2004, p. 2). Since 2004, similar Indigenous rights–based positions have advanced Indigenous educational self-determination (Justice, 2004) and Indigenous educational sovereignty in higher education (Aguilera-Black Bear & Tippeconnic, 2015; Battiste, 2018; Deer, 2015; RCAP, 1996; TRC, 2015; United Nations, 2007). While there is a growing recognition of Indigenous constitutional and global human rights in higher education (Battiste, 2018), some scholars have outlined the limits of using settler colonial legal frameworks to assert Indigenous sovereignty (Coulthard, 2014). Instead, these scholars assert the need to return to Indigenous forms of governance through Indigenous resurgence (Corntassel, 2012; L.B. Simpson, 2014).

Since the TRC, Indigenization, decolonization, and reconciliation discourses have proliferated in Canadian university policy discussions and processes aimed at organizational change (Cote-Meek, 2020; Davidson & Jamieson, 2018; de Leeuw et al., 2013; Elson, 2019; Gaudry & Lorenz, 2018b; Hanrahan, 2013; Ottmann, 2013, 2017; Pete, 2016, 2018; Sasakamoose & Pete, 2015; Pidgeon, 2016; Rigney, 2017). Mi'kmaq scholar Michelle Pidgeon (2016) defines institutional Indigenization as "meaningful inclusion of Indigenous knowledge into the everyday institutional policies and practices across all levels, not just in curriculum" (p. 79). Torres Strait scholar Lester-Irabinna Rigney (2017) describes Indigenization as "institutionalized change efforts towards Indigenous inclusion that uses a whole-of-university approach underpinned by principles of recognition and respect for Indigenous peoples, knowledges and cultures" (p. 45). In the university context, institutional Indigenization is intended to transform universities, to go beyond the Westernized university and Indigenization-inclusion approaches that focus on increasing Indigenous students' access and assimilation, and to move toward the reform of universities at a broader system level (Cote-Meek, 2020; Ottmann, 2013; Pidgeon, 2016; Rigney, 2017). As such, Indigenization-reconciliation, as a system-wide process of organizational change, is intended to transform the university across broad areas including academics; student affairs; personnel, planning, and policy; structural development; relational strategies; and approaches and philosophies (Minthorn & Chavez, 2015; Ottmann, 2013, 2017; Pidgeon, 2016).

The academic literature is rich with discussion of Indigenization in universities in the areas of policy (Axworthy et al., 2016; Battiste, 2018; Cote-Meek, 2020; de Leeuw et al., 2013; Elson, 2019; FitzMaurice, 2011; Gaudry & Lorenz, 2018a, 2018b; S. Johnson, 2016; Marker, 2017; Mawhiney, 2018; Ottmann, 2013, 2017; Pidgeon, 2016; Sasakamoose & Pete, 2015; D. Smith, 2017); curriculum and teaching (FitzMaurice, 2010; Gaudry & Lorenz, 2018a; Pete, 2015, 2018; Tanchuk et al., 2018); student affairs (Pidgeon, 2008; Shotton et al., 2013; Waterman et al., 2019); and research (Canadian Institutes of Health Research et al., 2014, 2018; FNIGC, 2014; Stiegman et al., 2015). While few studies have focused specifically on approaches to Indigenization, an increasing amount of academic writing (Bopp et al., 2017; Cote-Meek, 2018a, 2018b, 2020; Debassige & Brunette, 2018; Greenwood et al., 2008; Lavallee, 2020; Newhouse, 2016), policy briefs (Barnard, 2015; CAUT, n.d., 2016a, 2016b, 2018; Davidson & Jamieson, 2018; Mawhiney, 2018; Universities Canada, n.d., 2018), and media and social media coverage (Gaudry, 2016; Lavallee, 2019; MacDonald, 2016; Sterritt, 2019) has surfaced in the Canadian context in recent years.

INDIGENOUS REPRESENTATION IN UNIVERSITIES

Over the course of the four-part timeline outlined above, Indigenous people's participation in universities has grown. Exclusion and forced assimilation have given way to assumed assimilation, which has in turn given way to Indigenization-inclusion. Despite a steady increase in Indigenous participation, however, Indigenous people continue to be chronically under-represented when compared to non-Indigenous people in universities, and are thereby continuously marginalized at every representational level of the university—as students, staff, faculty, and administrators. Moreover, Indigenous people in the academy often struggle with experiences of racism shaped by the ongoing and violent nature of colonialism (Cote-Meek, 2014).

Indigenous Students

Although Indigenous representation in universities varies by institution and geographic region, on average, Indigenous undergraduate students now comprise approximately 5 percent of all students attending Canadian universities (CUSC, 2017). But while their numbers are increasing, the gap between the proportion of Indigenous and non-Indigenous students who attain university degrees is large and widening in Canada. In 2022, for example, only 10.3 percent of Indigenous people attained a degree, compared to 27.4 percent of non-Indigenous people, a startling 17 percent gap (Statistics Canada, 2022).

Indigenous students at both the undergraduate and the graduate levels face unique and often compounded barriers related to access, child care, relocation, transportation, family responsibilities, health, employment, and financial needs (Mendelson, 2006; Paquette & Fallon, 2010; Restoule et al., 2013). These complex and compounded barriers often require Indigenous students to "stop out" and take a break from their studies, an interruption that interferes with typical transition and graduation rates (Pidgeon, 2014). As well, Indigenous students often report negative experiences in their classrooms linked to anti-Indigenous racism and colonial biases (Clark et al., 2014; Cote-Meek, 2014; Gallop & Bastien, 2016).

Indigenous women are under-represented in universities compared to non-Indigenous women: only 13.1 percent of Indigenous women are reported to possess a university education, compared to 29.2 percent of non-Indigenous women—a 16 percent gap (Statistics Canada, 2022). At the same time, important differences also exist between Indigenous male and Indigenous female student groups. Indigenous women are nearly 6 percent more likely than Indigenous men to earn a degree (Statistics Canada, 2022). While Indigenous women represent a higher percentage of university students than do Indigenous men, they also tend to face unique financial needs connected to additional family responsibilities. Little research has focused on the gendered differences between Indigenous women and men attending Canadian universities, and especially on understanding Indigenous men's low participation (Brayboy & Solyom, 2017). There is even less academic literature examining the needs of LGBTQ2S Indigenous students.

Indigenous Faculty Members

Indigenous faculty members make up on average only 1.4 percent of the professoriate across universities in Canada (CAUT, 2018b). While the overall rate of Indigenous faculty members has increased four percentage points since 2006, Indigenous faculty members overall continue to be chronically under-represented, and experience higher rates of underemployment and lower earnings than non-Indigenous faculty members (CAUT, 2018b). When it comes to equitable earnings, Indigenous women professors earn 26.7 percent less than non-Indigenous women in the academy, and Indigenous male professors earn 26.3 percent less than non-Indigenous male professors (CAUT, 2018b). Moreover, important differences exist between Indigenous faculty member groups: Inuit are the least represented among Indigenous faculty, at only 0.03 percent; Métis representation is 0.54 percent and First Nations is 0.76 percent. While important distinctions were made between Indigenous groups in prominent reports on Indigenous faculty members, these reports did not distinguish between Indigenous men and women faculty members (CAUT, 2018b).

Beyond chronic under-representation of Indigenous faculty members, some literature has begun to identify unique challenges that universities face in attracting, hiring, and retaining Indigenous faculty members (Deer, 2020), and in particular, challenges that Indigenous professors face in the hiring process (Sensoy & Diangelo, 2017) and in the promotion and tenure process (Louie, 2019).

Indigenous Staff Members

Indigenous staff members are neither faculty members nor students, yet they are vital contributors to the enactment of Indigenization policies within Canadian universities. This employee group's representation, however, remains startlingly low at many universities. Under Canada's Federal Contractors Program, which began in the 1990s, all publicly funded institutions were mandated to collect workforce data on four designated groups: women, visible minorities, Aboriginal people, and people with disabilities. While most Canadian universities participated in the Federal Contractors Program, and approximately 3.8 percent of the general workforce (which includes staff and faculty members) was reported to be Indigenous (CAUT, 2018b), there is currently no university-specific Indigenous staff member data that can be used to compare Indigenous staff member representation rates across the higher education context specifically. This lack of adequate comparable Indigenous staff member workforce data in Canadian universities contributes to making this group and the labour they perform invisible.

Indigenous Administrators

The number of Indigenous administrators in Canadian universities is on the rise. Nevertheless, a survey conducted on the diversity gap in Canadian universities in 2019 reported a notable absence of Indigenous people in leadership roles in universities (Academic Women's Association, 2019). This intersectional diversity study examined the representation of Indigenous men, Indigenous women, and Indigenous non-binary people in U15 institutions (the top fifteen research-intensive universities) working at the levels of senior executive, dean, associate dean, departmental chair and director, and program chair and director. Malinda S. Smith, a black scholar and equity leader, reported that Indigenous people face chronic under-representation in leadership overall, although Indigenous women were represented at much higher levels compared to Indigenous men (Academic Women's Association, 2019). For example, 1.2 percent of senior executives identified as Indigenous women, whereas the numbers of Indigenous men and non-binary Indigenous people at this level were so low that they were unreported. Representation of Indigenous men, women, and non-binary groups was noted as nearly absent at the decanal level. At the associate dean level, Indigenous men and women were equally represented at 0.7 percent. At the departmental chair level, Indigenous women comprised 1.9 percent of administrators, while Indigenous men made up 1.1 percent. At the program chair level, Indigenous women were reported to make up 0.3 percent of administrators and Indigenous men, 0.1 percent, while the non-binary proportion was unreported. Overall, it is undeniable that Indigenous people are abysmally represented at all levels in Canadian universities—as students, staff, faculty, and administrators.

LIMITS OF REPRESENTATION

While Indigenous representation is one important indicator of the levels of equity and inclusion experienced by Indigenous people in Canadian universities, several issues persist concerning the use of representational data alone to measure levels of Indigenization. Beyond lack of culturally congruent institutional standards for gathering and reporting on Indigenous representational data, the numbers of Indigenous people in university settings, when collected, are often so low they go unreported. Not reporting low numbers is a common practice in quantitative studies in order to avoid the possibility of compromising individual identities, but this nonetheless contributes to the "asterisk phenomenon" (Shotton et al., 2013)—and thereby reinforces Indigenous people's invisibility, essentially erasing them from the representational data altogether. Other limits of the data on Indigenous representation include a lack of intersectional approaches to data analysis, a lack of comparative data on Indigenous staff members across the Canadian university sector, and a lack of data and reporting on non-binary Indigenous faculty members across the university sector.

In addition to gaps in the statistics describing Indigenous representation, it is important to recognize that Indigenous representation alone does not capture the full experiences of Indigenous people navigating the academy. Nor does representational data alone equate to deeper levels of Indigenization, such as structural changes and epistemological shifts in curriculum, which put the focus back on educational systems rather than individuals. As Gaudry & Lorenz (2018b) suggest, Indigenization work in Canadian universities takes place on a three-part continuum, and Indigenization-inclusion, the first step in this process, often focuses on "merely including more Indigenous peoples [as] it is believed that universities can indigenize without substantial structural change" (p. 219). Research in other settler colonial contexts has called for broad and culturally relevant approaches to evaluating Indigenous policies in higher education (Smith J., 2018).

INDIGENOUS EXPERIENCES OF LABOURING IN THE ACADEMY

Beyond using representational metrics to measure institutional Indigenization, very little academic literature focuses on Indigenous people's work experiences in universities. Some scholars have documented the anti-Indigenous racism faced by Indigenous people in the academy (Bedard, 2018; Brayboy, 2005; Brayboy et al., 2015; de Leeuw et al., 2013; Henry, 2012; Henry & Tator, 2009; Henry et al., 2017; Louie, 2019; Mohamed & Beagan, 2018; Monture, 2009; Pete-Willett, 2001). Anishnawbe scholar Renée Mazinegiizhigo-kwe Bédard reports on her own experiences of racism in the Euro-Western academy, which, she argues, attempts to make Indigenous people into token "Indians in the cupboard" to be brought out and displayed on settler colonial terms (Bedard, 2018). Other scholarship, in Canada (de Leeuw et al., 2013; Greenwood et al., 2008; Henry, 2012; Louie, 2019; Yahia, 2016), the United States (Almeida, 2015; Brayboy, 2005; Brayboy et al., 2015; Waterman, 2007), and Australia (Bunda et al., 2012), focuses on how Indigenous people experience ongoing racism in the academy and deal with additional expectations placed on them, expectations that often result in inequitable workloads and poor working conditions.

Yahia (2016) reported that Indigenous and racialized senior administrators in Canadian universities face continual racial microaggressions that complicate their leadership experiences and practices. Microaggressions are "the daily verbal, behavioural, or environmental indignities, whether intentional or unintentional, that communicate hostile, derogatory or negative racial slights and insults toward people of color" (Sue et al., 2007, p. 278).

In another US-based study of Native American staff members working in higher education, Deirdre Almeida (2015) documents five common expectations placed on Indigenous university leaders: (1) to overcommit in their positions and respond to all Indigenous-related matters; (2) to conform to predominantly white institutional cultures and ideologies, despite the cultural conflicts this may cause workers; (3) to not speak out or challenge policies, decisions, or mandates from their supervisors or senior administrators; (4) to live up to the dominant colonial biases placed on Indigenous people; and (5) to fulfill all of the above without any willingness on the part of the institution to understand systemic barriers and/or recognize Indigenous leaders' contributions (p. 163). Almeida links these five expectations to "racial battle fatigue" and burnout, which she argues is exacerbated for Indigenous people as it is intertwines with their intergenerational experiences of historical trauma.

In an analysis of the additional expectations often placed on Indigenous workers in the academy, Canadian settler scholar Sharon Stein (2019) argues that these expectations are connected to deeper forms of colonialism. "Conditional inclusion" places the responsibility for changing the university on Indigenous people themselves, implying that Indigenous people are still the problem. Stein suggests that the ultimate goal of this conditional form of inclusion is

> not to change the system, but [to] change individuals to ensure that the system runs more fairly and efficiently. This also includes individualistic interventions at the institutional level such as cultural competency training as a means to combat racism, hiring more counsellors as a means of addressing declining mental health, and offering more workshops and training at careers centres as a means to prepare students to face the competitive job market. (2019, p. 9)

Settler colonial conditional inclusion imposes change on Indigenous people through individualistic rather than structural or radical transformation. Scholars have described these types of inclusion-based approaches as "exploitative inclusivity" (Greenwood et al., 2008). I further connect them to the reproduction of "emotional labour," an affective economy (Hochschild,

1983) in which Indigenous people are expected to manage their feelings and expressions in order to fulfill settler colonial work expectations. This form of emotional labour for Indigenous and racialized people working within the settler colonial academy has been documented in the literature and associated with a sense of "fatigue" (Ahmed, 2017), "racial battle fatigue" (Almeida, 2015), and "reconciliation fatigue" (Anderson et al., 2019).

THE COLONIAL, GENDERED, AND RACIAL NATURE OF RECONCILIATION

Several scholars have documented the problematic expectations placed on Indigenous peoples working in the academy in the Indigenization-reconciliation period, specifically outlining how Indigenous peoples face and endure reconciliation fatigue associated with the increased demands placed on workplaces in the wake of the TRC. More troublingly, part of the fatigue results from the expectations placed on Indigenous peoples to continuously educate non-Indigenous people (Anderson et al., 2019; Greenwood et al., 2008; Stein, 2019; Styres et al., 2022). Inspired by the feminist concept of "emotional labour" (Hochschild, 1983), which refers to the undocumented and unpaid expectations placed on the members of certain professions to manage their emotions in the workplace, I argue that Indigenization-reconciliation work operates in a similar way. Indigenization-reconciliation places an additional emotional pressure on Indigenous peoples who work in the academy to lend their time and share their experiences as a type of emotional labour that is not necessarily part of their formal roles and responsibilities. When looking at the administrative work of Indigenous women in this book, I argue that reconciliation efforts become an institutionalized response that is deeply colonial, gendered, and racialized, and that places Indigenous women at the nexus of complex and ongoing colonial problems.

CHAPTER 3

NAVIGATING THE DISCURSIVE TERRAIN

In Canadian universities, the discourses of decolonization, **Indigenization**, reconciliation, and, more recently, Indigenous resurgence are often invoked interchangeably, even though vitally important distinctions exist between these key concepts and their specific lineages, goals, and intentions.

DECOLONIZATION

Calls to decolonize the academy can be linked to broader global political decolonization movements that have emerged in areas of the world impacted by Eurocentric dominance, including the Americas, Africa, Australia, and New Zealand, where Indigenous peoples have long been fighting colonial subordination and oppression. The term "decolonization" is often used in the academy to describe institutional transformative changes that challenge the dominance of Euro-Western ways of knowing in educational settings—in specific disciplines, in research, and, more recently, in institutional structures and policies.

Decolonization is, therefore, considered a transformative praxis in education—a combination of theory and practice that decentres and deconstructs the assumed supremacy of Euro-Western knowledge and ideologies in academia (Battiste, 2013) and, most importantly, attempts to divest the academy of colonial domination (D. Smith, 2017, p. 101). The decolonizing movement emerged in academic contexts in Canada well over twenty years ago (Battiste, 2002; Battiste et al., 2010) in relation to broader global Indigenous movements (L. Smith, 1999). While some scholars have attributed decolonization to a post-colonial theory grounded within a critical paradigm (Denzin et al., 2008), others recognize that there are important distinctions between post-colonial theory and decolonial praxis (L. Smith, 1999; G. Smith, 2003). In particular, (1) decolonization recognizes that colonization is an ongoing and pervasive structure and ideology in settler colonial contexts, and (2) decolonization is not merely a theory but a praxis-centred methodological approach intended to destabilize the dominance of Euro-Western white colonial supremacy through transformative action and to make room for Indigenous knowledges (L. Smith, 1999).

While decolonizing the university does not necessarily require the total rejection of Euro-Western knowledge and structures (Battiste, 2013; L. Smith, 1999), it does involve unsettling the dominance of Euro-Western knowledge hierarchies. Moreover, there are many debates around decolonial approaches in education, including strong critiques of discursive tendencies toward a metaphorization of decolonization that acts as a "settler move toward innocence" (Tuck & Yang, 2012, p. 1). Within these criticisms of decolonization, scholars argue against the common disassociation of the term "decolonization" from its meaning: the repatriation of Indigenous land and life. Moreover, scholars such as Tuck and Yang (2012) assert that when metaphorization of decolonization occurs in education, Indigenous educational projects get trapped within dominant white liberal frameworks of education, which are complicit in reproducing settler colonial power. In the context of education, some scholars have argued, however, that decolonizing our thinking and curriculum in universities must occur first; only then can Indigenization work emerge (George, 2019; Grafton & Meloncon, 2020). The political purpose of decolonizing the academy in this sense is to transform the education system, to decentre colonial ideologies, structures, and systems of power, and to create space that not only elevates Indigenous voices and agency but advances Indigenous languages and ways of knowing (Battiste, 2000; L. Smith, 1999) and asserts Indigenous educational sovereignty (Gaudry & Lorenz, 2018b).

Indigenous leadership and policies in universities can play a powerful role in advancing decolonial and Indigenizing agendas; however, they are constrained by the structurally embedded nature of ongoing settler colonialism within universities and nation-states. Considering these constraints, scholars like Lynn Lavallee (2020) and others (Andreotti et al., 2015; Grande, 2018a, 2018b; Tuck, 2018) have questioned whether decolonization as an institutional reform process in universities is even possible. Lavallee argues that decolonization is an "overly ambitious and unrealistic" institutional project (2020, p. 120). Nonetheless, calls to decolonize the university have been used by many scholars, leaders, and activists alike to demand change and a more equitable allocation of space and resources for Indigenous people and Indigenous ways of knowing in higher education. According to one policy document focusing on the social sciences and humanities, decolonizing work is defined as "unsettling the impacts of colonial histories, ideologies, experiences and legacies on disciplines, archives, canons, curricula, methodologies, and pedagogies, as well as on structures of governance, institutional design, and cultures, symbols, and ceremonies" (AC-EDID, 2021, p. 6).

INDIGENIZATION

Indigenization in the university refers to the naturalization of Indigenous epistemologies and ways of knowing (Battiste & Youngblood, 2009).

Unlike decolonization, which is grounded in a critical paradigm, Indigenization emerges within an Indigenous paradigm—within Indigenous epistemology, ontology, and axiology (Absolon, 2011; Chilisa, 2012; S. Kovach, 2009; S. Wilson, 2008). Shawn Wilson (2001) defines an Indigenous paradigm as a set of beliefs about the world and the acquisition of knowledge that is in stark contrast to Western ways of knowing. Although some scholars have problematized structuralist and essentialist tendencies of Indigenization discourses, which position Indigenous and Western ways of knowing in blunt opposition to each other, others have argued for a post-structural dialogue that permits fluidity between these ways of knowing (FitzMaurice, 2011; Nakata et al., 2012). For example, two-eyed seeing frameworks advocate for bringing the strengths of Western and Indigenous world views together (Marshall et al., 2006). This braiding approach to Indigenous research is prominent in Indigenous health, but it is not without its tensions as research continues to be taken up in colonial contexts where Indigenous knowledges are often misinterpreted and reduced to sub-levels of knowing (Broadhead & Howard, 2021). Despite these tensions, other scholars have asserted the need for "strategic essentialism" to understand the rationale for transformative change (Spivak, 1998). Strategic essentialism calls for temporarily advancing simple, static notions of, for example, Indigenous and Western knowledges, in order to demonstrate how distinctly these overarching paradigms operate, how dominant colonial power privileges Western understandings over Indigenous, and, more importantly, how Western colonial ideologies continue to Other Indigenous people and ways of knowing in higher education.

In deepening Indigenizing approaches to education, many scholars have taken nation-specific approaches to theorizing Indigenization (Battiste, 2018; Kovach, 2009; L. Smith, 1999), mapping out complexities and multiple diversities across Indigenous ways of knowing, Nations, and languages, and thereby pushing back against essentializing and pan-Indian understandings. Other scholars have outlined common relational ontologies across Indigenous epistemologies that counter Western anthropocentric ways of knowing (Battiste, 2002).

Lori Campbell (2021), Nehiyaw Apithakosisan scholar and leader, problematizes institutional-Indigenization approaches in universities, especially when Indigenous strategic plans do not properly define Indigenization. She argues that this lack of definition in some strategic documents opens the door to co-optation and misinterpretation by non-Indigenous people. Despite the troubling ways that Indigenization work operates in the academy, I argue that Indigenizing approaches to education must assert Indigenous autonomy over Indigenous projects. While Indigenous ways of knowing must be recognized as ontologically distinct, approaches to change in the university must strive to move toward Indigenous educational sovereignty in academic oversight, theorizing, research methodologies, and pedagogies.

RECONCILIATION

Since the TRC began its work in 2008, reconciliation discourses have been on the rise in Canadian institutions. Truth and reconciliation processes, however, have broader global connections with movements that aim to undo damage enforced by colonial governments. In Canada, the TRC defines reconciliation as a process of "establishing and maintaining a mutual respectful relationship between Indigenous and non-Indigenous peoples" (TRC, 2015, p. 1). The National Centre for Truth and Reconciliation, affiliated with the University of Manitoba, aims to document the history of, and educate Canadians about, this country's ongoing colonial relationship with Indigenous peoples. Through processes of education, establishing safe spaces, and working toward respectful relationships between Indigenous and non-Indigenous peoples, reconciliation, as Métis scholar and leader Ry Moran (2016) argues, must be more than conversations; it must accompany significant action and the assertion of an Indigenous rights–based framework. According to *Calls to Action Accountability: A 2020 Status Update on Reconciliation*, a report compiled by Anishnawbe scholar Eva Jewell and settler scholar Ian Mosby (2020), three barriers remain to implementing the TRC's Calls to Action: (1) a vision among policy-makers of the "public interest" as generally excluding Indigenous peoples; (2) the deeply paternalistic attitudes of politicians, bureaucrats, and other policy-makers; and (3) the ongoing legacy and reality of structural racism.

Like decolonization discourses, reconciliation discourses are rife with conceptual ambiguity, generate much debate, and are widely contested by scholars and activists alike. The concept of reconciliation has been critiqued for its roots in Christianity and the project of atonement (Lavallee, 2020), which centres on healing relationships between Indigenous and non-Indigenous people without necessarily attending to power inequities and ongoing colonial structures. By far the most pervasive critique of reconciliation is that the settler colonial state continues intact, and reconciliation discourses get misused by political actors to advance white liberal settler and assimilationist agendas. As Tuck and Yang (2012) assert, "reconciliation rescues settler normalcy." Thus, scholars have critiqued reconciliation in Indigenizing policies in universities for falling prey to performative approaches and "reconciliation rhetoric" (Gaudry & Lorenz, 2018b). Some scholars have attributed reconciliation to a "politics of recognition" that fails to grapple with the impossibility of separating policies from the ongoing structures of settler colonialism (Coulthard, 2009; Daigle, 2009; Gaudry & Lorenz, 2018b). Indeed, Mushkego Cree scholar Michelle Daigle has argued that reconciliation in universities is often just a performance—a spectacle where "public, large-scale and visually striking performances of Indigenous suffering and trauma [occur] alongside white settler mourning and recognition" (2019, p. 706).

Despite widespread contention, some leaders and scholars have also recognized that polarizing dichotomous views associated with reconciliation often hinge on problematic binaries between the colonizer and colonized, and, according to Asch et al. (2018), sometimes justify a totalizing, rejectionist stance based on the assumption that all approaches fall prey to co-optation and recolonization. In similar ways, in their edited book *Troubling Truth and Reconciliation in Canadian Education: Critical Perspectives*, Sandra Styres and Arlo Kempf (2022) argue for the need to critically problematize reconciliation discourses, not dismiss them altogether. These scholars argue against a rejectionist stand on the usage of reconciliation, as this does not nuance reconciliation in practice, nor does it complicate different approaches, different actor positions, or the complex interdependences that Indigenous people have with settler systems.

RESURGENCE

More recently, academic discourses emerging around Indigenous resurgence have focused on revitalizing Indigenous ways of knowing, Indigenous languages, land-based education, and Indigenous nation building (Corntassel, 2012; Gaudry & Lorenz, 2018b; L.B. Simpson, 2014). In this educational context, Indigenous resurgence work in universities actively resists Indigenous people's and Nations' dependencies upon the settler colonial state's education system. According to Gaudry and Lorenz (2018b), decolonization and resurgence can work in parallel to re-centre Indigenous ways of knowing and rebuild political orders through education. Cherokee scholar Jeff Corntassel (2012) agrees that decolonization and resurgence can be intimately interconnected.

Like Indigenization, resurgence in education strives to revitalize Indigenous ways of knowing as well as Indigenous nation-building projects. Two powerful examples of Indigenous resurgence work are happening within the Dechinta Bush University and the Yellowhead Institute. The Dechinta Bush University is a partnership between Yellowknives

Dene First Nation and the University of British Columbia. It is dedicated to supporting self-determining and sustainable Indigenous communities rooted in Indigenous knowledge by offering an array of university accredited and non-accredited programs on the land. The Yellowhead Institute is a First Nations–led research centre supported through Toronto Metropolitan University that focuses on policies related to First Nations lands and governance. Both initiatives, while housed in and supported through universities, ensure that Indigenous communities govern the educational priorities.

While resurgence work offers some powerful ways to redirect university educational aims and research agendas, Indigenous resurgence work, like decolonization work, is not immune to settler colonial structural challenges and a "politics of distraction" (G. Smith, 2003)—that is, the ways in which settler colonial agendas infiltrate and constrain Indigenous educational priorities. Thus, Corntassel (2012) advocates Indigenous resurgence as an everyday practice, which calls on Indigenous people to be vigilant and willing to assert acts of resistance to the settler colonial status quo. He further warns Indigenous people to be continuously aware of how settler co-optation can become a distraction that occurs when Indigenous people become overly consumed with settler priorities that do not serve Indigenous educational priorities and needs. I, too, assert that Indigenous resistance as a refusal is a necessary leadership and policy disposition that is useful in guarding against ongoing settler dynamics and the politics of distraction.

NAVIGATING CONCEPTUAL AMBIGUITY AND DISCURSIVE APPROACHES

In this research, Indigenous women administrators attested to conceptual debates and ambiguities, which produced embodied tensions and challenges for them in their leadership practices in universities. The common either/or positioning of Indigenizing and decolonizing rhetoric created ambivalence for leaders doing Indigenizing work. For example, participants identified binary discourses that positioned Indigenizing policy work inside the academy as reformist, and Indigenizing (or resurgence) work outside the academy as revolutionist. Indigenization as reformist tended to be cast simply as supporting the maintenance of universities, and therefore complicit in reproducing settler authority and power. Indigenization as revolutionist, on the other hand, was often depicted as simply occurring outside the academy and as more radical, not complicit with colonialism, and concerned with the total rejection of settler power in favour of advancing Indigenous goals.

To interrogate these absolutist and binary discourses, I return to Asch et al.'s (2018) scholarship on reconciliation and resurgence in legal reform work in Canada, scholarship in which those authors identified similar separatist discourses occurring in their field that they argue polarizes and fosters divisions in Indigenous communities. They claim not only that these positions contributed to divisions within Indigenous communities, but that dichotomous and simplistic thinking obscured the nuances of Indigenous people associated with the academy doing Indigenous resurgence work in different places and at different levels. I argue that similar dichotomous discourses shape our understandings of Indigenizing leadership and policy work related to the university. Furthermore, the discursive nature of positioning Indigenizing work in dichotomous ways invisibilizes Indigenous women administrators' labour; it undermines the complex and intersectional positionalities that stem from their working in between as well as within, against, and outside the university (Kelley, 2016). Moreover, this simplistic way of framing Indigenous work conceals larger systemic conditions of global capitalism, patriarchy, and settler colonialism, which are at play in all facets of Indigenous life. It is therefore important to recognize the conceptual complexities that underpin Indigenous work occurring both within and outside the academy; otherwise, I argue, we risk covering up complex systems of power, position, and experience, and we risk covering up the work of Indigenous women and others who are struggling to transform educational systems.

CHAPTER 4

INDIGENOUS WOMEN *in* EDUCATIONAL LEADERSHIP

Considering the history and ongoing nature of settler colonialism in Euro-Western universities in general, it is unsurprising that Eurocentric gendered conceptions of leadership are not only embedded in academic structures but are taken for granted in daily administrative practices and norms. The field of educational leadership is well-known for its deep roots in administrative science, a theoretical grounding that privileges an "ontology of hierarchy" (Malott, 2010). An ontology of hierarchy favours the relationship that leaders have with formal bureaucracies, which are often driven by underlying scientific management as well as behaviourist and systems theories, all of which are entrenched within taken-for-granted notions of managerialism. Dominant leadership discourses rooted in administrative scientific reasoning have long defined notions of "good leadership" through individualist and masculinist norms that portray leadership as a politically neutral practice with universal characteristics easily applied to any context.

Looking at women in educational leadership, white feminist scholar Jill Blackmore's (1999) research has been helpful in terms of highlighting the gendered ways in which women in general are often troubled in educational administration. Blackmore traces this troubling back to masculinist ideologies of leadership that are connected to larger structures of patriarchy embedded in administrative theories and organizational practices that tend to place men in leadership roles, on the assumption that men are more objective, assertive, and confident in their decisions and characteristics.

Arguably, similar patriarchal colonial leadership tropes have infiltrated Indigenous women's representations in leadership. Consider, for example, the ways that Indigenous leadership has been portrayed in historical accounts involving great male Chiefs and warriors who fought against colonial invasion. These representations, although often colonial and racist in nature, have tended to exclude Indigenous women's and nonbinary people's contributions to political and social life. We can also point to the ways that hetero-patriarchal and settler colonial policies, such as those stemming from the *Indian Act*, have long permeated Indigenous communities and eroded Indigenous women's political, religious/spiritual, and economic positions inside and outside Indigenous communities (Anderson, 2000; Lajimodiere, 2013; Sunseri, 2010; Thomas, 2018; Voyageur, 2008). Eurocentric colonial and masculinist ideas of leadership have infiltrated both Indigenous and non-Indigenous communities, perpetuating false notions that only Indigenous men, and not Indigenous women, can be leaders. For example, under Canada's patriarchal *Indian Act*, Indigenous men were automatically granted the status of heads of households, thereby displacing Indigenous women's traditional roles in many families, communities, and Nations (Lajimodiere, 2013). This displacement had particularly devastating impacts on matriarchal Indigenous societies (e.g., Haudenosaunee) in which Indigenous women held prominent governing positions, such as that of Clan Mother

(Sunseri, 2011; Thomas, 2018). Moreover, when Indigenous women married non-Indigenous or non-Status men, they lost their Indigenous legal rights, and they and their children were systemically removed from Indigenous communities, denied access to the Nation, to land, and forced to relocate into settler-dominated contexts where they often struggled to survive (Thomas, 2018). Indigenous women were further disenfranchised under settler colonial laws through the denial of their participation in settler-imposed political governance and formal leadership positions both in First Nations community contexts, between 1869 and 1951, and in non-Indigenous societies until the 1960s (Thomas, 2018). Such sexist colonial policies have long eroded Indigenous women's political voices and access to leadership positions in different contexts. Indeed, such notions of Indigenous women are still prevalent today, and still reinforce false beliefs that Indigenous women are not capable, deserving, or effective in different leadership contexts.

In educational leadership research, the "double bind" has been associated with Indigenous women's educational leadership experiences (Fitzgerald, 2003a). Indigenous and other racialized women become marked as the "Other-within" (Blackmore, 2010), a notion that draws on an original concept put forth by Black feminist scholar Patricia Hill Collins (1986). Settler scholar Tanya Fitzgerald (2006) elaborates on the double bind to propose a "triple bind" related to three intersecting barriers experienced by Indigenous women leaders working in (1) a predominantly white world, (2) an educational system that values patriarchal leadership (and cognitive imperialism), and (3) a context where Indigenous women tend to be Othered. Fitzgerald argues that the triple bind places Indigenous women educational leaders at the margins in educational leadership contexts, and in impossible dichotomous positions (i.e., they are themselves when working with Indigenous communities, but the Other when working within settler institutions). The experience of being Othered in academic spaces has been similarly theorized by

Sara Ahmed (2000) in her articulation of "embodying strangers," which describes the Othering experience of racialized women when confronting the "phenomenology of whiteness" (Ahmed, 2007b), which is pervasive in academic spaces, and which causes racialized bodies to feel "out of place" (Puwar, 2004). Ahmed argues that the experience of non-white bodies encountering a phenomenology of whiteness, while it is often difficult to convey in words, is nevertheless felt by the way such bodies are received, questioned, marked, obstructed, and disciplined in academic spaces.

For Indigenous women leaders, Othering can also conjure up complex racial, colonial, and gendered stereotypes unique to an Indigenous phenomenological (embodied) experience, which is further related to the infamous "princess/squaw" binary that can be traced back to early colonists' depictions of Indigenous women (Green, 1975; Lajimodiere, 2013). The princess stereotype tends to portray Indigenous women as good, seeking alliance with white men and institutions, and generally supportive of the settling process. The princess stereotype, however, makes Indigenous women traitors to Indigenous communities, and paints them as white and assimilated (Green, 1975). On the other hand, the squaw stereotype is associated with notions of Indigenous savagery (as opposed to civility); the squaw is depicted as resisting change and standing in the way of progress. In an academic administrative context, I argue that these long-held tropes continue to mark Indigenous women's experiences.

Mohawk scholar Audra Simpson (2016) writes about the perceptions and misrepresentations of Indigenous women leaders in settler colonial contexts, affirming that "when you are an Indigenous woman, your flesh is received differently" (p. 22). To argue this point, Simpson exposes the violent mistreatment of Mushkego Cree Chief Theresa Spence by the mainstream media during her six-week hunger strike as part of the Idle No More movement in Canada, in the winter of 2012–13. During this time, Chief Spence fasted on Parliament Hill to bring attention to deplorable housing conditions in her far northern Attawapiskat First Nation community. During Spence's fast, the mainstream media often criticized and objectified her body, accusing her of "cheating" because she drank fish broth during the hunger strike. The media comments that followed often centred on Chief Spence's body, in oppressive and violently gendered, racialized, and body-shaming ways. Her leadership was further questioned with reference to the "crooked Indian" stereotype (Palmater, 2014), a common myth based on notions of corrupt band governance that is often used as a settler colonial tactic of distraction and a way to pathologize Indigenous leaders who seek to interrogate the colonial system. With Spence's life on the line, the online discourse clearly surfaced deeply engrained anti-Indigenous racism and sexism, which in turn reaffirmed settler colonialism's pervasive and often hidden pathological desire to disappear Indigenous women (NIMMIWG, 2019).* Damaging racial, colonial, and gendered stereotypes have long been imposed on Indigenous women generally; they also surfaced in my research. The imposition of these ongoing settler colonial markings on Indigenous women, I argue, infringe upon women's "embodied sovereignty" (L.B Simpson, 2017). Embodied sovereignty within Indigenous epistemology is a relational and collective ontology rooted in Indigenous storytelling and is connected to one's relationship to one's community, to the land, and to a holistic way of knowing. As Leanne Betasamosake Simpson (2013b) asserts, it is the freedom to take control of our bodies, to feel at home in our skin, to express our embodied experiences. I extend that to argue that embodied sovereignty is also about being holistically present in our bodies, and moreover, about having agency over our experiences in and out of academic spaces.

Despite the horrific colonial and gendered dimensions of Indigenous experience in leadership, the field of educational leadership has done

---

* "NIMMIWG" refers to the National Inquiry into Missing and Murdered Indigenous Women and Girls, an official body whose mandate was to investigate and make recommendations to address the epidemic of missing and murdered Indigenous women, girls, and Two Spirit people in Canada.

little to disentangle and critically complicate the underlying patriarchal forces that perpetuate dominant leadership assumptions, which has had massive consequences on women in leadership in general, and devastating impacts on Indigenous women leaders in particular. While feminist leadership research has challenged gendered assumptions prevalent in dominant educational leadership research (Acker, 2012; Ah Nee-Benham & Cooper, 1998; Blackmore, 2010, 1999; Blackmore & Sachs, 2007; Ngunjiri & Gardiner, 2017), Indigenous researchers recognize the dominance of white women's voices in feminist leadership discourses (Ah Nee-Benham & Cooper, 1998; Ambler, 1992; Blackmore, 2010; Faircloth, 2017; Fitzgerald, 2003a, 2003b, 2004, 2006, 2010, 2014; V. Johnson, 1997; Johnson et al., 2003; Lajimodiere, 2011; Santamaría, 2013; Warner, 1995).

In the Indigenous scholarly circles of Turtle Island, scholars have focused on the erasure of Indigenous women in research in general (Anderson, 2000; Anderson & Lawrence, 2012; Maracle, 1996; Monture-Angus & Mcguire, 2009), the experiences of Indigenous women working in the academy (Archibald, 2009b; Mihesuah, 2003; Monture, 2009), and, more recently, Indigenous women in leadership (Anderson, 2009; Cote-Meek, 2020; Faircloth, 2017; Fitzgerald, 2003a, 2003b, 2004, 2006, 2010, 2014; V. Johnson, 1997; Johnson et al., 2003; Lajimodiere, 2011; Lavallee, 2020; Maracle et al., 2020; Santamaría, 2013; Sunseri, 2011; Thomas, 2018; Voyageur, 2008; Warner, 1995).

Settler scholar Tanya Fitzgerald (2014), in a study that focused on Indigenous women educational leaders in settler colonial contexts, including in Canada, reported two ongoing myths associated with women's leadership in higher education: (1) that women's increasing representation has resolved inequities, and (2) that women's presence in leadership has solved the gender problem in leadership. Fitzgerald argues that despite women's access and participation in educational leadership contexts, ongoing organizational practices and cultures persist, and continue to have a negative impact on women's experiences. In other words, while women may be given access to leadership roles in higher education, they are still expected to lead in dominant white, masculinist ways and to conform to Euro-Western administrative norms and expectations. Métis scholar Lynn Lavallee (2020) concurs with the existence of gendered dynamics in administration in Canadian universities, and explicitly adds colonial dimensions of leadership among the experiences of Indigenous women in the academy. Lavallee argues that, while universities are eager to promote Indigenous women to senior leadership roles, in practice they often position these women as "exotic puppets" to be manipulated and pressured under dominant colonial and gendered norms. She also exposes the ways that age-old colonial tropes around the "Indian problem" surface in Indigenous women's leadership experiences: "There is an expectation that [Indigenous women leaders] socialize and mould other Indigenous people who do not fall in line. You are meant to deal with what is often perceived as the Indian problem on your own" (2020, p. 27).

In other studies, Indigenous women leaders often talked about the gender-related forms of oppression they experience in educational leadership roles (Ah Nee-Benham & Cooper, 1998; Ambler, 1992; Cote-Meek, 2020; Faircloth, 2017; Fitzgerald, 2003a, 2003b, 2004, 2006, 2010, 2014; V. Johnson, 1997; Lajimodiere, 2011, 2013; Lavallee, 2020; Tippeconnic-Fox et al., 2015; Santamaría, 2013; Voyageur et al., 2015). Anishnawbe scholar Denise Lajimodiere (2011) uncovered various gender biases, including resistance from Indigenous men in relation to patriarchal male discomfort and from other Indigenous women, identifying the latter as a form of lateral violence. Scholars associate these experiences of Indigenous women leaders with the patriarchal nature of colonialism, which is omnipresent within dominant educational environments and Indigenous communities.

In this study, I found that troubling colonial and gendered authenticity discourses would occasionally surface as some participants talked about Indigenous women's leadership. Some participants talked about the characterization by others of Indigenous women leaders working in the academy as assimilated and therefore less than Indigenous. There is no doubt that Indigenous women struggled with and expressed threats of colonial assimilation and co-optation when leading in the Euro-Western academy; however, automatically positioning all Indigenous women working in university administration as assimilated is to fall prey to troubling colonial authenticity discourses. Such colonial depictions not only undermine Indigenous women who occupy leadership roles (and prevent others from taking on formal leadership roles altogether), they suggest that Indigenous women lack agency. This positioning of Indigenous women in leadership falsely perpetuates distorted colonial and gendered stereotypes based on the infamous princess/squaw binary, which positions the Indigenous woman labouring inside the university as a type of princess-servant to be instrumentalized by the white patriarchal institution. Furthermore, such positioning ignores the possibility that Indigenous women leaders are agentic and can be politically motivated, strategically astute, and independent in their thinking, capable of engaging in various spaces and through various methods of leadership while continuing to be uniquely and authentically Indigenous. Moreover, this simplistic positioning fails to recognize that Indigenous women administrators in the academy can be deeply invested in the Indigenous collective project of advancing Indigenous educational sovereignty.

Aside from reports of the gendered and colonial experiences of oppression among Indigenous women educational leaders, a growing body of work has deliberately shifted away from a deficit way of thinking about gender and Indigeneity to one that acknowledges Indigenous women's epistemic strengths and resilience in the face of colonialism (Ah Nee-Benham & Cooper, 1998; Cote-Meek, 2020; Faircloth, 2017; Johnson et al., 2003; Krumm & Johnson, 2011; Lajimodiere, 2013; Lavallee, 2020; Maracle et al., 2020; Santamaría, 2013; Sunseri, 2010;

Thomas, 2018; Tippeconnic-Fox et al., 2015). These strengths are associated with Indigenous women's epistemic-informed gender identities and Indigenous epistemologies (Ah Nee-Benham & Murakami-Ramalho, 2010; Johnson et al., 2003; Maracle et al., 2020; Santamaría, 2013), and with the reclamation by Indigenous women of traditional leadership roles and responsibilities (Ambler, 1992; Krumm & Johnson, 2011; Lajimodiere, 2013; Tippeconnic-Fox et al., 2015). For example, Krumm & Johnson (2011) explored Indigenous women presidents of tribal colleges in Canada and the United States. In this study, the authors connected Indigenous women's leadership to their traditional roles as matriarchs, caregivers, and nurturers, and found that gender barriers related to leadership were often a result of mainstream educational environments, which are not as prevalent in tribal educational institutions. Additionally, Lajimodiere (2013) has written powerfully about the role that Indigenous women play as teachers and leaders in Indigenous societies, and how women are the heart of a Nation's sovereignty.

BEING CALLED TO INDIGENOUS EDUCATIONAL LEADERSHIP

While the concept of leadership has proliferated in academic discourses across many disciplines over the last forty years, Indigenous epistemic perspectives on leadership across disciplines and in the context of educational leadership are vastly under-represented, and even silent. Researchers have thus called for an increase in Indigenous leadership perspectives in education overall (Ah Nee-Benham & Murakami-Ramalho, 2010; Fallon & Paquette, 2014; Hohepa, 2013). Globally, scholars have examined Indigenous educational leadership in universities in some settler colonial contexts, including Australia (Coates et al., 2022), New Zealand (Povey et al., 2021), and North America (Minthorn & Chavez, 2015). In the United States and Canada, literature has emerged from different educational contexts—the mainstream K–12 level (Bird et al., 2013; Santamaría & Santamaría, 2012); within First Nations, Métis, or Inuit community settings (Blakesley, 2008; Fallon & Paquette, 2014; Goddard & Foster, 2002; Ottmann, 2009; Robinson et al., 2019; Umpleby, 2007); in tribal college settings in the United States (Ambler, 1992; Crazy Bull et al., 2015; Johnson et al., 2003; Krumm & Johnson, 2011); and in mainstream higher educational environments (Brower, 2016; Cote-Meek, 2020; Faircloth, 2017; Ford et al., 2018; Gomes, 2016; Gunstone, 2013; Hardison-Steven, 2014; Lavallee, 2020; Minthorn & Chavez, 2015; Ottmann, 2013, 2017; Pidgeon, 2008; Santamaría, 2013; Warner, 1995; Yahia, 2016).

As a result of complex historical and contemporary forces playing out in universities, dominant educational leadership theories and practices tend to privilege apolitical scientific and instrumentalist positions of leadership over critical positions (Gunter, 2001). In other words, leaders tend to be invested in maintaining educational systems rather than transforming them. Gunter (2001) outlines four main positions prevalent in educational leadership practices: scientific, instrumentalist, humanistic, and critical. She argues that scientific and instrumentalist approaches dominated by positivist ontology and epistemology are widespread in educational leadership research and practices. Scientific and instrumentalist approaches tend to be invested in meeting standardized organizational and educational outcomes, whereas critical positions prioritize redressing power imbalances and advancing emancipatory aims for marginalized groups. In the fields of social justice research, similar research in the areas of organizational change and educational leadership asserts that structural functionalist and interpretivist epistemologies dominate organizational change theories over critical paradigms, forming what Colleen Capper (2019) has described as a critical "epistemological unconsciousness." Structural functionalism tends toward improving on the system's efficiencies and effectiveness (Capper, 2019). A structural functionalist approach to leadership operates within a limited notion of change and tends to advance managerialist ideologies. Furthermore, this approach to leadership is generally apolitical or neutral when it comes to acknowledging structural and interpersonal power imbalances and tends to be more invested in maintaining the current social order. An interpretivist approach to leadership is similarly oriented toward changing people, often through education at the individual level, as opposed to deep structural change. Generally, interpretivism is based on the assumption that if one simply educates people about colonialism, for example, that problem can be solved; however, this stance is severely limited as it does not factor in material redistribution or issues of governance, which are necessary in order to increase Indigenous people's educational sovereignty.

In my research, I have discovered few critical studies of educational leadership based in decolonial theoretical approaches (Bird et al., 2013; Khalifa et al., 2019; Minthorn & Chavez, 2015). Even fewer studies focus on Indigenous leadership in higher education or on leadership from an Indigenous epistemological perspective (Bird et al., 2013; Minthorn & Chavez, 2015). The gaps in critical Indigenous decolonial approaches to educational leadership are striking when we consider the colonial roots of education, and the ways that educational administrators have acted as instrumental tools in the colonizing process.

Beyond Indigenous women leaders facing the triple binds connected to gendered, racialized, and colonial leadership experiences, five other recurring themes concerning Indigenous people in educational leadership are evident in the literature: (1) the value of Indigenous leaders drawing on their Indigeneity and experiences in colonial educational environments; (2) the expectations placed on Indigenous leaders to navigate different worlds; (3) the expectations Indigenous leaders face to work toward Indigenous educational sovereignty within an inherently colonial educational context; (4) the expectation that Indigenous leaders will be relationally accountable to Indigenous people (past, present, and future) and Indigenous ways of knowing; and (5) the call for Indigenous leaders to critically "Indigenize" their leadership.

Indigeneity and Educational Leadership

Indigenous leaders' ability to draw on their Indigeneity is a critical, strength-based factor in Indigenous educational leadership research (Chavez & Sanlo, 2013; Cote-Meek, 2020; Faircloth, 2017; Hohepa, 2013; Minthorn & Chavez, 2015; Moeke-Pickering, 2020; Tippeconnic, 2006; Santamaría, 2013; Santamaría & Santamaría, 2012). "Identity-based leadership" fosters congruence between leaders' values and beliefs and organizational missions, visions, and activities (Tippeconnic, 2006). Some scholars point to the need to take an intersectional approach to identity-based leadership that complicates the multi-faceted nature of identities (Chavez & Sanlo, 2013). Chavez and Sanlo (2013) assert that it is important for educational leaders to reflect on their various identities across the interlocking systems of power that create compounded barriers, in order to make conscious efforts to challenge leaders' internalized assumptions, and to learn to understand and relate across complex differences in order to influence emancipatory change.

Literature also affirms that Indigenous leaders find storytelling an effective way to share their identities and experiences in educational settings (Ah Nee-Benham & Cooper, 1998; Chavez & Sanlo, 2013; Cote-Meek, 2020; Minthorn & Chavez, 2015; Santamaría & Santamaría, 2012). The sharing of stories often helps Indigenous leaders develop relationships and lead equitable change to improve outcomes for Indigenous students and communities (Santamaría & Jean-Marie, 2014; Santamaría & Santamaría, 2012; Ah Nee-Benham & Cooper, 1998). Indigenous leaders' identities and associated stories often become a powerful pedagogical tool that enables them to reclaim their Indigeneity in colonizing educational contexts and transform their Indigeneity from a misperceived deficit to a source of strength.

Navigating Different Worlds

While the literature testifies to both the strengths and barriers related to leading with one's Indigeneity, it also points to the tenuous position that Indigenous leaders occupy when enacting their roles within dominant Westernized educational settings. As such, much literature in educational leadership addresses the need for leaders to walk in more than one world (Ah Nee-Benham, 2003; Barkdull, 2009; D'Arbon et al., 2009; Fitzgerald, 2010; Goddard & Foster, 2002; Johnson et al., 2003; Kenny & Fraser, 2012; Muller, 1998; Ottmann et al., 2010; Santamaría, 2013; Santamaría & Santamaría, 2012; Warner, 1995). Walking in different worlds requires Indigenous leaders to "code-switch," a practice of alternating between two or more cultural contexts, such as between the dominant Westernized administrative context, with its policies and norms, and an Indigenous community context, with its cultural protocols. This ability has been described in academic literature as an important factor in Indigenous educational leaders' success (Santamaría & Santamaría, 2012). The notion of different worlds, however, highlights and enhances the gap between the culturally disparate contexts represented by Westernized universities and Indigenous communities, and points to the different ways in which Indigenous and Westernized leadership is often conceptualized and assigned (Bryant, 1998; Cajete, 2016; Hallinger & Leithwood, 1996; Turner & Simpson, 2008; Warner & Grint, 2006).

The experience of walking in multiple cultures and contexts has not just been reported in the literature, it has been fully recognized by leaders themselves as a challenge, a challenge that creates ambivalence, isolation, and alienation, thereby reinforcing "insider and outsider" (Goddard & Foster, 2002) role expectations, and creating conflicts between worlds and among leaders themselves (Ah Nee-Benham & Cooper, 1998; Faircloth, 2017; Santamaría & Santamaría, 2012). One Indigenous educational leader shared the pain she experienced as a result of being perceived by some Indigenous community members as a "traitor" because she worked within the non-Indigenous school system (Santamaría & Santamaría, 2012). Other researchers have identified intermediary roles that call on Indigenous leaders to act as cultural interpreters—to translate dominant educational policies for Indigenous communities (Goddard & Foster, 2002), and translate Indigenous worlds for dominant institutional communities. The experience of being "caught" in the middle of two often competing and unequal worlds is a common narrative in the literature (Aguilera-Black Bear & Tippeconnic, 2015; Fitzgerald, 2003a; Kenny & Fraser, 2012; Minthorn & Chavez, 2015). In an academic context, there are debates as to whether leaders should succumb to code switching. For example, Jeff Corntassel (2011) asserts that Indigenous people doing resurgence work must avoid mediating between worlds, must challenge Euro-Western domination in academic settings, and must be willing to become warriors of Indigenous truth and ways of knowing.

Indigenous Educational Sovereignty

Considering the enduring nature of settler colonialism in Westernized educational systems, and institutionalized education's role in attempting to eliminate Indigeneity, Indigenous educational leadership research often focuses on advancing Indigenous rights in education (Aguilera-Black Bear & Tippeconnic, 2015; Hohepa, 2013; Smith & Smith, 2018), and on achieving educational sovereignty and self-determination (Ah Nee-Benham, 2003; Bird et al., 2013; V. Johnson, 1997; Kenny & Fraser, 2012; Minthorn & Chavez, 2015). Aguilera-Black Bear and Tippeconnic (2015) define Indigenous educational sovereignty as

> decolonizing the system of a solely Western educational worldview and specifically developing culturally responsive educational systems to replace assimilationist models of education. It is considered imperative to the cultural sovereignty and survival of Indigenous communities. (p. 5)

Indigenous educational sovereignty highlights the problems with the historical and enduring nature of colonial education; it aims to counter explicit and implicit assimilationist approaches through resistance and reaffirm Indigenous rights, perspectives, languages, and knowledges in educational institutions (Minthorn & Chavez, 2015). Sovereignty for Indigenous peoples is often defined within Indigenous intellectual and legal traditions, which are inconsistent with the Canadian nation-state's tendency to locate Indigenous educational aims within a settler colonial framework (Coulthard, 2014). According to Leanne Betasamosake Simpson (2014), Indigenous sovereignty should advance Indigenous ways of knowing through stories and a pedagogy of the land. For Simpson, a pedagogy of the land privileges Nishnaabeg stories as theory and as a process of generating Nishnaabeg thought. Because of the inherently colonial and racist nature of Euro-Western universities, however, enacting Indigenous sovereignty is an ongoing struggle shaped by the unequal settler colonial structures of power and relations that characterize universities.

Some noteworthy tensions emerge from the academic literature between Indigenous educational sovereignty work and equity and diversity work in higher education. While Indigenous work in the academy shares many common objectives with equity and diversity initiatives (e.g., removing barriers, increasing access, addressing under-representation), Linda Tuhiwai Smith and Graham Hingangaroa Smith (2018) argue that Indigenous work in the academy, especially that related to self-determination, is unique on several important fronts: (1) implementing a unique constitutional and global Indigenous rights framework across many areas, and including leadership, curriculum, and research among those areas; (2) implementing long-standing Treaty agreements; (3) responding to reconciliation agendas across various disciplines; (4) supporting Indigenous community- and nation-building efforts in various forms; and (5) advancing Indigenous languages and knowledges in curriculum and research priorities (p. 13).

Relational Accountability

In the context of Indigenous educational leadership, the need to be relationally and ethically accountable to local Indigenous Nations and communities and ways of knowing also surfaces in the literature. Researchers increasingly call for more localized approaches to working with Indigenous communities through community-engaged processes (Ah Nee-Benham & Murakami-Ramalho, 2010) that are both relational and accountable to the land and the political locality of the university (Cote-Meek, 2020; Kirkness & Barnhart, 2001; Ottmann, 2013, 2017; Pidgeon, 2008). In higher-educational settings, relationship building is highlighted as key to institutional leadership approaches (Ottmann et al., 2010; Pidgeon, 2008). Community engagement and relationships with Indigenous communities informed how leaders in one study understood Indigenous knowledge and improved their abilities to work respectfully with Indigenous communities (Pidgeon, 2008). Several publications focus on moving accountability beyond anthropocentric values and toward the valuing of relationships between humans and non-humans, including land and place (Ah Nee-Benham & Murakami-Ramalho, 2010; Kenny & Fraser, 2012; Marker, 2015; Ottmann, 2005; Warner & Grint, 2006), relationships with Elders (Jules, 1999; Minthorn & Chavez, 2015; Young, 2012), and spirituality (Ah Nee-Benham & Murakami-Ramalho, 2010; V. Johnson, 1997; Marker, 2015; Minthorn & Chavez, 2015).

Call for Indigenizing Leadership

Finally, much literature addresses the significance of the privileging of Indigenous conceptions of leadership (Aguilera-Black Bear & Tippeconnic, 2015; Ah Nee-Benham, 2003; Ah Nee-Benham & Murakami-Ramalho, 2010; Fallon & Paquette, 2014; Fitzgerald, 2010; Johnson et al., 2003; Hohepa, 2013; Lajimodiere, 2011; Minthorn & Chavez, 2015; Santamaría, 2013). This literature often distinguishes between Western and Indigenous concepts of leadership, with Western models described as privileging hierarchical structures rooted in positional power and formal bureaucracies, while Indigenous models are described as relational and collectively tied to community needs and driven by different types of leaders and their persuasive techniques (Turner & Simpson, 2008; Warner & Grint, 2006). Gregory Cajete (2017) describes the role of Indigenous community leaders as intimately tied to one's relationship with Indigenous knowledges. Most importantly, the recognition of individual Indigenous community leaders is often talked about as needing to be chosen and determined by Indigenous communities, not institutions. As a result, many times Western and Indigenous conceptions of leadership are described as at odds with each other, pointing to a troubling binary depiction that places Indigenous leaders in impossible positions (Hohepa, 2013).

While many scholars underscore problems with the dominance of Westernized, individualistic, and hierarchical conceptions of educational leadership (Blakesley, 2008; Fallon & Paquette, 2014; Fitzgerald, 2003a, 2003b, 2004, 2006, 2010; Goddard & Foster, 2002; Hohepa, 2013), they also sometimes argue against creating a unitary Indigenous leadership approach or style (Fallon & Paquette, 2014; Fitzgerald, 2014; Hohepa, 2013) as this would obscure the diversity that exists across Indigenous Nations and languages. Māori scholar Margie Hohepa (2013) in particular has warned that creating a unitary approach would be a universalizing trap. Hohepa cautions scholars against falling prey to essentialist and authenticity discourses in Indigenous educational leadership, discourses that place added constraints on Indigenous leaders. She instead asserts the need for Indigenous leaders to draw from a range of different leadership methods—different theories and approaches—but to do so critically and cautiously and from within their Indigeneity—through an Indigenous epistemic and political lens. In asserting this position, Hohepa argues for the need to "Indigenize leadership" carefully using an ongoing, critical self-reflexivity in relation to existing forms of colonialism. She also suggests that leaders draw on a broad base of leadership tools and technologies in order to avoid uncritically adopting hegemonic colonial administrative norms and reducing Indigenous ways of knowing in leadership settings. In this way, Hohepa asserts that Indigenous women in leadership must grapple in their leadership practices with tensions between being assimilated and co-opted by colonialism.

Like other scholars, she warns against imposing Euro-Western ways of leading onto Indigenous people as this can become a form of recolonialization (Grande, 2015). At the same time she argues, like others, that Indigenous people benefit from embracing new technologies and knowledges in order to achieve political aims in a complex global context (Hohepa, 2013; Turner & Simpson, 2008). Hohepa (2013) asserts that Indigenous leaders should be able to do both, and, at times, to "do things the same but differently" (p. 617). Hohepa argues that Indigenous leaders should be able to "draw on Western approaches to leadership but also be able to adapt them (Indigenize them), guided by Indigenous knowledge, values, and practices, in order to realize Indigenous education priorities" (p. 619). Hohepa also cautions scholars about falling into gendered essentialist discourses around Indigeneity in relation to educational leadership. She asserts that Indigenous people should be able to engage with various spaces and methods but, in doing so, avoid uncritically adopting Euro-Western approaches and priorities that may harm and reduce Indigenous people and knowledges. Certainly, according to some participants in this book, the struggle to express one's Indigeneity in academic leadership practice can be stifled and often deemed unsafe within dominant settler colonial academic administrative norms and contexts. Findings point to the challenges of fully Indigenizing Indigenous women's leadership in the academy as it is often an unsafe and dangerous act for Indigenous leaders working in predominantly white settler academic spaces. Nonetheless, Hohepa advocates—as do I—for the complicated and layered work of engaging in ongoing critical reflexivity about various leadership practices through an Indigenous decolonial lens.

CHAPTER 5

An INDIGENOUS FEMINIST STORIED DECOLONIAL LOOK *at* EXPERIENCE

An Indigenous feminist theoretical lens is an important aspect of this research. Indigenous feminism has surfaced in academic literature over the last fifteen years (Arvin et al., 2013; Barker, 2017; Goeman, 2009; Goeman et al., 2009; Green, 2007, 2017; Suzack et al., 2010). Positioned in stark contrast to white liberal feminist modes that focus on gender and sex within settler colonial and imperial constructs, Indigenous feminisms, while diverse, generally centre on a critique of settler colonialism and its hetero-patriarchy (Arvin et al., 2013). As articulated earlier, settler colonialism is a structure loyal to the nation-state (Coulthard, 2014; Wolfe, 2006). Hetero-patriarchy is another construct that positions heterosexual men over women and LGBTQ2S people, at the top of the social and cultural hierarchy. Hetero-patriarchy also narrowly defines masculinity and femininity, treating them as binary categories

Figure 2. My Theoretical Lens

and subordinating and excluding a plethora of fluid genders and sexualities, in turn naturalizing male and female constructs and heterosexuality as the norm. It is worth noting that prior to the imposition of colonial patriarchy, Indigenous communities observed and respected a number of gender expressions. An Indigenous feminist lens not only challenges the limits of these Eurocentric gender binaries, it focuses on a decolonizing project as a "politically self-conscious activism" (Green, 2007, p. 25) with an allegiance to restoring Indigenous knowledges and advancing Indigenous sovereignty and self-determination (Barker, 2008, 2017).

Acknowledging the complex interconnections between hetero-patriarchy, racism, and colonialism, my Indigenous feminist lens recognizes that associated ideologies are pervasive both in dominant institutions such as the academy and in Indigenous communities. I draw on the scholarship of Torres Strait scholar Aileen Moreton-Robinson (2015) to put forth the notion of "patriarchal white sovereignty" as an overarching "regime of power, operat[ing] ideologically, materially, and discursively to reproduce and maintain its investment in the nation," a regime that positions Indigenous peoples as a white possession and that "operationalize[s] as a discourse of pathology that legitimates the subjugation and disciplining of Indigenous subjects" (p. xxiii). Moreover, patriarchal white sovereignty, according to Moreton-Robinson (2015), operates on a possessive logic founded on the continuous desire of the nation-state (and all its public institutions, including universities) to own, control, and dominate Indigenous people, and thereby undermine Indigenous knowledges and Indigenous educational sovereignty.

Despite important theoretical contributions, ongoing tensions remain in the area of Indigenous feminist thought, including a "caution about claiming the [feminist] label" (Green, 2017) among many Indigenous scholars (Anderson, 2010; Arvin et al., 2013; Grande, 2015; Lindberg, 2004; St. Denis, 2007). Indigenous scholarly distancing from white liberal feminism can be traced back to the historical exclusion of Indigenous women in early feminist research and activism, along with white liberal feminist tendencies to ignore the intersections of whiteness and colonialism (Arvin et al., 2013; Grande, 2003; Moreton-Robinson, 2006). Consequently, universalizing discourses in feminism have not only obscured colonial histories and ongoing political structures, they have also silenced Indigenous women and Indigenous epistemologies and helped to motivate many Indigenous women to avoid associating their scholarship and work with feminist activism and alliances. While I respectfully recognize these positions and tensions in the Indigenous scholarly field, I position my work within an Indigenous feminist lens. In doing so, I aim to explicitly interrogate the co-constituted nature of hetero-patriarchal, settler colonial, global capitalistic, and racial ideologies pervasive in both Euro-Western academic administrative contexts and Indigenous communities. As previously outlined, Indigenous communities are not immune from internalizing patriarchal colonial ideologies that continue to adversely subordinate Indigenous women in various contexts. Considering that this study centres on Indigenous women administrators' experiences, Indigenous feminist theory is critical if we are to take gender seriously as a social organizing process located within hetero-patriarchal colonial societies and structures (Green, 2017). I choose an Indigenous feminist lens as a political tool to make these complex forces visible and to emancipate Indigenous women from the co-constituted nature of our subordination.

INDIGENOUS RED INTERSECTIONALITY

In the present study, I also draw on the Indigenous feminist concept of "red intersectionality" (Clark, 2016) to understand Indigenous women's complex positionalities within interconnected systems of power. As Métis scholar Natalie Clark (2016) describes it, a red intersectional framework moves beyond the ways in which intersectional frameworks are often used today. The concept of intersectionality was first conceived by Black feminist legal scholar Kimberlé Crenshaw (1989) as a mode of analysis to understand how multiple forms of oppression—most importantly, gender and racism—intersect to disadvantage Black women engaging in the legal system in the United States. A red intersectional framework draws inspiration from the concept of intersectionality but privileges the intersectional realities of Indigenous people at various micro (individual) levels, and how they embody multiple, converging, and interwoven positionalities (i.e., non-binary genders, sexual orientations, races, connections to land, historical traumas, socio-economic statuses, abilities, etc.). These micro-positionalities intersect with larger structural systems (i.e., hetero-patriarchy, global capitalism, settler colonialism) to create complex experiences of privilege and oppression. Further, Clark's (2016) red intersectional framework centres the ongoing settler colonial relationship that Indigenous people have with the settler nation-state. That relationship shapes unique experiences of disadvantage—disconnections from Indigenous communities, dispossession from Indigenous lands, languages, and ways of knowing, and experiences of intergenerational trauma—which Clark asserts often get obscured and overlooked within mainstream understandings of intersectionality. Beyond recognizing how colonialism has historically and currently affected—and effected—Indigenous women, a red intersectional framework recognizes how Indigenous women resist such oppressions and uphold the role and responsibilities of reclaiming Indigenous ways of knowing and asserting Indigenous sovereignty (Stinson, 2018).

Intersectional Indigeneity is more than a theoretical concept; it is a "lived, practiced and relational" embodied and space-specific ontology (Hunt, 2013, p. 29). Through this embodied practice, Indigenous women leaders navigate dominant masculinist administrative and white settler colonial academic spaces where they confront norms and are often forced to participate (though they sometimes refuse) in ontological shifting (Hunt, 2013) between their intersectional identities (i.e., as Indigenous community members and as university administrators) and ways of relating to the world (i.e., through Western epistemic frames as well as Indigenous epistemic frames). In doing so, Indigenous women's bodies navigate dominant institutional norms and negotiate ontological limits that can create an internal sense of dissonance and ambivalence. I argue that this dissonance contributes to a "dual consciousness" (also known as the double bind), which can be linked back to the seminal work of W.E.B. Dubois (1903), a Black male sociologist who first described the sense of division and dissonance experienced by Black people operating within white-dominated contexts.

BORDERLAND THEORY

To explain the ontological shifting that Indigenous women administrators contend with when navigating predominantly white settler spaces, I draw on border theory. Border theory can help us understand the complex, in-between space that Indigenous women administrators navigate in the intermediate areas between Indigenous communities and ways of knowing and Euro-Western institutions and knowledges. Borderland theory was originally put forth by Indigenous-Chicana lesbian scholar Gloria Anzaldúa (1987, 1999) as a spatial boundary imposed on Latina people living along the US-Mexico border. While some of Anzaldúa's theories (that concerning Mestizaje in particular) have received some scholarly criticism, specifically over the romantic representation of an Indigenous past and silencing of contemporary Indigenous realities (Saldana-Portilla, 2001, cited in Ortega, 2016), Anzaldúa's contributions to establishing borderland theory as a field of its own is undeniable. Moreover, borderland theory has expanded across "geographic, ideological, sociological and identity borders" (Aldamma & Gonzalez, 2018, p. 25), demonstrating how people are placed in between different worlds, where they are often forced to negotiate processes of transformation, exchange, and resistance (Aldamma & Gonzalez, 2018).

While Anzaldúa's theory emanates from her own complex identity and Mestiza consciousness specific to living in the United States on the US-Mexico borders, the notion of working on a type of borderland, I argue, can be applied to Indigenous women administrators in this study, who operate in a complex, in-between space that straddles Indigenous communities and the Euro-Western academy. Latina feminist scholar Mariana Ortega (2016) describes the borderland as an in-between space where racialized women experience a multiplicity of selves that in turn bring forth contradictions, ambiguities, and a thick sense of "not-being-at-ease" (p. 12). Walter Mignolo (2000) similarly draws on border thinking to assert that the academy is underpinned by both geographic and epistemic borders marked by imperialism/colonialism and Eurocentric thinking. I draw on Mignolo's epistemic border theory to assert that Indigenous women leading Indigenizing work in the academy confront and negotiate complex spatial and epistemic borders in their academic leadership work.

TRICKSTER (WEESAKECHAHK) THEORY

Another central aspect of my larger theoretical lens is Cree storytelling, and in particular the Weesakechahk story—a type of Trickster story—which I included in my prologue and take up in chapter 7. The positioning and privileging of Indigenous stories as theory has been well articulated in academic research (Barker 2017; Borrows, 2013; Goeman, 2013; L.B. Simpson, 2013a, 2013b; Sinclair, 2010). Indigenous stories contain Indigenous knowledge (Archibald, 2009b; Kovach, 2009), which often structures and guides human relationships with and responsibilities to Indigenous worlds (Snyder et al., 2015). Among Mushkegowuk Cree, two general types of stories are often told: atalohkan (sacred stories related to mythological figures) and tipacimowin (historical life events related to humans) (Bird, 2007; Ellis, 1995). Robert Alexander Innes (2014), a Plains Cree Nehiyaw scholar, has further complicated these two overarching categories by asserting their complexities and interconnections across time and memory. Nonetheless, among the Mushkegowuk Cree, atalohakan stories have centred on mythological figures, including Weesakechahk (and others) as a teacher. Jo-ann Archibald Q'um Q'um Xiiem (2009b) has written extensively about Trickster as a teacher in both research and education in her foundational book *Indigenous Storywork*. Archibald has also asserted that every Indigenous Nation has their own Trickster figures, including Coyote, Glooscap, Raven, and Weesakechahk.

In the field of Indigenous studies, several Cree scholars have drawn on Weesakechahk (also known as Elder Brother) to assert a Cree theoretical framework (Innes, 2014, 2017; McLeod, 2007; A. Wilson, 2016). Innes has offered an in-depth look at Elder Brother as a means for teaching theory and as a source of Cree kinship knowledges. Ininew Two Spirit scholar Alex Wilson (2016) and Cree Two Spirit playwright Tomson Highway have both critiqued the ways in which Weesakechahk has been taken up in Eurocentric and hetero-patriarchal ways that reinforce the gender binary, which they associate with mistranslations of Weesakechahk from the Cree into English that are marked by anglophone and Eurocentric male bias. Wilson (2016) suggests that "Weesakechahk" in Inninewowin most accurately means Wandering Star and is best understood as an "ongoing creator of the world," one who comes into being in various shapes to teach humans about life through a Cree cosmology. Highway's (2003) use of Trickster has been directed at subverting dominant colonial thinking through the use of humour and irony in his plays.

In the context of Indigenizing the academy, some Indigenous scholars have drawn on Trickster characters like Coyote to tell uncomfortable truths about university administration (Ottmann, 2017; Pete, 2018). For example, Saulteaux scholar and administrator Jacqueline Ottmann (2017) describes Trickster in Indigenizing work as a transformative figure who shows up to "draw people to truth" (p. 96–7). I draw on Trickster humour, in particular Weesakechahk, in similar ways to expose the paradoxical nature of policy-enactment processes and to share Indigenous women administrators' embodied stories in an Indigenous (Cree) way. Like Anishnawbe scholar and artist Leanne Betasamosake Simpson (2013a), I see cultural figures such as Weesakechahk as a pedagogical tool for advancing critical Indigenous thought in the academy.

While several intellectuals have drawn on Trickster in their research, scholars have also warned against the "trickster trope" (Fagan, 2010). The Trickster trope among researchers has been linked to early anthropological researchers (Womack, 2008), along with an increasing number of post-structuralist scholars who co-opted and over-generalized Trickster discourses in literary studies throughout the 1980s and '90s (Reder & Morra, 2010). During the later decades, many non-Indigenous scholars drew heavily on Trickster theory to analyze Indigenous literatures in pan-Indigenous ways that obscured linguistic and cultural distinctiveness, ignoring underlying social, political, and cultural dimensions of Indigenous storytelling and research in their analyses.

The "spot the Trickster" movement has therefore been heavily criticized for overlooking Indigenous epistemologies (Fee, 2010) and Indigenous storytellers' intellectual sovereignty (Baldy, 2015), in turn contributing to an intellectual colonialism. In the present study, I draw on my own location as a Cree woman, and on the specificity of Weesakechahk among the Cree Nation of which I am a member. In so doing, I avoid settler co-optation, pan-Indigenous archetypes, and the metaphorization of Trickster (Baldy, 2015).

THE TRICKY NATURE OF POLICY ENACTMENT

While drawing on Weesakechahk as a character to help tell women's stories, I also apply the notion of "tricky" to academic administrative spaces as they are imbued with colonial power relations that create unstable grounds. Māori scholar Linda Tuhiwai Smith (2005) uses the word "tricky" to describe the invisible yet powerful ways in which colonial power is operationalized in research. In my research, the notion of trickiness is used to expose the invisible and deceptive ways in which settler colonialism functions in neoliberal and neo-colonial contexts where policy-enactment processes, policy documents, and policy actors' politics and positionalities inform administrative practice. Stephen Ball (1990) first developed the concept of "policy enactment" as involving discursive practices that "embody claims to speak with authority, [that] legitimate and initiate practices in the world and...[that] privilege certain visions and interests" (Ball, 1990, p. 22). Similarly, Taylor et al. (1997) have added that "there is always a political struggle over whose voices will be heard and whose values will be reflected in policies" (p. 27). Unlike rationalist and instrumentalist approaches to policy that assume policies are politically neutral and can be implemented in straightforward and unproblematic ways, Ball (1990) asserts that "policy enactment" is complex, contested, and messy in practice, and, furthermore, linked to policy actors' diverse positionalities, assumptions, and biases. These are tricky spaces where Weesakechahk likes to play around.

I take the typical critical policy enactment understanding a step further by explicating the historical and ongoing ways that settler colonialism shapes Indigenizing policy practices. For example, I expose the colonial lineage of educational policies in relation to Indigenous people, policies that have acted as tools to control, dominate, and dispossess Indigenous people of their lands in order to naturalize settler colonial authority. I also argue that universities as public institutions and arms of the settler colonial state (Tuck, 2018) continue to reproduce settler colonial dynamics, often in ways that conceal colonial violence, naturalize settler authority, advance settler economies, misappropriate Indigenous knowledges and land, and deny decolonial possibilities (Steinman, 2015, p. 222).

To help explain the stealthy ways that settler colonial dynamics are operationalized in policy-enactment processes, I point to the critique of "policy rhetoric" (Gaudry & Lorenz, 2018b) and the tendencies of universities to embrace "recognition politics" (Coulthard, 2014). Through my proposed critical decolonial policy-enactment lens, I strive to make visible the underlying settler colonial dynamics at play in university policy enactment, and to interrogate whether a "colonial fantasy" is perpetuated—a fantasy based on the underlying assumption that with the "right policy approach, the right funding arrangements, the right set of sanctions and incentives, Indigenous [educational] lives will somehow improve" (Maddison, 2019, p. xvii). From this settler dreamland, policy actors obfuscate the need for settler colonial structures and underlying ideologies to change. While Indigenous people are sometimes included in Indigenizing university policy work, their inclusion is often "conditional" (Stein, 2019): Indigenous people remain the ones in need of changing; they remain the "Indian problem." Settler colonialism as a structure remains intact, and Indigenous administrators continue to struggle, operating within tricky, messy, and contradictory policy-enactment spaces that inevitably surface the incommensurability of decolonization and the academy (Tuck & Yang, 2012).

Within an ongoing settler colonial context, university policies tend to "metaphorize decolonization" (Tuck & Yang, 2012). This is an evasive practice that proclaims decolonial commitments to Indigenous people and to reconciliation, but which does not necessarily attend to the issues of Indigenous repatriation of land and Indigenous futurity. Policies become discursively performed as symbolic gestures that disguise ongoing colonial erasures and violence. Sara Ahmed (2006a), in her work on university equity policies in the United Kingdom, describes these types of tendencies as "politics of declarations." Drawing on the notion of "Performativity" (Butler, 1993), Ahmed argues that the university is performative in its discursive practices as its policies strive to produce the impression (the tricky illusion) it names (Ahmed, 2006a). Ahmed (2009) further argues that diversity policies act as "institutional speech acts" that are non-performative because, although they give the impression that universities are committed to equity and diversity (in this research, in Indigenizing and reconciliation policies), they do not necessarily achieve the change they claim to embody. Instead, Ahmed (2006a) argues, "institutional speech acts" operate as a brand, a corporate image of organizational pride that exudes good performance but that in practice puts the bodies of the very people doing diversity work at odds with institutional performative narratives.

Beyond her contributions to the non-performative nature of diversity policies in universities, Ahmed (2009) also offers important understandings of the e/affects of "embodying diversity" policies for marginalized groups, understandings that some Indigenous scholars have also identified (de Leeuw et al., 2013). Ahmed (2009) has described the tension that racialized diversity workers experience when doing diversity work—when they are expected to smile and show gratitude for having been received by the academy. In *Living a Feminist Life*, Ahmed (2017) describes how racialized bodies are used as evidence of good institutional performance. She further argues that when racialized women resist this positioning and do not play the institutional game of "being diversity," they become problematized, labelled as "killjoys," and are heard to be angry, disruptive, and even self-motivated. Anishnawbe scholar Lynn Lavallee (2020) also describes some of the ways in which Indigenous administrators are perceived as angry when they challenge the settler colonial status quo, underscoring the unique position of *doing Indigenization work and being reconciliation* among Indigenous women administrators in Canadian universities.

INDIGENOUS REFUSAL

To explain how Indigenous women administrators in the present study negotiate the political messiness of policy enactment and embody the non-performative tendencies of reconciliation, I draw on the concept of "Indigenous refusal" (Grande, 2018a, 2018b; A. Simpson, 2014; Tuck & Yang, 2014b). Indigenous refusal is used to explain how, as part of their leadership work within universities, Indigenous women administrators resist the settler colonial academy. Tuck and Yang (2014b) describe Indigenous refusal as

> the stance that pushes us to limit settler territorialization of Indigenous/Native community knowledge, and expand the space for other forms of knowledge, thought-worlds to live. Refusal makes space for recognition, and for reciprocity. Refusal turns the gaze back upon power, specifically colonial modalities of knowing persons as bodies to be differentially counted, violated, saved and put to work. It makes transparent the metanarrative of knowledge production—its spectatorship for pain and its preoccupations for documenting and ruling over racial difference. Refusal generates, expands, champions

representational territories that colonial knowledge endeavors to settle, enclose, domesticate. We again insist that refusal is not just a no, but a generative, analytical practice. (p. 817)

Tuck and Yang assert that Indigenous refusals are a useful part of decolonial research praxis related to both the ongoing settler colonial project and the inter-subjective nature of settler colonial power dynamics at play within research. I use the concept of Indigenous refusals to help expose Indigenous women administrators' agency in their intermediary positions—in between the Euro-Western university and their Indigenous communities—where they are often forced to speak uncomfortable truths and challenge Euro-Western hegemonic norms. In the present study, Indigenous women participants shared diverse and complex stories about leading and refusing in the settler colonial university. Such stories emerged as participants talked about the nuanced ways in which they lead in the academy. At times they shared stories about rejecting normative administrative activities that contributed to their own oppression, and about disputing hegemonic leadership practices and refusing to be neutral or less political in their leadership approaches.

Participants also enacted refusals when they exposed and deconstructed the hegemonic nature of the settler colonial academy and its underlying structures, ideologies, and norms, which tended to operate in invisible, normalized, and rationalist ways. Though participants described how hegemonic norms were labelled by some settlers in the academy as "the way things are done," participants did not always accept those rationales, and sometimes described "stepping up," "speaking out," and "taking a stand" as a necessary aspect of their leadership work.

When Indigenous women administrators reported refusing to adhere to established norms in the university, they often reported being cast by some white settlers in anti-Indigenous and stereotypical ways reminiscent of Ahmed's concept of the feminist killjoy. They faced racialized and colonial stereotypes and were often labelled as "too political" and "uncollegial." By being stereotyped in this way, these Indigenous women administrators were portrayed as problematic, political, and divisive in their leadership, a portrayal intended to silence and discredit them and naturalize settler colonial authority and norms. Like several Indigenous critical scholars, I refuse to accept this Othering positioning and misrepresentation of Indigenous women's leadership, and instead position their refusals as courageous, generative, and even productive in advancing decolonial aims and interrupting white settler colonial common sense in the academy.

While I privilege the concept of Indigenous refusal, I also acknowledge similar concepts put forward by Ahmed, specifically in *On Being Included* (2012) and *Willful Subjects* (2014), which focus on equity workers in universities in the United Kingdom. Ahmed employs the term "willfulness" to describe how diversity workers resist the dominant white norms of the academy in their equity work. Ahmed connects willfulness to the paternalistic ways in which children have been historically marked as unruly under Euro-Christian, hetero-patriarchal, and paternalistic frameworks and applies its usage to diversity workers in universities. Anishnawbe scholar Brent Debassige and I drew on the notion of willfulness to describe Indigenous people's Indigenizing work in Canadian universities as a "reaction to and against unquestioned biases inherent within white colonial systems of power, which do not serve the goals of Indigenous educational sovereignty" (Debassige & Brunette, 2018, p. 123). In the present study, I privilege Indigenous refusal over willfulness because it both centres settler colonialism as an ongoing invasive structure and logic that consolidates whiteness in universities and, more importantly, provides support for the resurgence of Indigenous ways of knowing in education (L.B. Simpson, 2014).

In examining refusal, I also draw on the scholarship of US-based African-American historian Robin D.G. Kelley (2016), who describes refusal in nuanced ways as complexly situated and occurring within, against, and outside the university. Kelley's ideas are useful because they challenge simplistic binary ways of thinking that tend to position Indigenous refusal as an all-or-nothing orientation, and as occurring in single spaces such as in or out of the university. This anti-binary and anti-simplistic orientation is worthwhile not only when thinking about Indigenous administrators who enact Indigenous refusals in their Indigenizing policy work in universities, but also when thinking about Indigenous women's work on the borderland between worlds.

Finally, I draw on the concept of the "politics of distraction," first described by Māori scholar Graham Hingangaroa Smith (2003) as a tricky process that involves settler colonizers continuing to control activities and priorities, and to keep Indigenous people busy with tasks that tend to serve and reproduce settler privilege rather than Indigenous peoples' educational needs and priorities. The politics of distraction is a deceptive, co-optative process that surfaces in policy-enactment processes, and is, I argue, something that Indigenous people must identify and at times refuse as part of an ongoing leadership practice in order to exercise collective voice and agency in higher education and to assert Indigenous educational sovereignty.

CHAPTER 6

MY APPROACH *to* RESEARCH

begin this chapter by sharing my Cree floral research design (figure 3). This design outlines and makes visible some of the epistemological and theoretical underpinnings associated with my research. I have chosen to use Cree floral beadwork because beadwork is deeply rooted in Indigenous, and particularly Cree, ways of knowing. Moreover, a "fluidity exists between the practices of beading and storytelling because patterns cannot be distinguished from stories" (Ray, 2015, p. 368). Prior to the colonization of Turtle Island, beads were made of shell, bone, and stone, but glass beads were quickly embraced by Indigenous people after the arrival of settlers, when they were traded between Indigenous and settler groups. Glass beads thus symbolize, for me, complex intercultural exchanges between settlers and Indigenous people, and the preservation of Indigenous people's agency and ways of knowing and being in the intercultural exchange process. In the context of the ongoing violent imposition of settler colonialism on Indigenous people, and the incessant pressure it places on us to assimilate into dominant Euro-Western ways of knowing, the adoption of glass beads reminds me of the ways that

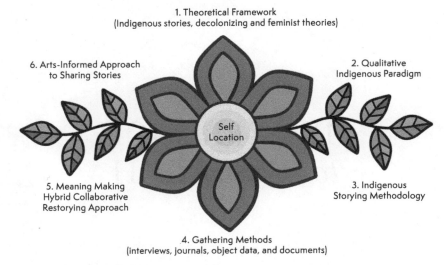

Figure 3. My Cree Floral Research Design

Indigenous people, particularly but not exclusively women, simultaneously resist and adapt new technologies that have sustained Indigenous storying traditions. Among the Cree, glass beads have been embraced; they have been embedded into our designs and adorn our mukluks, mitts, coats, hoods, and bags. The designs often pass on familial, land-based, and community-centred stories that tether Cree people to our cultural identities, sense of responsibility, and connections to land. For me, beadwork therefore reflects how Indigenous women have remained open, adaptive, creative, and resilient in the face of ongoing settler colonial domination.

According to Cree/Saulteaux scholar Margaret Kovach (2009), frameworks such as my floral research design (figure 3) play a useful role in Indigenous inquiry as they illustrate the holistic structural symbolism contained within one's research and make visible the complex interrelationships that shape a researcher's inquiry process. My research design comprises seven interrelated parts that come together to form the flower image:

1. The yellow seeds in the centre of the design represent my subjective role as the primary researcher; these include my Mushkego iskwew (Cree woman) epistemological, ontological, and axiological lenses (expanded on in figure 4).
2. Petal 1 at the top represents my theoretical framework, which combines critical Indigenous feminist decolonizing theories and Indigenous stories.
3. Petal 2 on the upper right represents my qualitative Indigenous research paradigm.
4. Petal 3 on the lower right represents my methodological approach, which draws on Indigenous storying.
5. Petal 4 at the bottom represents four open-ended ways of gathering stories: through conversational interviews, field notes, object data, and documents.
6. Petal 5 on the lower left represents my methods of analyzing stories using a combination of thematic, storying, and collaborative approaches.
7. Petal 6 on the upper left represents an arts-informed approach to sharing stories through performance writing. The new knowledge co-created in this process is also represented through twelve leaves, one to represent each of the women involved in this study.

SELF-LOCATION: MY MUSHKEGO ISKWEW EPISTEMOLOGICAL LENS

Within my research design, the yellow centre of the Cree floral beadwork design references my subjective lens as the primary researcher. This centre gestures toward another associated design—shown in figure 4, which is not featured in figure 3 as it is too small to be included—that I created at the beginning of my research project and that stories my own Mushkego Cree epistemology. I first created this design when I

Figure 4. My Mushkego Epistemological Lens Design

was writing the proposal for the present study; it was a way of expressing my culture and representing important tenets of my Cree Indigeneity while reclaiming Indigenous epistemology in research. Later, while I was gathering stories, I delivered a presentation on my research in which I shared this preliminary design along with a beadwork project with my Becoming Educational Leaders graduate class, a course I have taught for several years as part of an Indigenous community-based professional educational leadership program. Later that year, the Indigenous graduate students who had been part of that class unexpectedly presented me with the beaded design as a medallion necklace—a gift to me at their year-end symposium. Beyond the meaningful and powerful tradition of gifting within Indigenous communities, the medallion represents not only my Cree identity, but, reinforced through the act of gifting, my responsibility to work with Indigenous students and communities to nurture the next generation of Indigenous educational leaders.

Within the design appear several important symbols: a goose, the moon, the waterways, and the bush. The goose symbolizes the roles and responsibilities geese play in sustaining Cree ways of life; geese remind me that people (and all creation) need to work together to travel far distances, and of the value of gathering and visiting among each other. Such social acts build relationships and mutual understanding. Moreover, geese inevitably remind me of Weesakechahk, and of the fact that Cree stories can be one of our greatest teachers when we pay attention and reflect on them. The moon reminds me of the unique gifts of iskwewak—Cree women. Within Mushkegowuk and Nishnawbe epistemologies, women are intimately tied to the moon and water cycles through our child-bearing capacities. In undeniable ways, these responsibilities shape my own interest in focusing on the lived experiences of Indigenous women leaders labouring in universities. The waterways illustrated in the goose's wing symbolize my ancestral northern homeland, and the land where I come from. The bush line portrayed inside the goose's belly signifies Cree people's relationship to the bush and our intimate reliance on the land and communion with animals. As a researcher, therefore, my own epistemology (beliefs about the nature of thinking or thought), ontology (beliefs about the nature of reality), and axiology (beliefs about morals and ethics) are tethered to my Cree epistemology, and are integral components of my methodology and ontology, which is made visible in figure 3 as part of this research process (Absolon, 2011; Kovach, 2009; S. Wilson, 2008).

A THEORETICAL FRAMEWORK

The first petal of the Cree floral research design includes my theoretical framework, which I presented earlier in chapter 5 as comprising a combination of complementary theories including Indigenous feminist theory, Weesakechahk Trickster, and Indigenous decolonial theories, including the concept of Indigenous refusal in understanding Indigenous women administrators' leadership experiences.

A QUALITATIVE INDIGENOUS PARADIGM

The second petal of my research design refers to my research paradigm—an Indigenous qualitative research paradigm. According to Anishnawbe scholar Kathleen E. Absolon (2011), "paradigms are frameworks, perspectives, or models from which we see, interpret, and understand the world" (p. 53). Cree scholar Shawn Wilson (2001) uses the term "paradigm" to talk about the researcher's world view and beliefs. Wilson (2008) and Kovach (2009) argue that an Indigenous research paradigm is based in Indigenous ways of knowing. The academic project of articulating an Indigenous paradigm has led to the emergence of Indigenous methodologies in research, methodologies that are distinguished from dominant academic research paradigms such as positivist/post-positivist, interpretivist/constructivist, critical, post-structural, and pragmatic paradigms. Indeed, an Indigenous research paradigm is epistemically distinct (Kovach, 2009; L. Smith, 1999; S. Wilson, 2008). It is grounded in an Indigenous ontology and epistemology in which reality and knowledge are understood as relational and the researcher's responsibilities to the Indigenous collective are recognized. It is vested in gathering and sharing knowledges in ways that are consistent with Indigenous epistemologies (Kovach, 2009). As Shawn Wilson (2008) posits, there is no one definitive or objective reality; instead, sets of relationships make up an Indigenous ontology. Stories are an integral entry point into an Indigenous relational ontology.

A STORYING METHODOLOGICAL APPROACH

Beyond grounding this study in an Indigenous paradigm, I take an Indigenous methodological storying approach to research. Narrative inquiry is a way to understand experience (Clandinin & Connelly, 2000). I am interested in understanding the embodied experiences of Indigenous women administrators. I draw on narrative research because it offers distinct approaches to understanding experience, composing research texts, and sharing knowledge, approaches that I believe are congruent with Indigenous epistemologies and ways of knowing. Aligning my thinking with that of Hawaiian scholar Maenette K.P. Benham (2007), I also assert the need to Indigenize narrative inquiry in order to attend to issues of Indigenous ethics and sovereignty. Thus, I do not define my research approach as one of narrative inquiry, but rather as an Indigenous storying approach. Storying is "the act of making and remaking meaning through stories" (Phillips & Bunda, 2018). The Indigenous distinction observes the unique ethical and political significances of attending to Indigenous issues of colonial power in terms of asking who is telling and retelling Indigenous stories, how they are telling Indigenous stories, and for whom they are telling Indigenous stories (Benham, 2007). From my Indigenous (Mushkego Cree) standpoint, I respond as follows: Indigenous women administrators are telling each other Indigenous stories; I am an Indigenous (Cree) woman researcher taking responsibility to retell our stories in a Cree way; I am telling our stories drawing on Weesakechahk; and I am telling them primarily, but not exclusively, for Indigenous peoples.

Participant Group

This study took a national look at Indigenous women's leadership experiences in Canadian universities after the release of the TRC's final report in 2015. I began recruitment of participants in late 2018 and completed my research in early 2021. My study centred on the stories of twelve Indigenous women administrators, of whom I am one. As part of the participant selection process, each participant self-identified as an Indigenous woman who had worked in an administrative appointment in either an academic or non-academic unit in a Canadian university in the last five years. Their administrative positions included a range of senior executives (vice-provosts, vice-presidents, senior executive directors, etc.) and departmental and program chairs as well as interim leadership positions, including special advisers.[1]

Despite the common practice of naming participants in Indigenous research (Canadian Institutes of Health Research et al., 2014, 2018), maintaining participants' anonymity in this study was a priority for two reasons: (1) the study focused on Indigenous women's resistance in their leadership roles, meaning that identifying them could have negative impacts on their careers; and (2) Indigenous women working in administration comprise a relatively small yet high-profile population in Canada at the time of this study, and for this reason certain information, such as their geographic region, Nation, educational background, etc., could make them traceable and lead to their identification.[2] In order to protect their anonymity, I used pseudonyms, and instead of preparing individual profiles, I offer a composite description of the collective group, identifying diverse characteristics observed across the twelve participants.[3] When quoting participants, I selected pseudonyms from the Ininimowin language that specifically draw on words for the twelve-moon calendar cycle: Opawahcikanasis (frost-exploding moon), Kisi-Pisim (great moon), Mikisiwi-Pisim (eagle moon), Niski-Pisim (goose moon), Athiki-Pisim (frog moon), Opiniyawiwi-Pisim (egg-laying moon), Opaskowi-Pisim (feather-moulting moon), Ohpahowi-Pisim (flying-up moon), Nimitahamowi-Pisim (rutting moon), Pimahamowi-Pisim (migrating moon), Kaskatinowi-Pisim (freeze-up moon), and Thithikopiwi-Pisim (hoarfrost moon).

While the participants all identified as Indigenous women, they also expressed diverse Indigenous intersectional positionalities across an array of Nations and cultures. They differed in age, stage in life, tribal background, educational background, sexual orientation, and career progression. Many of them held various responsibilities both inside and outside the academy—as mothers/grandmothers/aunties in their families, and community leaders in various contexts, including on reserve, in ceremonies, and in urban contexts. While all participants located themselves within a particular Nation, they came from diverse cultural backgrounds, and often (but not always) worked in universities outside their home Territories.

As a result of background variations, Indigenous women administrators often expressed their Indigeneity in multiple and complex ways. For example, some had strong relationships with their cultures, families, and ways of knowing, while others were painfully disenfranchised by settler colonialism and only reconnected with their families and communities as adults. As a result of land dispossession connected to colonialism, some participants had grown up in urban centres, disenfranchised from their Territories and home communities, while others had been born and raised in First Nations, Métis, or Inuit community contexts. All participants had completed university graduate degrees, and thereby benefited from the privileges that higher educational and social status offers. Despite their educational attainment, however, several participants shared negative stories about their early experiences in public education (K–12) and the challenges they faced accessing and navigating the dominant Euro-Western post-secondary system. Several participants testified that their own earlier negative experiences in K–12 and higher educational settings had precipitated or strengthened their desire to change the education system.

APPROACHES TO GATHERING STORIES

I drew on four main methods for gathering stories: (1) conversational interviews (Kovach, 2010);[4] (2) personal journals and field notes;[5] (3) objects;[6] and (4) documents.[7] My primary sources of data (i.e., stories) were interviews, field notes and personal journals, and object-related data. I gathered documents to use as a secondary source of data for triangulation purposes.

APPROACHES TO ANALYSIS AND MAKING MEANING

To make meaning from the stories and other data I gathered, I applied an overlapping and complementary hybrid approach that drew on both an Indigenous storying approach to analysis and a thematic approach to analysis. I was, in this study, a participant, an embodied observer, and an interpreter of Indigenous women's stories. This was a complex role that required me to engage in critical, ongoing self-reflexivity within both approaches. To complete this hybrid mode of analysis, I relied on my subjective, epistemological/relational, and theoretical lenses to make meaning.

Indigenous Storying

"Storying is the act of making and remaking through stories" (Phillips & Bunda, 2018, p. 7). For Phillips and Bunda (2018), stories are alive and in continuous movement as humans story with them. Influenced by narrative-inquiry methodologists D. Jean Clandinin and F. Michael Connelly (2010), I drew on a "three-dimensional space of inquiry" to explore Indigenous women's experiences—their experiences of being in the three dimensions of social and cultural context, place, and time. I examined stories as units of specific experience, using an inductive, interpretive, meaning-making, iterative process. I Indigenized the meaning-making process by applying Hawaiian scholar Maenette K.P. Benham's (2007) three-pronged approach to analysis. Reflecting on how Indigenous women's experiences reflected embodied tensions between Indigenous and Western ways of knowing and doing, I uncovered ecological features (physical and organic aspects of place), socio-cultural features (familial, cultural, political, economic, educational, and spiritual dimensions of experience), and institutional features (school systems, communication systems, and political and judicial systems, including policies) that were important to understanding their experiences. During this stage of meaning making, I deliberately attended to the uniqueness of different participants' stories, the characters and scenarios they encountered, and the tensions they endured so that I could later draw upon these experiences as sources of inspiration in creating fictional dramatic texts. I also drew on my own journal reflections, where I answered all the interview questions myself and reflected after nearly every interview.

Thematic Analysis

As part of my hybrid approach to analysis, I used a coding process to identify common experiences shared across several participants. This type of analysis identifies the complex contextual and structural factors that shape experiences, rather than simply showing that the experiences occur. To complete this thematic analysis, I undertook four phases of open coding of the stories shared in the interviews.[8] To increase the trustworthiness of the research, I used three different methods: triangulation, verisimilitude checks, and critical self-reflexivity.[9] In qualitative narrative methods, criteria other than validity, reliability, and generalisability are used to determine trustworthiness (Connelly & Clandinin, 1990).

REPRESENTING AND TELLING OUR STORIES

While I decided to organize some of the findings thematically, I also applied an Indigenous "arts-informed approach" (Knowles & Cole, 2008) in order to develop several dramatic scenes. Dramatic scenes were developed by identifying salient experiences and recurring themes across participants' experiences and composing interim texts and fictional scenes to show *how* Indigenous women experienced challenges to their leadership and policy enactment. Drawing on my previous playwriting experiences in Indigenous community-based theatre, and fuelled by my unwavering passion for Indigenous stories as theories, I also explored re-storying (Phillips & Bunda, 2018) Indigenous women's experiences drawing on Weesakechahk storytelling traditions. Arts-informed research is "a mode and form of qualitative research in the social sciences that is influenced by but not based in the arts broadly conceived" (Knowles & Cole, 2008, p. 59). The purpose of arts-informed research is to embrace new understandings of experience and reach diverse audiences (Knowles & Cole, 2008). In my arts-informed re-storying process, I created four fictional characters, two of whom were women: Maria and Heather, and Weesakechahk and Nokum/the Moon. As an Indigenous storyteller and researcher, it was important for me to develop research texts that were not only meaningful, culturally relevant, and respectful of Indigenous ways of knowing and sharing knowledge through stories, but that also embodied and captured the metaphysical nature of Indigenous ways of knowing, including mythological teachers such as Weesakechahk. In the performance text, Weesakechahk is a narrator and character in the metaphysical space of Indigenous storying who drops Indigenous truth bombs, pokes fun at settler normativity, and reminds Indigenous women characters in subtle and invisible ways of their responsibilities to the Indigenous collective.

Collaborative Re-storying

I also strived to engage in what Māori scholar Russell Bishop (1999) calls "collaborative storying," following principles that increase participants' influence over how they are represented in the research process. I did this by informing participants at the beginning of the study that I would invite them to review and provide feedback on interim texts. While Bishop (1999) writes about collaborative storying in comprehensive ways, involving working with participants from early conceptualization of research questions all the way to dissemination of findings, I strived to embody his principles in the ways in which I engaged Indigenous women in reviewing interim texts.[10] I invited participants to independently review seven fictionalized performance texts and to answer and expand on two questions: (1) Are aspects of your experiences reflected in these performance texts?; and (2) do the fictionalized characters (i.e., Weesakechahk and the two women) and dramatic scenarios resonate with your experiences or the experiences of other Indigenous women administrators you know? Eight of eleven participants responded with generally favourable feedback, explaining that the dramatic scenes resonated with their professional experiences. This feedback acted as a combination of collaborative re-storying and verisimilitude checks. In narrative research, verisimilitude checks are commonly used as a way to assess the authenticity of narrative texts. This approach involves checking in with participants on whether they have a vicarious experience when reading the interim texts. Employing verisimilitude checks helped me observe a

MY APPROACH TO RESEARCH

collaborative storying process and reduce any risk of misrepresentation and/or conflating my own experiences and interpretations during the re-storying process.

INDIGENOUS ETHICS

Considering that Indigenous ethics is a core pillar of Indigenous research and methodologies (Kovach, 2009), I turned to Indigenous Salish education scholar Jo-ann Archibald (2009b) and her seven principles of Indigenous storywork: (1) respect for cultural knowledge; (2) responsibility to carry out the roles of teacher and learner; (3) reciprocity to give to each other in order to continue the cycle of knowledge from generation to generation; (4) reverence to honour spiritual knowledge and one's spirit being; (5) holism to recognize the four mental, emotional, physical, and spiritual realms of learning and to situate oneself in relation to the knowledge gained from family, community, and Nation; (6) interrelatedness vis-à-vis all of creation; and (7) a synergistic call that maintains the relationship between the storyteller and the listener. Hawaiian scholar Meanette K.P. Benham's scholarship (2007) also provided me great insight and direction in the ethical handling of Indigenous oral narratives. Both Benham and Archibald warn of the dangers of taking Indigenous sacred stories out of their contexts and writing about them in ways that may be appropriative and recolonizing. Both scholars call on researchers to assume greater accountability, responsibility, and ethical care throughout the research process. They call on researchers like me to be attentive to Indigenous cultural protocols and avoid falling victim to Western approaches to storytelling that tend to misrepresent, Other, stereotype, and even harm Indigenous peoples.

To deal with some of the ethical questions surrounding the use of Indigenous stories, I applied Archibald's seven storywork principles to my research, especially in relation to working with Weesakechahk stories in ethical ways. For example, in an effort to respect the words of the opening story's original storyteller, Xavier Sutherland, I chose, when retelling that story, to reference this original source of inspiration explicitly. As a way to honour Indigenous stories as teachers, I also invite readers in the concluding chapter to reflect for themselves on what the Weesakechahk stories mean to them. As Leanne Betasamosake Simpson (2013a) reminds us in *The Gift Is in the Making*, "As Nishnaabeg, we are taught to see ourselves as part of these narratives" (p. 3). Archibald emphasizes that this relational learning happens in the context of our holistic lives in relation to family, community, and Nation. And to honour cultural protocols for telling Weesakechahk stories, I recognize in my prologue how some Elders warn against telling Weesakechahk stories during the summer. These various efforts aim to respect various traditional storytelling approaches and cultural protocols in storytelling.

To attend to Archibald's and Benham's concerns around misrepresentation, I also incorporated a number of critical and culturally responsive activities into my research process in an effort to safeguard against the inadvertent surfacing of harmful colonial dimensions of power. My activities included engaging in an ongoing, critical self-reflexivity that examined my own rights and responsibilities around the use of a Weesakechahk story, retelling Cree stories in my own ways, and using Cree stories as a theoretical frame. I also invited Nishnawbe scholar and storyteller Leanne Betasamosake Simpson to review my retelling of the opening story. I shared my cultural background, the original story source upon which I was drawing, and my version of the story. I also shared my journey in recovering Cree stories over my lifetime, including my earlier graduate and artistic work with the Cree community. Simpson's feedback helped me more critically and explicitly locate myself in relation to the Weesakechahk story and think through some of the ethics concerning how to attend responsibly to power dynamics. Throughout this research process, I have maintained ongoing critical reflexivity and engagements with Indigenous community members, scholars, and participants on these matters, and through this difficult work I have refined my approach and deepened the way I locate myself in this research. I am deliberately transparent about my learning journey, and my connections to and disconnections from my Indigenous (Cree) community, language, land, and knowledge.

An Indigenous storying approach to qualitative research surfaced some other ethical considerations and tensions for me as the primary researcher and as a participant in this study. In retrospect, I recognize that my conversational approach to interviews (Kovach, 2010) along with my pre-existing relationships with some participants helped to build trust and make it easier for participants to share their stories more candidly with me. Correspondingly, I confronted anxiety and tensions as I re-storied our conversations and operated in the tricky space of interim texts; I did not want to violate my participants' trust, or inadvertently misrepresent Indigenous women leaders in stereotypical ways that could be harmful. My collaborative re-storying approach helped me avoid any unintended harm or negative outcomes. At times, I also grappled ethically with my own desire to centre my own experiences and stories, and to write about my findings in overly generalized and reductionist terms that made definitive claims about the world. Throughout the research process, I turned to ongoing critical self-reflexivity to unpack my assumptions, biases, and ethical role as the primary researcher and a participant, and to confront my power over the representation of women's stories.

When it comes to representing Indigenous women's stories, I strived to combat misrepresentation by being explicit about my interpretative role and by inviting participants to review and offer feedback on interim performance texts, thus employing more collaborative approaches to Indigenous re-storying. My attention to these ethical concerns emanates from my Indigenous methodological framework, which calls on me to be relationally accountable when working with Indigenous people and ways of knowing. Relational accountability aims to maintain a sense of responsibility and answerability to Indigenous people and communities (Kovach, 2009; S. Wilson, 2008). From this axiological stance, I have explicitly outlined the ways in which I have tried to mitigate any risk of harm or misrepresenting Indigenous experiences and knowledge. Although I have done my best from my location in my learning journey, I end by taking full responsibility for the choices and consequences of my actions and inactions in this research.

CHAPTER 7

A Play
FLIGHT: JOURNEYING
for CHANGE

CHARACTERS

Heather Rice: An Anishinawbe woman from Odjig River living in her home Territory in southern Ontario, where she works at the University of Manitou as the inaugural vice-provost of Indigenous affairs.

Maria Thunderchild: An Oji-Cree woman with mixed Oji-Cree and French ancestry originally from Caribou Falls, in northern Manitoba, but raised in Toronto, where she works as an Indigenous special adviser at the University of Canada.

Nokum: The moon and female entity that guides Weesakechahk and women.

Weesakechahk: A non-binary, metaphysical being and narrator who appears at the beginning of the play and, unexpectedly, in various scenes (Weesakechahk is invisible to non-Indigenous people in certain scenes) to guide Indigenous women administrators in their leadership work in the academy.

SETTING AND SET DESCRIPTION

The play is set at the University of Manitou (in Manitoba) and the University of Canada (in southern Ontario) during the spring of 2017, two years after the release of the TRC's final report. Scenes take place on the doorstep under a wooden archway in front of a Gothic-style building with gargoyle features; in a performance hall on campus; and around a rectangular boardroom table inside a meeting room with an exposed brick wall.

PLAYWRIGHT NOTES

The two central characters, Maria and Heather, and the universities at which they work, are fictitious creations inspired by the lived experiences of twelve Indigenous women administrators, including the primary researcher, who participated in the present study. The play draws on the legendary Cree storyteller Weesakechahk, and is inspired by an oral story, "Weesakechahk Flies South with the Waveys," originally told by Xavier Sutherland.

SCENE 1

Opening music. Sounds of whistling winds. Night falls, a full moon appears, and soon its shadow transposes a star constellation overhead. A spotlight on the stage reveals Weesakechahk lying on a snowbank wearing snowshoes and looking up at the night sky.

> WEESAKECHAHK
>
> Wow, this never gets old, eh? Looking up at that big old sky. *(A dark cloud covers the moon.)* Old lady? You still there?
>
> NOKUM
>
> Yeah, I'm here. You're listening, that's good.
>
> WEESAKECHAHK
>
> Did you say something? Ah, just kidding.
>
> NOKUM
>
> Always fooling around, Weesakechahk. Some things never change.
>
> WEESAKECHAHK
>
> Who said we can't have any fun? You're so serious.
>
> NOKUM
>
> You better get going now. You have work to do.

Music starts again. Weesakechahk stands up and starts walking across the hard snow making squeaky, crunchy sounds and slowly transforming into the shadow of a goose.

> End of scene.

SCENE 2

The lights come up. Birdsong on a brisk fall morning. It's not snowing, but it is freezing cold outside and Weesakechahk can see their breath vapour in the air.

TRICKY GROUNDS

WEESAKECHAHK
It's cold!!! I hate this place. *(Kicks a rock, stubs a toe.)* Damn it. I can't wait to get the hell out of this hole. *(Weesakechahk's stomach growls with hunger and they hear honking in the distance.)* Mmmm...I'm hungry. Sagabon, maybe? *(Weesakechahk sniffs their way to a large flock of geese gathering by the bay. Unbeknownst to the niskak, Weesakechahk watches them working away, visiting and gathering together.)* I wonder where they're off to next? Wouldn't it be fabulous if I went along, maybe even led this time? Surely it can't be that hard. *(Weesakechahk pounces out of nowhere upon a couple of niskak.)* What ya doing?

NISKA 1
Geez, you damn near give me a heart attack.

NISKA 2
What do you...want?

WEESAKECHAHK
I was wondering *(pointing and circling a toe in the snow)*, what you're doing? What you're eating? Where you're going? Who is the okimaw, anyway? Can I come? I could really get out of this place.

NISKA 2
(under breath) Who does this one think they are anyway?

Both niskak look at each other, look away, and ignore poor Weesakechahk by just keeping on eating.

NISKA 2
This pondweed is delicious, isn't it?

NISKA 1
OMG, have you tried the cattail stems? They are absolutely delicious with a bit of swamp juice. The earthy tones and fragrant combinations are divine.

NISKA 2
Here, try the horsetail.

NISKA 1 & 2
Mmmmmmmm!!!!!!!

WEESAKECHAHK
Do you know who I am? How rude? Mmmm, how can I get these niskak's attention? *(After a good long while of thinking, hesitating, and thinking again, Weesakechahk is interrupted.)*

NISKA 1
Pepoon's coming! We're leaving tonight. It's going to get even colder out here—freezing temperatures. Like -40; with the wind chill it'll go to at least -55. We've got to fatten up. We need an extra layer. We need energy for the flight.

WEESAKECHAHK
The flight!? Right. Well, you should have said something, I'm always in for a trip and a good feast *(Weesakechahk gets comfortable and starts gorging on the feast food)*,

followed by a nice long nap. Did you know that some of the most brilliant minds napped every day? I'm feeling pretty sleepy. Where can a cool cat like myself catch a couple zzz's around here anyway?

The niskak point with their noses toward a nearby nest. Weesakechahk gets comfortable inside the big comfy nest, starts dozing off, then goes into a heavy slumber, and soon enough starts snoring away.

          NISKA 1

Great, look what we have to put with now. I don't know why you were nice to them.

Weesakechahk's snoring rises to new heights. Unexpectedly, Okimaw Niska appears. All the birds straighten up quickly, clear their throats to put on a good show.

          OKIMAW NISKA

What are you doing?

          NISKA 1 & 2

Just eating; preparing; you know.

          OKIMAW NISKA

We leave at sundown sharp!

All the niskak start cleaning themselves feverishly, one by one diving into the water.

          NISKA 1

Look out below! *(Loud splash.)*

Weesakechahk gets all wet but just keeps on sleeping. Meanwhile, the niskak are plucking and cleaning their goose down. Feathers are flying everywhere, all over Weesakechahk, who is still sleeping. Then, the niskak break into some yoga stretching, opening their wings and beaks, and warming up their throats.

NISKA 2
Mama mama mama mama
Nana nana nana nana
Brrrrrrrrrrrrr brrrrrr brrrrrrr
Lala lala lala lala

NISKA 1
A skunk sat on a stump and thunk the stump stunk but the stump thunk the skunk stunk.

NISKA 2
Ha ha ha...*Honk!*

Weesakechahk is awakened by the loud honk. The Okimaw Niska is standing in front, quite unimpressed with Weesakechahk.

OKIMAW NISKA
Mm. Do you mind? *(Weesakechahk scrambles out of the nest, and up onto their feet with the other niskak, who are eagerly waiting to please the Okimaw Niska.)* Okay, everyone. I need us to remember to stay in formation, to stay focused up there, and whatever you do...

NISKAK *(all together)*
...don't look down! *(Looking discriminately at Weesakechahk.)*

OKIMAW NISKA
I'm not sure about this one. Well, we've got little time to waste, so let's go!

Adventure music starts, signalling the flock to get into formation. Soon a cacophony of honking fills the evening air and the flock fly up one by one until they are in a V formation in the sky.

NOKUM
Now, there are stories about being in formation, and there are stories about dropping out, into darkness, free-falling past sparkling lights. Whatever version of the story is told, every journey has a lesson, every story is worthwhile.

End of scene.

SCENE 3

Band music begins. Weesakechahk is dressed as a goose and enters the performance hall wearing a robe and ridiculous beefeater cap. Weesakechahk walks down the centre aisle toward the stage, where a podium stands stage left. The music softens once Weesakechahk reaches the podium.

WEESAKECHAHK *(speaking as narrator)*
October 11, 1870, marks the University of Canada's Founders' Day. On this day nearly 150 years ago the University of Canada welcomed its first class of students—*(under breath very fast)* of white male students—who would pave the way for this country and breed a generation of Canadian policies.

FLIGHT: JOURNEYING FOR CHANGE

Hello; my name is Weesakechahk. Yes, that's me, the one and only—almighty, heroic leader of the Innewak-Mushkegowuk, also known as Whiskey-jack. Neh. Ayee!!! They've made legends about me, you know? Passed them down from generation to generation in oral t-r-a-d-i-t-i-o-n.

Truth is, stories about me don't float around in the ether. They come alive in the telling and retelling of 'em through breath *(breathes out and watches it)* and body *(shakes the booty)*. Nokum taught me that one. But my stories are not usually told in this stuffy old place. Look around, they can't even see me.

What Nokum told me a long time ago—well, not that long, really, in the grand scheme of things—was that Mushkegowuk people stopped telling our stories. A lot of our people were told that our stories were just "children's stories, folklore, myth, fairy tales." I guess Innewak-Mushkegowuk got tired and beaten down by those black robes, Indian agents. Maybe some just went to sleep, I dunno. *(Shrugs shoulders.)*

But some people told our stories anyways, sometimes in secret to family during the long cold winter nights through shadows on the prospector tent walls.

Some told 'em to anthropologists, historians, ethnographers connected to these places who thought Innewak-Mushkegowuk were dying off—a race vanishing. Mushkegowuk stories were often taken and translated into English, put into books; flat, thin, frozen in time. Those books became really powerful. Ininew iskwewak were usually ignored in these books, erased from the official record, the colonial archive.

But you know, white storytellers who wrote down our stories got them all twisted up, wrote our stories through their crooked eyes. Some of our stories got turned upside down, mixed up inside out.

Interesting places for old Weesakechahk to get into some trouble, eh?

You know what Nokum told me too? She told me to help Mushkegowuk find those books, read 'em, learn 'em, and start telling our stories again through Mushkegowuk eyes.

This next series of stories is inspired by the old Weesakechahk style of telling stories, telling iskwewak's versions, of entering the academy, finding themselves in the old book stacks, reclaiming what was taken, and being left by the side. *(Sound of faint drumming and singing echo in the distance.)*

End of scene.

SCENE 4

On the doorstep of a Gothic-style university building with gargoyle features, under a wooden archway. Weesakechahk transforms into the gargoyle statue.

MARIA
Sometimes I wonder how a girl like me, Maria Thunderchild, Oji-Cree from Caribou Falls, ever ended up in a place like this.

Okay, I grew up in the city too, "the Big Smoke." After Mom met Dad up in Lightning Bay, we moved to Toronto. She was forced to leave 'cause she married a white guy; she married out. I'm one of those "urban Indians," Bill C-31 half-breeds.

But Mom worked hard as a waitress in a small diner downtown. I still remember how we'd go there every Friday before school for pancakes. *(Weesakechahk perks up on stage.)*

WEESAKECHAHK

Did someone say pancakes? Mmmm. I'm hungry. Where's that fork? *(Starts rummaging through a bandolier bag.)* It's gotta be around here somewhere.

MARIA

And mom would drink a lot of coffee.

But I grew up in a time when it was not in vogue to be "an Indian," so I learned how to pass in white spaces. I clearly wasn't white, and it was just easier to go along with being Spanish, Italian, or Portuguese, anything but "an Indian." *(Sigh.)* I guess I learned how to blend in when I could in order to survive.

WEESAKECHAHK

Ah. Here it is. Everyone needs a fork and plate in their bundle.

MARIA

We didn't have much growing up, but Mom did the best she knew how, and I helped whenever I could. After her and Dad split, we were always going back 'n forth from the city to Caribou Falls. Always on the move. In and out, never in one place. Different schools, apartments.

Never fitting in. I dropped out of high school at sixteen. Got a real job. It paid the bills, put a roof over my head, enough food in my belly. Then I had my son, and everything changed. *(Sound of a crying baby.)* Sh sh sh *(gesturing as if rocking a baby).*

WEESAKECHAHK
(Standing over Maria's shoulder, singing a soft Cree lullaby to calm the crying baby.)

MARIA
You know, I wanted more for my kids. So I went back to school in my thirties. It was hard to get in, so I found my way through the back door—a bridging program. Found a place in Native Student Services and Native studies. Those were the early days of Indian control of Indian education.

WEESAKECHAHK
(smacking lips loudly) Hungry for justice.

Weesakechahk stands up and starts singing the American Indian Movement (AIM) drum song and signalling a Red Power hand gesture.

MARIA
That's where I started to learn my language, unravel the secret shame I carried inside. That's when I started my healing journey, letting go of that lie that we are just stupid dirty welfare Indians. That's when I returned to my teachings, to Elders, and started finding my voice. My voice was faint and trembling in the beginning.

University was terrifying. I still remember the first time I saw a Native professor in class.

WEESAKECHAHK
Ahhhhhh *(praying gesture)*. Neh. Don't get too full of yourself, eh. Damn professors think they are all-knowing. *(Weesakechahk guides Maria through the doorway, into the building, and into the library stacks.)*

MARIA
It was cool, though, cause there weren't a lot of Native professors teaching Native studies back then. But my professor got it, and just her being there told me I belonged. We belonged. My fire for learning was ignited so strong in her class. I loved learning, especially about our people, history, and colonialism. *(Weesakechahk pulls the RCAP four-part series off the shelf and drops them one by one down on the table.)*

The library was so big and daunting. I'd always get lost in the stacks. Sometimes security would stop and question me. I still remember sitting down on the cold concrete floor in some dark row, the smell of old books all around me. I didn't always understand the coding system, so I'd sometimes pull titles off the shelf, open them up to some serendipitous page. *(Weesakechahk flips the pages of the book and passes it to Maria.)*

It was like someone was guiding me. There weren't a lot of books written by us back in those days. But I read what I could even when it was written by old white guys or girls with twisted tongues. It's all I had. I took what I could get.

You know, I would never have imagined myself to be an intellectual. Never mind a "leader" sitting here, one day. Me? That girl from the sticks? The call to lead didn't come right away. After my undergrad, I started working with Chiefs in different communities. Then I went back to do my master's and then my PhD. I focused on education. Two decades after the RCAP, the TRC hit. Someone approached me from a university down South about an administrative position. I was like, "I don't want to do that right now; I can't; I'm not done my PhD yet." I have so many things that I still want to do. But it was hard for them to find someone to do the job. I'll confess. No one like me dreams of one day becoming an administrator *(laughs)*. It's almost *(starts whispering)* tantamount to being...

MARIA & WEESAKECHAHK
...an Indian agent.

MARIA
But I kept getting this nagging feeling, a deeper sense, you know? *(Weesakechahk poking her shoulder.)*

WEESAKECHAHK
Someone's got to do it for the next generation. You could make a difference; make it easier for the ones coming after you.

Faint echoing of the drum and a women's voice singing in the distance.

MARIA
So I took on the role; temporarily, of course.

MARIA & WEESAKECHAHK
That was five years ago.

End of scene.

SCENE 5

At the front of the wooden archway on the doorstep of the Gothic-style building.

WEESAKECHAHK (*transformed into a photographer taking Maria's photo for the local press*)
A little to the left, right; no, back to the left. Yes, right there. Smile. A little happier. That's it. *(Snap.)*

Extra, extra, read all about it. *(Maria's walking, and her iPhone alerts her to a newsfeed that appears on a screen on stage.)* "The University of Canada appoints Maria Thunderchild as special adviser Indigenous initiatives—a historic moment for the university signalling its commitment to reconciliation."

MARIA
Being the Indigenous face of reconciliation is not quite what I bargained for. It's a surreal feeling to become the epitome of the solution and the problem at the same time. Reconciliation commitments and all sorts of promises, but you still get the feeling like you're there, but you don't quite fit in. Maybe it's the way people look at you, the assumptions they make about how you got the job, what you don't know, the ways they include you and don't. Or just forget. The words sometimes start

feeling empty. Sometimes you find yourself worrying that HR and security will just someday walk you to the door, and you'll vanish into the night. Not a word of how or why. Just erased.

WEESAKECHAHK
Poof. Sound familiar?

MARIA
Embodying reconciliation promises comes at a cost. Daily triggers, emotional loads. It takes a toll on your well-being, your relationships with family and community. You feel distant from them. People don't treat you the same anymore. Some people think you are just a traitor assimilated. The load gets heavy, and after a while you find yourself questioning everything, if you're not careful.

You try different ways to make change to be heard inside the university. Use the facts, reference university policy—develop new policies, revamp old ones, use legislation, constitution, OCAP, UNDRIP. If you bring in the right evidence, like statistics, quantitative surveys, literature…But if *you* weigh in, you get overlooked, dismissed, ignored, labelled a problem, you talk too much or with that tone, you're too political, don't do that. What's this? You start thinking maybe I'm being too sensitive. Maybe I'm just overreacting. Eventually you start getting fed up.

At one point, it became abundantly clear how I was seen and heard by one colleague. It all happened when we were co-planning this panel on "Indigenizing the academy." A refreshing change from the regular annual offerings, right? My colleague, the lead organizer, asked me to recommend some panelists. What about so-and-so, I say. Without skipping a beat, they respond, "She's a bit too activist, don't you think?"

Long, uncomfortable pause.

                 WEESAKECHAHK
(Taking a picture, but it sounds faintly like a gun shot.)
Nice.

                 MARIA
I'm stunned. Like I'm floating above my body trying to find the right words to respond. I didn't see it coming. I've since learned to be vigilant, to be better prepared. To be on the defence.
    "What about Donald so-and-so?" she responds.

                 WEESAKECHAHK
(Taking another picture) Come on! White male? *(Throws arms up in the air.)*

                 MARIA
By this point, my anger is rising, boiling. My nervous system has been kicked into full throttle. Sitting above myself looking downward, trying to find productive right words, to not overreact.
    My colleague tries to recover herself. "I heard him speak at a conference. As a president, I think he will have credibility here."

WEESAKECHAHK
Anger, guilt, shame, denial, dismissal, minimization, and violent rejection equals exhaustion.

MARIA
I deal with these kinds of interactions. Every. Day.

WEESAKECHAHK
(Takes one last picture.)

End of scene.

SCENE 6

Heather is driving in her car heading to work. She turns on the radio. Weesakechahk transforms into the radio host.

WEESAKECHAHK
Welcome to CMH31. It's a beautiful spring day in Manitou Zibbing. The sun is peeping over the eastern horizon. It's going to be a great day, folks.

And now for the news. The University of Manitou finds itself in hot water this morning after the administration hired a non-Indigenous person into an Indigenous director role. Local Indigenous communities are enraged about the appointment, claiming it undermines reconciliation.

HEATHER
(Sigh.) It's going to be a long day.

                    WEESAKECHAHK
Good morning. Welcome to Tim Hortons. How can I
help you?

                    HEATHER
Extra *extra* large double-double, please.

                    WEESAKECHAHK
Mmm. Nothing like a fresh cup of kwaahpii to start the
day, eh?

Heather pulls into the campus parking lot. She walks past carefully manicured gardens. As she gets closer to Convocation Hall, she notices a goose; it's Weesakechahk standing on the edge of the building, tormenting the gargoyle statue.

                    WEESAKECHAHK
Honk, honk, honk. Damn academic administrators. I
could tell them a thing or two about organization, about
biodiversity, astronomy, sustainability, physics.

Heather's cell phone rings.

                    HEATHER
Hello.

                    SARA
Hi, Heather; it's me, Sara. I'm calling to let you know
I just heard the students are planning a demonstration
outside of the dean's office tomorrow.

HEATHER

I guess we saw this coming, eh? What did they expect when they hired a non-Nishnawb to run an Indigenous program? I will never know. *(Sighs.)* This is going to get messy. Okay, do you know what time they're gathering?

SARA

Eleven a.m. Oh, yeah, and I think community members are coming too. Some students asked if you'll be there. *(Pause.)* Will you be there?

Maria's cell phone signals a new email. The stage projector shows her screen and the email subject line: "Emergency meeting re: student protest."

HEATHER

I gotta go.

End of scene.

SCENE 7

Heather arrives at the doorway to a room where a meeting is clearly already in session. Six administrators are sitting around a rectangular boardroom table; there is a brick wall in the background. Four of the six administrators are visibly white men, one is a white woman, and the last is Heather, a visibly Indigenous woman.

PRESIDENT

Thanks for coming, Heather. Come on in. *(Heather sits down.)* It's come to our attention that Indigenous students are planning a protest about the hiring of the Indigenous studies director.

VICE-PRESIDENT OPERATIONS
Yes, Heather, we are worried about the situation escalating, and other groups co-opting the protest, not to mention the negative publicity this brings to the university. We'd like to get your advice on how to manage the situation.

DEAN
Heather, this hire was such a challenge for us. *(Weesakechahk appears outside the meeting room window on a ledge, clearly eavesdropping.)* We had a failed search the first round, and we really needed to put someone in place.

WEESAKECHAHK
Even after she warned you. You didn't listen! Serves you right.

DEAN
Now the media are at my door asking a lot of questions on why we didn't hire a Native person. It seems it's becoming a racial issue. I haven't accepted an interview with the media, but I'd like to get in front of this story, and control the messaging, you know?

WEESAKECHAHK
So let me get this straight: now you want her to clean up your mess? The house cleaning never ends. And they think my shit droppings are a problem?

HEATHER
First off, we really need to stop talking about Indigenous people demonstrating as a violent protest.

WEESAKECHAHK
Right!

HEATHER
Indigenous people are too often cast in negative ways. I'd like for us to look at this as an opportunity to build relationships and open dialogue with community. Indigenous students are trying to tell us something. They're engaged in the university.

DEAN
But have you read the online criticism by some of our students and community stakeholders? I don't think threatening us is ever an effective way to build relationships, to be heard and influence change. The university is about civilized and respectful dialogue.

WEESAKECHAHK
Honk. *(Accidentally honks at the word "civilized.")*

PRESIDENT
Can someone close that window? The geese are a real pest this year. This one literally started a nest on my window ledge; was here when I arrived this morning. I had to call campus security to remove the damn thing.

WEESAKECHAHK

What so-called civilized society removes children from their mothers? Honk, honk. *(Someone closes the window.)* Honk.

DEAN

Those geese can get so aggressive. It's dangerous.

HEATHER

I really think political activism is a healthy part of students' learning. Plus, it's not just students participating in the demonstration; community and faculty members will be there too, maybe even administrators. *(Awkward silence.)*

I think we need to find ways to listen to the students, be responsive to what they are trying to communicate to us.

DEAN

But who's leading this demonstration anyway? Can we bring them in? What do you think they expect from us?

HEATHER

The Indigenous Students Association seems to be taking a lead role. But you know it's not one person. Let's see if we can set up a meeting with some key people across different areas.

DEAN

Their concerns are about the appointment of the Indigenous studies director, right? If they want to talk about that, our collective agreement clearly states that we cannot divulge details about that search. I won't be able to even give many answers. I can assure you, though, we followed the policy, the process. Our appointments committee hired the most qualified person for the job.

WEESAKECHAHK
The book, the policy, ya, ya, the written word. Who wrote those rules anyways?

HEATHER
I think students expect to see an Indigenous person in the role, and more importantly, to be included in the decision process. Being Indigenous brings all sorts of skills and competencies that aren't defined or understood in typical hiring processes. Community want a voice in the decision. They expect to be part of the process. I understand this is a big issue for people.

PRESIDENT
Okay, I don't want to get into the hiring process right now. Let's focus on managing the protest—sorry, demonstration—first. As a next step. *(Everyone turns and looks at Heather.)*

Heather, can you talk with the CBC reporter along with Dean Smith? Let's also bring the Indigenous Student Association in for a meeting to hear them out.

All the administrators close their binders at the same time, agree, shake hands, and leave the room.

End of scene.

FLIGHT: JOURNEYING FOR CHANGE

SCENE 8

Performance hall. Weesakechahk walks up onto the stage toward the podium, holding a paper, adjusting necktie nervously, clearing throat, looking down toward the rattling page, ready to recite a land acknowledgement verbatim, mispronouncing many words.

    WEESAKECHAHK
Welcome to the University of Manitou. My name is Dean Fowl. I am happy that you could be here with us today. The University of Manitou is proud to acknowledge that it sits on the land of the Anashubeeek people, the original stewards of this place. The university is ppppproud of its work in the area of reconciliation. We welcome you. Enjoy the show.

An awkward silence fills the auditorium as Weesakechahk exits backstage right. The stage light dims and flickers. A faint light shines into the audience, searching for someone. It stops at Heather, an Anishnawbe, sitting in the second row. Suddenly she realizes that the light is lingering on her. The sound of a faint drum starts up with a woman's voice singing softly. Heather stands. She starts talking to the audience from her place in the audience.

    HEATHER
The truth is. Any Indian under the *Indian Act* who may have been admitted to this university with the degree of doctor of medicine, or with any other degree by any university of learning, would have been ipso facto enfranchised up until the 1950s. So it's hard for me to sit here and listen to this hypocrisy that the university is committed when it cannot even admit that they

systemically denied me and my relatives from attending for generations. You know this place that we stand on—the earth beneath your feet. Yeah. Feel your feet, take a breath. Under this very building are my ancestors' bones. We have stories about the Odjig River, the one that flows right through this campus and that's older than this building. I bet not one of you knows any of those stories, eh? Yet we're a house of learning.

Nimki kwe nintishnikaas. *The light shines brighter.* My name is Lightning Woman. My grandmother named me, because on the day I was born there was a big, big storm and lightning hit a maple tree while my mother was in labour. That's where my name Nimki kwe comes from. I've carried the name and story ever since. My mom buried our placenta by the same old tree. Our lineage is tied to this land back generations. I still visit that tree, now and again, especially when I'm tired. I need to go there a lot these days.

I am Anishnawbe. I've been working in this university for too long, well over thirty years banging my head against brick walls. I was around when the first Native Student Services office was created back in the 1990s. I started part-time in a small office. We eventually grew into a room in the basement. After twenty-seven years, we finally got our own space, and I got a promotion to special adviser, it only took a commission for that one to happen. I'm still only just "a staff member" and seconded on a one-year contract.

Since the TRC hit, like a tidal wave, the system has been forced to look at itself. Some administrators are listening, stepping up like never before. The TRC, I guess, has opened some eyes. I gotta believe that most Canadians are good people, and when faced with the truth, they want to change. The Liberal federal government's reconciliation promises have helped make some room, but the provincial Conservative government still controls the post-secondary funding. Short-term, insecure funding. First Nations funding backlogs haven't gone away. Disputes over education as a right versus a social policy linger on. Education is political, and jurisdictional divides are real problems for us "Indians."

All we know is that this moment won't last forever; it never does. Up and down. In and out with new governments and their campaign promises. Here on campus, we realized that we needed to move when the door was open. Some of us have been around long enough to know that much. So we Native folks on campus, the five of us, got to work. Don't get me wrong: we were working hard before, but now we went into overdrive, you know. We just did it; no more asking. We took the lead cause no one else is going to do it for us. So I stepped up as a staff. But us staff aren't always seen or heard like faculty members are around here.

At one point, I realized that it was unfair I was doing all this extra work and not getting paid. I was burning out. I was getting resentful. So I approached the president and said, "Listen, I think we need another arrangement. The work I'm doing is like another full-time job." So they created this adviser role. I guess it's a start, right?

So the university is trying. Land acknowledgements like Dr. Fowl's. *(Weesakechahk perks up on stage left, looking proud.)* The university is about to release an Indigenous action plan, a plan we've worked on for over three long years. More promises on paper. We spent so much time educating administrators and writing words on pages, I wonder when we'll start seeing the benefits. We still don't have structures, full-time leadership, or deep understandings of how to interpret the promises. Policies without the right system or document risk becoming another set of empty words on pages, sitting on some website, giving the appearance that the university has changed. Or, worse yet, getting taken up in bureaucratic ways, by people with good intentions, who just don't know, don't understand our world, our needs.

End of scene.

SCENE 9

Heather walks out of the building and down to the river. She passes by Weesakeechahk outside on the window ledge. As she reaches the water, she hears drumming and singing again. She looks back at the campus buildings.

HEATHER.
This place has dissected and categorized us, frozen our images onto pages, possessed us in archives, cut off our tongues.

As a student, I found myself rummaging through scraps and remnants of field books, notes, colonial archival collections. Piecing fragments together, sewing some semblance of reflection of who we are.

FLIGHT: JOURNEYING FOR CHANGE

Today policy promises too easily just become empty words, not enough deep understanding and action. Institutional words still authorize power, draw lines between us on sovereign land. It's like they want to see me tired, angry, worn out. I've pretended and performed. Risked losing myself. I've lived in the margins. Endured the absence of my reflection on the white brick walls, worked with little resources under parental controls. Tried to change the system from within. Earned their letters, became earnest in their ways, found myself a "credit to my race."

Yet I'm still all too often not heard, not trusted, doubted, assumed to be unable to manage affairs. On the outside. Put in tokenistic positions. When collisions surface, and I speak up, I become "the problem." I have tolerated listening to suits and ties tell me how to control public images, manage Indian problems, increase efficiencies, measure success, close "the gap," get into new markets, move globally instead of locally.

I've quietly lived in between two worlds, twisted tongue ties, silently fearing that they could invade me from the inside. One day, to my horror, I was mistaken by my own tribe—called a traitor, assumed to be on the wrong side. In hearing this call, they will probably dismiss me, disdain me, debate me, talk about me when I'm not there, but I see their eyes, uneasiness with my cries. So excuse me, I don't mean to be "difficult"; I just can't live with myself if I don't stand up and use my voice.

Heather stands up and raises her arm up in a Red Power hand gesture and sings along with the women whose singing and drumming can be heard faintly in the background.

End of scene.

SCENE 10

Sound of wings in flight, and a sudden gasp; sounds of falling.

HEATHER
The last thing I knew, I was falling, falling from the sky. I had not only dropped out of formation, but when I looked back at the flock, I realized that I had drifted away somehow, got tired and distracted. I don't know for how long I was on my own. It was at that moment that my oxygen levels dropped, I got distorted, I could hardly breathe, I couldn't see straight. I lost my equilibrium. Hyperventilation. As I gasped for air, I wondered where it went wrong. Did I float away willingly? Did someone push me? Did I hit another invisible wall? Then my hubris kicked in, reaching for rationales; maybe the atmospheric levels I was moving in were too difficult for the flock to handle. A part of me wanted to try to return, to push my way back into position at the head of the formation. Then I remembered: being at the front cutting the force of the wind is exhausting.

It was at that very moment I hit an air bubble that forced my body into an uncontrollable downward spiral. Whirlwinds. After thirty seconds of free falling, I hit a patch of warm air that held me in suspension, and a butterfly appeared. I knew I had to be close. Close to hitting the ground.

Then I saw another niska and remembered that we look after each other. I am not alone. The thought of moving back, being a different way, surfaced another possibility where I could suddenly breathe again. And I remembered what I was taught about flying.

MARIA

I had some stamina to continue on the flight a few more trips anyways. I became good at anticipating what they needed to move along, maybe only temporarily and very slowly, but it was movement, it was change. Something in me enjoyed the strategy of it all. Secure in who I am, nothing can change that. I know I can't do this forever, but I'll do my part, one flight at a time. Sure, the travel is dirty, messy, damn near bloody at times, but we all deserve to fly, right?

WEESAKECHAHK

Aerial collective movement is nothing like you can imagine it to be; manoeuvring together at atmospheric heights, against unforeseen forces, you realize how really interdependent you are. You're nothing without the flock. Nothing. It's a lesson that can be learned the hard way. I know I did. And there's no doubt that the flight comes at great costs, maybe because flying in those conditions is so damn unpredictable. Its dangerous.

The theatre turns dark, and a star constellation is illuminated in the sky.

NOKUM
Now, there are stories about being in formation, and there are stories about dropping out, into darkness, free-falling past sparkling lights. Whatever version of the story is told, every journey has a lesson, every flight is worthwhile.

Blackout.

End.

CHAPTER 8

BEING *the* SOLUTION *and the* PROBLEM
Embodied Experiences of Indigenous Women Administrators

This is a story about Nishnawbe iskwew. How she got lured in, twisted up, and snared in a trap, like those wabush (rabbits) on Nokum's trapline. Sometimes those traps are hidden in plain sight. Sometimes those wabush don't get stuck at all—they find their way out—but sometimes they get stuck in a bind. But this story doesn't happen on the trapline; it happens inside the brick walls of the academy, inside the university. Don't be fooled; many of those Nishnawbe iskwew know what they're doing; they put up a good fight, and they can be slippery too.

In this chapter, I examine the stories of twelve Indigenous women administrators, and answer the question, How do Indigenous women administrators experience their leadership work amid increasing pressures to Indigenize and decolonize the academy? I organize my findings around their embodied experiences of feeling trapped by the "triple bind" (Fitzgerald, 2006) of their experiences—the triple bind associated with (1) working within a white settler colonial education system, (2) leading in an administrative world dominated by hetero-patriarchal notions of leadership, and (3) leading on the borderland between Euro-Western institutions and Indigenous communities.

Considering that Indigenous women are embodied human beings with lived experiences shaped by complex relations of power that are socially constructed and reinforced by normative approaches in administration and education, their embodied experiences are critical to understanding Indigenous reconciliation movements. Here, I examine how the Indigenous women administrators who participated in this study know and sense the administrative world of the university. As Roxana Ng (2011) aptly suggests, "Power plays are both enacted and absorbed by people physically as they assert or challenge authority, and the marks of such confrontations are stored in the body" (p. 236). Not only are power plays embodied experiences stored in the body, they are felt and responded to differently by different bodies. I hope to show that Indigenous women's bodies are sentient storehouses of policy-enactment stories as an Indigenous embodied reality.

I share women's embodied stories through fictionalized dramatic texts based on participants' experiences and through anonymized direct quotes from participants organized thematically. In chapter 7, "A Play: *Flight: Journeying for Change*," Maria expresses a complex intersectional Indigeneity, recounting her educational experiences and leadership journey in the context of the rising reconciliation movement in Canadian universities. Maria's narrative raises important issues related to the colonial, gendered, and racialized childhood experiences of Indigenous participants whose embodied experiences, like Maria's, have been grossly shaped by (dis)connections to land, language, Indigenous ways of knowing in education, and the community. Specifically, Maria's story points to the gendered discrimination of the infamous *Indian Act* (Bill C-31) and the ways in which settler state laws forcefully disenfranchised Maria and her family intergenerationally, disconnecting them from their community and land. Many Indigenous women, like Maria's mother, were forced to relocate to urban centres after marrying out and struggled in poverty and cultural dislocation in a predominantly white settler urban landscape. Maria's story also contextualizes how she began reclaiming her sense of Indigeneity and found herself becoming grounded in Indigenous community and Indigenous ways of knowing in the context of Indigenous studies and in Indigenous Student Services on her university campus. Her story further underscores how, over time and through experience, Maria found herself called to participate in Indigenous rights–based movements in the academy.

BEING LURED INTO ADMINISTRATION

The Indigenous women administrators who participated in the present study shared multiple and diverse stories about their leadership experiences, with many reporting that they felt called, sometimes even pressured, to take on leadership roles within the academy. Many said they had never imagined themselves doing administration, that leadership was not something they had aspired to, but that they felt compelled to do it in order to contribute to Indigenous communities. Several participants had been actively pursued by university administration and encouraged to apply for their leadership roles. One participant attested to this dynamic:

> I got here by accident, totally by accident. After the Truth and Reconciliation Commission broke, there was a shift suddenly, an increasing interest nationally, and the university asked me if I would take on the role, because they didn't have anybody else that was—you know, that they were interested in hiring. "Well, will you come in a

secondment for a year, to do this?" So it was an accident. I'd never been in an administrative kind of position, and certainly wouldn't have thought that I'd like it. (Kisi-Pisim)

Getting "here by accident" for this participant meant she had not pre-planned her leadership career trajectory; it was not something she desired; leadership was thrust upon her by a combination of institutional pressures and an underlying sense of responsibility to serve Indigenous communities.

Another participant shared a similar story:

The position [ad] comes out. I was like, "I don't want to do this right now. I can't. I have so many things that I still want to do, but there's no one else here to do it." I thought, "Crap, this is my responsibility now; I have to do this." (Niski-Pisim)

All Indigenous women participants felt a sense of responsibility to take on leadership roles in the universities and to step up for the younger generations of Indigenous peoples entering the education system.

BEING CAUGHT IN A QUAGMIRE OF POSITIONS

Policy demands for the hiring of more Indigenous people have resulted in universities appointing Indigenous leaders into various types of leadership roles, such as interim special advisers, seconded leads, executive directors, vice-provosts, and vice-presidents. Consequently, participants in this study held many different types of leadership positions and were located in the academic reporting hierarchy in various ways. Several participants reported directly to a provost, others to the president, and still others reported to an administrator who themselves reported to the president or provost. Beyond the quagmire of Indigenous leadership positions, beyond titles and reporting relationships, the most significant barriers to advancing Indigenous institutional change reported by participants was whether the units that Indigenous administrators oversaw were provided with proper scope and authority, adequate personnel, and sufficient budgets to drive university-wide Indigenization initiatives.

Another challenge that emerged for some Indigenous women leaders concerned the type of administrative appointment they occupied, and the academic credentials they brought to the work, especially marking at times the differences between staff and academic administrative roles. Recognizing that most senior administrative appointments are five-year, limited-term appointments with possibilities of renewal, some women recognized the security challenges associated with continuous renewal processes. Some women also debated whether this type of role required someone with academic credentials (namely, a PhD) in particular research experience. Those in academic administrative appointments recognized the value of having an academic appointment within a faculty to return to after their administrative term ended. A couple of women also spoke about how tenured faculty members in particular held more security in feeling free to speak up without facing the consequences of losing their jobs. Within the academy and within Indigenous communities, interestingly, opinions sometimes differed about whether Indigenous administrative positions needed a PhD at all. There were some women who carried master's-level education and performed well in academic environments and administrative roles.

Women were not immune to a variety of tensions around their leadership, particularly the perennial conflicts between administrators and faculty members which were described by some participants. Some participants reported that, despite their credentials (PhD or not), they were challenged by some faculty members. These challenges were often based in faculty members' resistance to the bureaucratization of education and to an increasing administrative bloat in the academy overall. The role-related tensions between administrators and faculty members can be linked to the different types of work that they tend to focus on, and can be connected to deeper, conflicting paradigms that often shape faculty work, which can be characterized as critiquing the system, whereas administrative work tends to focus on practice, and even arguably on preserving and improving the university system.

BEING CAUGHT IN THE TRIPLE BINDS OF THE EDUCATION SYSTEM

Several women shared stories about how, despite their entry into university administration, they continued to face pervasive systemic barriers in their leadership work, barriers related to the triple binds of white settler colonialism and the patriarchal nature of the academic system. The university, they said, is structured in a way that privileges a Eurocentric, androcentric, white notion of leadership that inherently undervalues and marginalizes Indigenous people, particularly Indigenous women, in policies, procedures, and daily norms and practices. One participant, talking about the role of universities, highlighted the need for universities to be a place for the mutual exchange of diverse knowledges. Yet she underscored the continued dominance of white men in academic administration, and pointed out that this history is a structural reality that has disadvantaged different groups:

> The whole question of administration—who gets to sit at the big table? And in many universities for many, many years, it has been men—white men in particular. It wasn't women, not even white women. It's been a lot of people battling at a lot of fronts, not just Indigenous peoples. I mean, Black people, women. I still remember being at [*name omitted*] University and with all the old white guys sitting at the boardroom table, and [the tables] were so high, because they were made for men, right?

And I said, "You can really see that you guys haven't had women around your tables—everything is made for men!" (Pimahamowi-Pisim)

In conversation with this participant, I shared my own experiences of first entering a large banquet hall at my own university and looking around the room at all the portraits of the past presidents and chancellors. In the interview, I reflected and shared my observation of the portraits and said, "They were mostly white men; only a couple of women, white women."

Beyond the issues of structural barriers and under-representation, many participants described how they felt pressured to assimilate and take on hegemonic administrative norms, and, in turn, how they were forced to code-switch in order to be effective and successful in their leadership within the academy. As one participant described it,

I was told that if you want to be successful in here you have to be like us. And I was like, I don't want to be like you. You've got a lot of you running around here already. And if I have to choose between being like you and protecting my own community, you will always lose. It's just the way it is. (Pimahamowi-Pisim)

This participant resisted the expectation to conform to apolitical norms in leadership because they did not always align with her values and sense of Indigeneity. She challenged the taken-for-granted expectations placed upon her to assimilate and be more neutral, like other administrators. Her refusal challenged unspoken settler normative assimilative expectations in administration, and demonstrated how Indigenous women push back and maintain their agency to lead on their own terms. Her resistance does not, however, mean that she never drew on Westernized methods of leadership to achieve particular aims; it does mean that she asserted her right to determine and choose how she leads based on deeper goals, values, and ethics.

Other participants reported challenges navigating and negotiating the explicit and implicit hegemonic administrative norms of the academy. One shared her challenging experiences of learning the dominant culture of power, specifically when it came to adhering to a hierarchal chain of communication, suggesting that she has had to learn these unwritten rules and tacit knowledge over time:

> I never quite understand all the protocols of the institution. So in my community, I have Chiefs; I have a couple Chiefs' phone numbers on my cell. And they say, "When you need something, phone me." But when I want the president [of the university] I have to make sure that I go through this person, who then will do this, and then will do that, and then they go decide. I don't always understand the protocols, and I break them all the time and get in trouble for it. (Athiki-Pisim)

Here, Athiki-Pisim's words reflect the divergent communication styles encountered when working in the hierarchal academy, which contrast with her experience working in a relational community context.

Beyond pressures to walk in more than one world, several participants remarked on the challenges of encountering increasing backlash and navigating anti-Indigenous racism in relation to their leadership and the Indigenization movement altogether. Anti-Indigenous racism as an ideology emerges out of settler colonialism to justify and resist Indigenous people's distinctive rights in higher education. Several participants shared examples of a rise in free speech policy movements on university campuses, which negatively impacted their leadership experiences. These movements were often associated with troubling assumptions that Indigenization and decolonization work were somehow a threat to free speech and academic freedom, assumptions based on a deep denial of the inherent Euro-Western structure of the academy, and of the ways in which Eurocentric whiteness and meritocracy are unfairly embedded in the academy. One participant said,

> For me, you know, it's just a ludicrous notion that universities are the embodiment of free speech, and have ever been. Like, to me that notion is so ridiculous. I just cannot even talk about it. It's just too like [*makes bomb-like sound effect*]. I mean, look at us. This is what we're doing. We're fighting to be heard here. We're fighting to have our point of view in institutions. What's free about that? And free speech for whom in this instance? All of this stuff is about allowing hate-mongers to freely speak. (Kisi-Pisim)

This participant described the rise of free speech policies emerging in universities across several Canadian provinces, including Ontario (2018) and Alberta (2019), as a conservative right-wing political movement against liberals in education that both distracts from and counters her Indigenization policy work. Other participants also maintained that free speech rhetoric is being used as a political device to argue against education reform, and that it maintains structural inequities that privilege Eurocentrism and whiteness. More troublingly, these political movements were described as giving rise to residential school denialism and sensationalist media coverage that verge on inciting hate speech against Indigenous peoples and Indigenization work on campuses. Indeed, participants reported that resistance to Indigenization and decolonization under the semblance of protecting academic freedom was on the rise by some faculty members in universities since the TRC, and that this served as a stark reminder of the dominance of the Eurocentric, Westernized, and colonial higher educational system that systematically favoured white settler voices.

Several participants described experiencing or observing explicit and violent forms of anti-Indigenous racism on university campuses since the release of the TRC. One participant said,

We've seen some of the pushback from settler students and faculty since the TRC. We've seen a rising up of racism and power and privilege in the classroom. I've heard more faculty members talk about the level of disrespect that they feel from some of their settler students when they try to focus on Indigenous ways of knowing and being. We've had graffiti on the Indigenous house. We have a board that lists all our events, and we had graffiti on there. We've even had to call campus security a couple of times to get them to escort people out. (Athiki-Pisim)

Another participant described being confronted by several non-Indigenous faculty members who challenged the Indigenous knowledge sources she referred to in a public presentation in order to discredit her and the university's approach to Indigenization; the participant felt ambushed.

Attacks on Indigenous scholars' work often drew on Eurocentric rationales. Some Indigenous women administrators' work was discredited because it did not reference literature in the European canon, a criticism that reveals the dominance of Euro-Western thought in the academy and the way in which the European canon continues to be used to push out Indigenous perspectives. While many participants acknowledged the value of Western knowledge and the university as a place of critical dialogue and systematic inquiry, they also noted that existing structures based within settler colonial rationales and ideologies often served to silence Indigenous people and prevent them from accessing and fully participating in dialogue and inquiry. Thus, participants reported needing to be prepared to be publicly challenged, and to be ready to engage in critical decolonial debates that deconstructed problematic Eurocentric and colonial assumptions. This reality was particularly daunting for participants, many of whom carried their own historical traumas associated with the violent and ongoing nature of settler colonialism within Canada's educational system.

BEING ILL AT EASE

The triple bind was an internalizing, embodied narrative that sometimes played out in participants' experiences, experiences in which they struggled to find a sense of ease and belonging in predominantly white settler, male-dominated academic administrative spaces. One participant candidly described it this way: "I still walk into a room with all these leaders, who are all white, pretty much, and I still don't feel like I'm, you know—they're not going to accept me the way they accept each other" (Kisi-Pisim). Another participant shared her struggle with her own internalized beliefs embedded in colonialism, sexism, and racism:

> You know, you're walking in and, you know, you were raised to understand oppression, like to understand that we are the oppressed. So, for us to walk into a room with sixteen white people who are very well-educated, and us seeming as if we're well-educated, and we are always left feeling like, "Um, you know, maybe I shouldn't be here." So we're carrying a feeling that we aren't necessarily legitimate, but it's there. It's scary stuff. You're up against people who, you know, look at you; they give you that look. (Opawahcikanasis)

The notion of "the look" refers to Indigenous bodies being perceived as Other in dominant white settler spaces such as the academy. Feminist scholar Nirmal Puwar (2004) talks about "the look" as inducing an ontological anxiety informed by the "psychic and physical boundaries that are implicit to the sense of Europeaness, and more specifically the sense of who men of knowledge and leadership are as well as where they are placed" (p. 39). Indigenous women in the present study experienced "the look" as an Othering embodied response to their presence in white settler administrative environments, an Othering that occurs when they are seen and perceived to be out of place. In this way, participants' bodies were perceived as "space invaders" (Puwar, 2004); they were marked as strangers (Ahmed, 2007b), which contributed to their feeling alien in academic administrative spaces.

BEING LABELLED A RADICAL

Participants often reported needing to confront colonial and racial stereotypes connected to long-standing ideologies about Indigenous people. In particular, participants encountered Indigenous stereotypes that depicted them as radical, resistant, divisive, and activist in their leadership, activism being seen as a contentious approach to leadership frowned upon by many university administrators. Participants also talked about ways in which they carefully navigated their leadership and monitored their behaviour to avoid being stigmatized with such racial and colonial stereotypes, and described how they sometimes resisted the university in less visible, subtler, and more subversive ways.

Despite their efforts to counter racial stereotypes, participants described several ways in which their leadership work was dismissed and even problematized and politicized. One participant described being pulled aside by a colleague who advised her that she was being "too political" in her approach and that she "needed to open up to non-Indigenous people" (Thithikopiwi-Pisim). Another participant shared her experiences confronting anti-Indigenous bias in her leadership:

> I think we always need to be thinking about what people are thinking based on stereotypes. We have to address those all the time. We're always on, because it's so, so deeply embedded in the Canadian consciousness....We're always up against the media, and how badly it portrays Indigenous peoples. (Pimahamowi-Pisim)

Several other participants talked explicitly of concerns about being labelled difficult, resistant, militant, and activist in their leadership. One participant described being problematized by a colleague at her university:

> I have a colleague. She slips and—I don't know if she thought I knew, but she made a comment like, "You know you're so great to work with." She was praising me, only to come to the fact that—"I don't understand when some people say you're so difficult to work with." And I was like, *interesting*. (Niski-Pisim)

Another participant admitted that she tried to dispel troubling colonial stereotypes by actively creating collaborative relationships: "I try to create trust with certain people who automatically assume that I'm going to be the big militant" (Thithikopiwi-Pisim). And yet another participant admitted she had become so concerned about being labelled an activist at her university that she literally changed the way she dressed and avoided wearing camouflage clothes to work to avoid negative associations and messages. The unseen dimension of participants' worrying about what to wear and how they might be misperceived in racialized ways contributes to the emotional labour they are forced to undertake—the management of one's feelings and expressions as a requirement of administration work.

BEING QUESTIONED

While many Indigenous leaders recognized that they had been hired partly because of their Indigeneity, lived experiences, and connections to Indigenous communities, they also acknowledged that their Indigeneity was used against them within the university and was becoming increasingly scrutinized by Indigenous communities due to the rise in national concerns around ethnic fraud. Within the university, administrators' Indigeneity was sometimes used against them by non-Indigenous people who held assumptions that Indigenous people were not qualified to take on senior academic leadership work, and that they were only hired because of their Indigeneity. One participant, for example, said,

> You're sitting in a position where they say, "Well, how come she got the position?" Or, you know, "Oh, you're only in that position because you're Native." And I'm like, "No, I'm actually here because I'm smart. That's why I'm here." But that whole "Why are you here? You shouldn't be here, because you're not the right *whatever*." (Pimahamowi-Pisim)

Despite being questioned about "how they got there" by some people in the academy, Indigenous leaders' Indigeneity was also commonly questioned by Indigenous communities. Considering the rise in cases of ethnic fraud in Canadian universities, this was a legitimate matter for the administrators interviewed, who recognized the importance of leaders being accountable and transparent with their self-locations. Indigenous women administrators' positionalities were often highlighted in their professional biographies online, and universities often referenced leaders' Indigeneity publicly. Documents collected for the present study included press releases from university public affairs offices marking inaugural appointments of Indigenous senior leaders to universities. A typical press release often read something like this: "[University] appoints the first Indigenous woman [administrative title] to help restore relationships with Indigenous peoples." In these types of celebratory communications, Indigenous women administrators are positioned as the solution to complex and deep systemic problems. The assumption that the presence of an Indigenous women administrator will somehow solve the "Indian problem" is striking.

Beyond the ways in which Indigenous women administrators were positioned as policy solutions, participants often talked about being questioned about their leadership advice, resulting in paradoxical tensions in their experiences. Their Indigeneity, on the one hand, brought them a certain level of credibility in the public's eye. On the other, their Indigeneity was not always well-received in administrative practice overall—in fact, it was sometimes explicitly used against them, leading to their being questioned on the assumption that, being Indigenous, they were somehow incapable of making decisions or were biased. As one participant reported, "I'm dismissed when I give advice even on Indigenous matters, like, 'Well, you are Indigenous; you have bias,' so therefore my voice can't be heard on that one" (Thithikopiwi-Pisim).

Participants also shared stories about how they were dismissed or ignored when they drew on their experiences. The dismissal of their experience pointed to a prevailing preference for objectivist, quantitative decision-making approaches over subjective and qualitative ones. Institutions' tendency toward positivist notions of knowledge and evidence is another example of the apolitical and managerialist nature of university administration. One participant said, "They want to hear from me, but then they don't believe I'm credible" (Kisi-Pisim). Another admitted, "There's always this angst in me, like, are people going to look at me and...think, 'What kind of quack is she, and where's her numbers?'" (Athiki-Pisim). Yet another participant recounted, "It's [like my advice is seen as] bias[ed]. It's not factual. We're faced with, 'Well, that's not really a fact.' We're challenged...about our own experience" (Opaskowi-Pisim). The normative assumption is that Indigenous women administrators should not draw on their experiences to lead, an assumption that created a burden of doubt that constrained and undermined their leadership and resulted in a deep sense of frustration among several participants.

On the other end of the spectrum, some Indigenous women described feeling micromanaged in senior leadership. One participant, commenting on observations she had made about another Indigenous woman administrator, connected the senior administration's tendency toward micromanaging to an internalized doubting of Indigenous leaders' capabilities. She said,

> They wanted to hire [an Indigenous person], but it was very challenging to actually let them [lead] because they didn't believe—I don't think they believed—that she was capable of leading. Because they micromanaged her. That's why she left. Like every decision she tried to make was second-guessed. (Opawahcikianasis)

BEING MARGINALIZED AND HYPER-VISIBILIZED

Participants reported that the scope of their leadership was often limited to predetermined areas such as Indigenous student services or community engagement, and that their Indigenizing contributions across academic disciplines and other operational areas of the institution were often overlooked and underestimated. As one participant commented, "So if you're Indigenous and you're doing anything Indigenous, you're actually quite marginalized in the institution. They don't see you doing anything else except Indigenous issues" (Kisi-Pisim). This participant explained that she felt limited in her ability to contribute by the way she was received by other administrators around the leadership table, especially when she gave advice outside of their preconceived notions about her knowledge and expertise: "I always feel like people are startled when I make comments on issues other than Indigenous issues" (Kisi-Pisim). Consequently, some participants reported feeling a sense of being restricted to certain university activities, which not only segregated and limited their contributions and influence, but also constrained their participation in broad-based institutional change processes. Indigenous women administrators were assumed to represent Indigenous issues only; they were not heard when they spoke about university issues more broadly.

Indigenous-specific senior administrative roles within a university are often highly visible, scrutinized, and even politicized. Despite universities often making public announcements of these new roles, colonial attitudes about Indigenous peoples as "Other" and "lesser than" persist. These surfaced in many participants' stories. Moreover, leaders' Indigeneity often generated a higher degree of scrutiny, which in turn created a felt sense of hyper-surveillance and vulnerability among some participants. One commented on these felt vulnerabilities:

> I was a single mom flying across Canada. That put me in a position where I didn't have the same kind of supports or protective factors, so I felt vulnerable. It was like people wanted to poke holes in my work. (Opahowi-Pisim)

The same participant described how she received emails that bordered on hate speech and impacted her feeling safe and supported in her leadership role.

The marginalization of Indigenous leadership is likely based on assumptions around such leadership founded in settler colonial, racial, and hetero-patriarchal notions of Indigenous people and ways of knowing. Good leadership is assumed to be white, settler, and male. Such notions are normalized, and anyone not subscribing to these norms is cast as political and divisive, unable to offer good leadership. Participants, because of their gender and Indigeneity, were often assumed to be less capable in their leadership than the white settler male norm. This presumed incompetence often included the assumption that Indigenous women could not separate their personal interests from Indigenous collective interests, and therefore could not make good decisions. Such an assumption fails to acknowledge that the academy itself, far from being systemically neutral, is built on long-standing Eurocentric, patriarchal, and settler colonial ways of knowing, and on norms that are inherently political and invisible (Battiste, 2018; Sandy, 2018; Smith & Smith, 2018). Invisibilization of the underlying nature of the university system, along with ongoing hetero-patriarchal and colonial administrative norms of leadership, have created the illusion that the educational system and non-racialized leaders are neutral. Hyper-visibilized Indigenous women doing Indigenization work, therefore, are seen to be "too political" and problematic in their leadership.

In scene 5 in chapter 7 (p. 131), Maria's story offers insights into the complicated ways in which Indigenous women administrators encounter the triple bind in their leadership in the academy. Maria's story highlights the ways in which Indigenous administrative leaders' Indigeneity is employed in university practices and is celebrated and promoted as part of the university's public image and reconciliation efforts. In her monologue, the performative nature of the university's public image is juxtaposed with Maria's own internal narrative and ambivalence at taking on a leadership role. The story is further complicated by Maria's attempts to be heard, along with her struggle to find credibility in the institution. Her monologue concludes with the sharing of a storied interaction between Maria and a colleague that reveals the latter's deeply engrained colonial, gendered, and racialized biases about who should speak about reconciliation. The colleague's biases support the subjugation of Maria's leadership voice and demonstrates one of the ways in which she experiences micro-aggressions in the workplace.

WORKING WITHIN PATRIARCHAL AND COLONIAL NOTIONS OF LEADERSHIP

Several participants described their sense that Indigenous women administrators in Canadian universities are often overworked and are less likely than non-Indigenous people and Indigenous men to be frequently and rapidly promoted to leadership. As one participant said,

> I think that there's a sense it's a little harder and you have to work a bit, you have to work harder to get that space, and if you are too strong, you know, we still get cast in the role of warrior. If you're too weak then you're too soft, then you're not regarded with authority or respect. It's the stereotype that, you know, very deeply in the Canadian consciousness, really the global consciousness, that Indigenous peoples are not that smart, or they are difficult, somehow. (Pimahamowi-Pisim)

Another participant shared a similar perception about the undervaluing of Indigenous women's labour compared to that of Indigenous men in Canadian universities:

> I see the way that Indigenous men are treated compared to Indigenous women. Honestly, not to take away from Indigenous men, I think they do work, but I think Indigenous women overwork. We're the leaders in the home. You look after kids, you look after organizing the home. Indigenous women do a tremendous amount of work compared to Indigenous men moving in the system, and they're [Indigenous men] rewarded quicker. (Opawahcikanasis)

While it is important to recognize that Indigenous men face unique racial and colonial barriers accessing universities, and that Indigenous men are chronically under-represented as students and leaders when compared to Indigenous women, Indigenous women administrators in this study did voice unique gender-related challenges. Some of these gendered challenges had to due with balancing work-life demands and dealing with a compounded fatigue that Indigenous women endured leading institutional-Indigenization work. For example, Opawahcikanasis's quote speaks to her observation that Indigenous women were being overworked in the university. She also highlights in the same conversation how many Indigenous women felt that the long-standing institutional neglect of Indigenous education that preceded the reconciliation movement had caught up with Indigenous women's sense of fatigue. There was also a feeling that Indigenous women were not rewarded as quickly or as equitably for their work in universities, and that they were often expected to overwork both inside and outside the academy, which I argue points to an exploitative colonial and patriarchal dimension of institutional-Indigenization work in the academy.

While participants reported experiencing barriers related to the gendered nature of the Westernized administrative system, barriers often imposed against them by non-Indigenous settler colleagues, their negative experiences were not limited to interactions with non-Indigenous colleagues in the academy. One participant expressed frustration around her experiences with an Indigenous male colleague who, she believed, was not contributing to Indigenization at her university. She argued that Indigenization should be a "shared labour and shared vision" among all Indigenous people in the academy, but, from her perspective, one particular Indigenous male colleague was quite comfortable stepping back and saying, "You go ahead and do that; I'm going to focus on my career. I've got a research agenda I'm going to fulfill" (Ohpahowi-Pisim). His attitude highlighted the patriarchal nature of colonization and how some Indigenous men in the academy do not always feel as compelled as many Indigenous women do to take on the same level of responsibility for Indigenization.

Additionally, many participants talked about troubling interactions with Indigenous community members, both within and outside the academy. Several participants described challenging encounters with Indigenous women colleagues, Indigenous male students, and Indigenous community members. In telling their stories, participants often associated these negative experiences with forms of lateral violence in Indigenous communities and with the internalization of settler colonialism, sexism, and racism that is alive within Indigenous people's consciousness. One participant found herself working at a new university outside her ancestral Territory. Coming from a matrilineal culture that honours Indigenous women's role and voices, she asked an Indigenous staff member at the university to help her invite a local Indigenous grandmother to conduct an opening ceremony at an event she was planning. She was, however, quickly approached by a male Indigenous leader in the local community who said, "You are in [insert Nation] Territory, and we don't have women open our events" (Niski-Pisim). Surprised by this position, the participant accepted the community member's feedback, apologized, and assumed she simply needed to learn more about the local Territorial context. She found out later, however, that Indigenous women in the local community were highly respected and did indeed conduct ceremonial openings. The participant reflected on her earlier experience with the male community member, linking it back to "patriarchal models of Chiefs" and the ways in which the patriarchal nature of colonialism has been internalized within Indigenous communities. Perhaps, she thought, the interaction reflected Indigenous male discomfort with her as an Indigenous woman in a formal leadership position. Indigenous male discomfort can be further traced back to white male patriarchy, which tends to disassociate women with formal leadership.

While Indigenous women in this study identified tensions between Indigenous men and women, they also noted that Indigenous women were mistreated in racialized and gendered ways by other administrators. One participant described her president asking her to co-chair an Indigenous committee with a white male colleague, yet the president often communicated only with her male counterpart, excluding her from important conversations. Such acts of exclusion formed an ongoing pattern with this president, to the extent that the participant approached her co-chair to seek support in addressing it. The president, she reported, rationalized his actions by saying that he wanted to protect and avoid overworking her. In interviews, other participants described times when they were excluded from conversations and decisions by colleagues, often under the pretense that these colleagues did not want to overwork them. Moreover, the decision by some non-Indigenous peoples to exclude Indigenous women from conversations resulted in removing Indigenous women's agency, which was based on a dangerous assumption that Indigenous women were not capable of prioritizing and making decisions for themselves.

EMOTIONAL LABOUR

Some participants described struggling to operate within dominant Euro-Western leadership norms, feeling that they could not show their emotions. Given the highly personal nature of Indigenization work, and Indigenous people's intergenerational trauma in colonial educational settings, many participants found this expectation particularly challenging and not in alignment with Indigenous ways of knowing and being. At the same time, some women worried that showing emotion to administrators would hinder their being taken seriously or discourage others from interacting with them. One participant said, "I think there is an expectation that you are to remove the personalized aspect [in leadership], and that is really hard to disconnect from in our work. It is very personal work" (Opiniyawiwi-Pisim). Another participant admitted that at times she regretted showing emotion with some colleagues because it was not respected and was so uncommon in the academy that she feared it could be used against her. The dominant split between the personal and professional is the focus of a long-standing feminist critique of masculinist leadership approaches, which are often viewed as superior because they are deemed assertive, strong, and capable. The split can be connected to an emphasis on the management of emotions in the workplace and the bureaucratization of feelings experienced by many women in leadership (Blackmore & Sachs, 2007). On the other hand, several participants shared how they drew on their subjectivity and emotions when working with Indigenous communities as part of a relational approach to Indigenous leadership.

Interestingly, one participant reported that a show of emotion helped her in one instance to lead a transformative change inside the university. Trying to advance an Indigenous student admissions policy with the registrar at her university, she was stymied by a colleague who was unwilling to compromise on the dominant institutional practice of prioritizing only grade point average in the admissions process. After several failed attempts to make headway on accessible admission policies, and the registrar's indifferent and callous responses, she said, "I started to cry." As she explained it,

> When I get really frustrated sometimes I cry if I can't find my words. I started to cry, and I was mad, but that was the turning point for him; my reaction that day made him think about things in a different way. He actually picked up the whole idea of Indigenous admissions and championed [it] across the university. (Mikisiwi-Pisim)

The combination of a show of emotion, coupled with an analysis of how institutional racism becomes embedded in normative admission policies that push Indigenous students out, formed a turning point for this male colleague, who then shifted his view of admissions practices to be more inclusive and look at potential beyond the meritocratic confines of the traditional grade point average.

WORKING ON THE BORDERLAND

Several participants described the conflicting tensions they sensed operating on the borderland—at the intersection of Indigenous communities and the university. These tensions contributed to a feeling of ambivalence around how they saw themselves and how they were seen by others in the academy. Participants commonly talked about drawing deep cultural meaning from their Indigeneity and Indigenous ways of knowing. They linked Indigenous collective values—the importance of serving Indigenous communities and serving the next generation—to their leadership purpose. They often linked negative colonial experiences in their own educations to their desire to advance Indigenization and decolonization. Paradoxically, however, they also felt that their Indigeneity was often used against them, as an excuse to question, undermine, and dismiss their perspectives, and even, at times, to resist their leadership. Ironically and contrarily, although their Indigeneity played a central role in informing their purpose, it also made them more vulnerable to being Othered in the academy under the colonial gaze. Some participants expressed ambivalence about working within a highly entrenched colonial system that often appeared to be incommensurable with achieving decolonial aims. As a result, many participants, from inside the settler colonial academy, reported a dissonance between their leading decolonial change and their Indigeneity. That dissonance was revealed by one participant when she was asked, "Where do you get inspiration from as a leader?" The participant said,

> I grew up in a very small village. One of the things that I remember, and [it] made a big impression on me when I was child, was the village was kind of run by the women. So the men were, you know, hunting and fishing and doing all that good stuff, and getting the wood, you know? But the women ran the social life of the village, and I guess what we would now call the political life of the village was women's work. My father got up at five a.m. to check his nets. He had his nets laid all summer long. And on the way home he would always—he had stops along the way where he stopped and dropped off fish to people; people who were elderly, couldn't fish, or whatever. And so everybody got looked after. So I think maybe [my leadership] comes from

seeing all of that when I was a kid, you know? It was not taught to me like this conceptual stuff.... It was just [life]. (Kisi-Pisim)

The same participant described how her leadership position was perceived through the colonial gaze in the academy:

I've been told that people [in the university] are scared of me. And so I think, well, you know, here I am, I'm about five feet tall, I'm older and therefore, you know, for me, if they're scared of me, it must mean that I represent something *Other* than what is sitting in this chair. (Kisi-Pisim)

This participant's comments juxtapose two disparate ways of seeing Indigenous women leaders; they also highlight the embodied dissonance of leading with one's Indigeneity within the university. In her first comment, the participant reflects on her early childhood experiences, on growing up in a small village where she felt grounded by a sense of family, community, and kinship ties to land. She reflected on the prominent role that Indigenous women played in guiding the political life of the community, and how this understanding informs how she sees herself and her work. In stark contrast, she described in her second comment how non-Indigenous people see her and even fear her as an "Other" in the university. Reflecting on being informed by a colleague that people in the university are scared of her, she associated the fear with an ingrained colonial mindset and an Othering of Indigenous people in the settler academy and in society more broadly. This contrast marked a felt dissonance between her own and others' perceptions.

Epistemic Borderlands

Several participants identified both possibilities and limitations that surfaced as they lead Indigenization on the borderland of disparate worlds, where they experience "epistemic ignorance" (Kuokkanen, 2007). Sámi scholar Rauna Kuokkanen (2007) describes epistemic ignorance as

> arising at both institutional and individual levels [and] manifest[ing] itself by excluding and effacing Indigenous issues and materials in curricula, by denying Indigenous contributions and influences, and by showing lack of interest and understanding of Indigenous epistemes or issues (p. 67).

Kuokkanen also describes this as "rooted in academic structures that are complicit in colonialism and that reproduce the inferiority of non-Western epistemes in order to protect the interest of those in power" (2007, p. 67).

Participants encountered epistemic ignorance in their leadership in a number of ways, often finding themselves betwixt and between competing epistemic realities. Tensions arose not only when they encountered differing conceptions of leadership, but also when they were expected to behave in particular ways in order to be effective in their roles. One participant described different ways of understanding and organizing leadership that reflect epistemic differences: "[In the university], there is a focus on hierarchy. We [in Indigenous communities] don't engage in hierarchy with our people; we work in circles, we consult, we work more laterally" (Kaskatinowi-Pisim). This participant contrasts leadership as conceived and assigned within the academy with leadership in Indigenous community contexts, shedding light on the divergent epistemic centres in which Indigenous women administrators must work. On one hand, Indigenous women administrators are expected to operate in the highly institutionalized contexts of the academy, a space that recognizes positional authority, credentials, and hierarchy; on the other, they are expected to work relationally within Indigenous community contexts that tend to observe a deep respect and reverence for self-in-relation or relational leadership approaches. Indigenous community leadership tends to support emergent and fluid types of leadership based in community needs rather than in positional authority (Cajete, 2016). Because of these differences, Indigenous women administrators operate on a borderland; moreover, they must cross these boundaries, which is not easy or even safe to do. Asked how she contended with differing community and university leadership expectations and contexts, the same participant responded,

> If you think about Indigenous leadership [in the university], we're having to negotiate not just the hierarchical relationships, but we're also having to navigate lateral relationships, and so it [conventional leadership training] doesn't prepare you for the work in Indigenous communities in terms of working with Indigenous faculty, community, and staff. (Kaskatinowi-Pisim)

This participant alludes to the fact that she did not always adhere to the dominant institutional rules of engagement when working with Indigenous groups. She adheres to relational ontology when working with Indigenous communities rather than to the "ontology of hierarchy" (Malott, 2010) upon which Western institutions are premised. Several participants noted that they do not lead with their professional roles when approaching Indigenous communities, but instead lead with their relationships in the context of Indigenous Nationhood, land, and place. One participant put it this way:

> When I am around Indigenous people I downplay the position. I mean, you have to try to be like everyone else, you know? Like, I promise you, when I go home, I guarantee nobody knows what I do at the university, you know? Don't even talk about that stuff. There's a word at home, they call it [in their Indigenous language] "big feeling." You're a big feeling. It means you think much of yourself, and you think you're

better than the rest of us—big feeling. You don't want to be known as big feeling. (Kisi-Pisim)

Complex Positions on the Borderland

Participants identified the need to be aware when crossing borders, especially in academic/institutional contexts. As university employees, participants did not always fit neatly into university contexts or into local Indigenous communities. They were conscious of their own complex positionalities, trapped as they so often are in liminal spaces on the borderland of different epistemic worlds.

To complicate matters, many participants found themselves working in university contexts outside their own Indigenous Territories, which involved adapting when working with local Indigenous people. Some participants realized they were sometimes marked by local Indigenous community members as outsiders because they were not from the local Territory. One participant explained,

> My most telling moment was at an Indigenous Council meeting when one of the community members stated quite categorically that we weren't Indigenous because we worked at the institution. Therefore, we didn't speak with an Indigenous voice; we were speaking as the institution. And that was really startling. But that's how she saw us. Well, [inside the institution] we are looked at absolutely as the Other. They don't see us as the institution. Because that's the other side of it, when you're meeting with, you know—like I attend meetings with senior administrators, and it's all the deans and associate vice-presidents, et cetera. I attend those meetings, but I am totally the Native person at the table. And you can see it. It's tangible. There's even kind of, you know, if somebody else brings up the word "Indigenous" and they are talking about something, everyone will turn and look at me, not them. (Kisi-Pisim)

From this participant's perspective, taking on an Indigenous administrative role within a university involved being positioned by certain Indigenous community members as the institution, even as an outsider.

Conflicting Educational Aims on the Borderland

Beyond Indigenous women's complex borderland positioning, participants also reported being at the interface of sometimes colliding expectations between the university and Indigenous communities. For example, the university administration often expect that leaders remain neutral and serve the majority consensus, whereas Indigenous communities often expect Indigenous leaders to advance initiatives that serve the Indigenous minority. As a result of this conflict, Indigenous women administrators are often placed in the middle or in an intermediary role. This conundrum, however, does not mean that Indigenous women administrators were non-agentic in the process; it does, however, imply that they found themselves at times in complicated positions in which they felt they had to choose sides—either that of the university or of the Indigenous community. Some participants reported feeling at odds with their positions on this borderland. One participant explained, "So in my view, I worked for the members of the Aboriginal Advisory Council. In the president's view, I worked for [them]." For most leaders, maintaining their integrity with Indigenous communities remained paramount in helping them decipher and navigate these difficult decisions. One participant declared,

> My number one principle coming into this position was maintaining my integrity with community. I can't choose to stand with the institution and stand against community. I listen and meet with community all the time. Then go and try to meet with administration and try to be that negotiator. (Opaskowi-Pisim)

While all Indigenous women administrators reported feeling a strong sense of accountability to Indigenous communities, their ethical positions did not mean they never encountered challenges in their work with these communities. After all, Indigenous communities are not unified or in agreement on all matters. One participant shared a story about how some community members criticized a decision her unit had made. The criticisms were grounded in assumptions and misinformation, and she was later able to explain, through her relationship with one particular community member, the important missing context around the unit's decision-making process, and its limitations. The participant also explained how she comes to terms with the inevitable emergence of Indigenous community criticism of her leadership role:

> So, you know, I get into those spats quite regularly, and again, you know, the one thing that I come back to is as long as I think I've done my due diligence, then I live with it, and I have no qualms about saying, "Hey, I've got no power here." (Athiki-Pisim)

While she helped advise in the handling of a decision that was publicly criticized by some Indigenous community members, she emphasized that she did not in the end make the final decision. She also emphasized that Indigenous community members do not always agree and understand how university decision-making processes occur, and that she does not necessarily have authority on all matters.

Dangerous Terrain on the Borderland

Several Indigenous women participants talked about the dangers they faced working on the borderland between Indigenous communities and the administrative academy. They experienced the "shaky bridge" of Indigenous equity work in universities, taking on what Bunda et al. (2002) describe as the back-breaking burdens of those striving for social spaces within institutions that can serve needs and aspirations of Indigenous peoples. Again and again, Indigenous people crossing into whitestream institutions find themselves on shaky "equity" bridges, in peril of tumbling into rivers of tormented history. The terrors of such risks can bring about paralysed stand-stills arms crossed on the brink. Not to be thrown off stride and balance entails a very different spirit of bridge-building: a pooling of Indigenous resources not just for survival but for "hope, love, self-nourishment." It requires a lighter-stepping labour, with freer agency to move in ways and directions that take up Indigenous needs and aspirations, felt and imagined together in the walking. (p. 943)

Several participants testified that they were expected to "act as bridges" and to remove long-standing colonial divides between universities and Indigenous communities. Being situated on unequal ground, or on the shaky bridge, was not only exhausting but often dangerous embodied work. One participant described the challenges she faced being a bridge at her university as follows:

[Sometimes] the community people don't know how the university works. They have no idea how the structure works; they just think it's like this faceless, nameless, hard-hearted institution that they have to fight and is up to no good. (Kisi-Pisim)

This participant highlights how Indigenous leaders often become trapped at the interface of long-standing conflicts and divisions between Indigenous communities and the university. She describes the embodied experience of trying to bridge historical and ongoing systemic gaps and patterns as extremely isolating, challenging, and even impossible. Another participant described similar impacts stemming from her labour on the shaky bridge:

I ended up going on a leave of absence. I found out that I needed to unplug from the emotional labour of this work and found myself, honestly, just hating my job. So there were three distinct moments that happened this year that were so exhausting to constantly fight for Indigenous peoples, you know, so it was hardly any policy-making but lots of advocacy this year. And it was really exhausting. I mean it was awful in a lot of ways, because it really showed the neutrality [of the university] to us, and their complicity in this type of hateful rhetoric that exists around campus. So, anyway, I went on leave, and I am basically wanting to come to a place where I can at least love to go to work again. I just hit a brick wall. (Niski-Pisim)

This participant affirms the dangers of falling from the shaky bridge. As Bunda et al. (2012) have asserted, "Those who dare to negotiate the double desire—to remain Indigenous and to participate in often inhospitable institutions for benefits they might provide—can feel tenuous and alienated, even while hoping to forge possibilities for moving forward" (p. 948). This passage, along with comments from several other participants in the present study, point to experiences of "racial battle fatigue" (Almeida, 2015) that place additional expectations on Indigenous leaders working under white settler, patriarchal, and borderland conditions, and that have adverse embodied impacts on Indigenous women leaders.

EMBODYING THE TRIPLE BINDS

Educational administration has undoubtedly acted as a colonizing tool for the settler colonial state. The history and ongoing structural reality of universities is based on white settler colonial and male-centric norms of leadership. The Indigenous women administrators featured in this book grappled with these hegemonic norms in their embodied experiences of the triple bind. They commonly testified to feeling a sense of dissonance and ambivalence in their leadership work, a dissonance that revealed itself when they compared how they understood and experienced their own leadership responsibilities with how they were often seen and treated by others in the academy. As a result of complex institutional lineages, Indigenous women reported becoming caught within the triple bind in their roles working within a settler colonial educational system and under dominant male notions of leadership. These predicaments created dissonance, embodied tensions, and ambivalences among Indigenous women leaders as they operated on the borderland between disparate worlds—the university and the Indigenous communities they served. Despite the undeniable privilege and positional power associated with their senior administrative roles, Indigenous women administrators described facing consistent challenges in enacting their leadership within dominant administrative contexts. Many talked explicitly about the multiple and interlocking barriers they faced when championing institutional change within highly visible and often politically charged roles. Under a normalized administrative culture that espouses hierarchy, neutrality in leadership, positional power, and structural functionalism—all aimed at the maintenance of the university system—Indigenous women administrators who led Indigenizing policies with their Indigeneity struggled not only to be seen and heard but to guide decolonial change. Consequently, they often talked about bumping up against the "brick walls" of the hegemonic administrative academy. Against the backdrop of these brick walls, participants talked about the danger of borderland work—as they navigated, negotiated, and sometimes challenged dominant settler colonial institutional structures and norms.

Despite these felt and embodied binds, women also described a sense that the struggle in which they were engaged was denied by the dominant group in universities and underappreciated by Indigenous communities unfamiliar with the university. University colleagues did not understand the unique challenges Indigenous women faced in their leadership work, nor did they appreciate the weight of the emotional labour they undertook and the reconciliation fatigue they endured trying to transform an inherently colonial institution. Several women recounted painful stories of being ostracized by Indigenous people, especially when they worked outside their ancestral Territories. These experiences revealed that internalized colonialism and lateral forms of violence are alive within Indigenous communities. While many women recognized that by holding administrative positions within the university, they were implicated in a Euro-Westernized way of conceiving and distributing leadership and power, they also recognized that leadership was often understood differently in some Indigenous community contexts (both within and outside the academy), and thereby that their work straddled different epistemic conceptions of leadership. Some women talked about how Elders occupied important leadership roles that were not always well understood or respected in formal educational hierarchies. At the same time, when working within Indigenous community contexts, women would sometimes downplay their formal leadership roles in universities. Indifference to formal leadership positions in some Indigenous communities can be linked to differing epistemic understandings and values.

CHAPTER 9

"IT'S NOT *as* EASY *as* IT SOUNDS"
The Trickiness of Indigenizing Policy Enactments

This is a story about the written word of policies, the promises they make, and the tricks they play when we try to put those words into action. This story unfolds in the slippery crevices between bricks and mortar that structure power in often invisible ways. But if we listen carefully from the margins, we can hear "Other" stories and how policy promises sometimes get questioned by the very group they claim to serve. In this story, I hope you can start to hear beyond the grand institutional narratives and listen to the embodied tensions experienced by those who are most expected to put words into action.

As part of the national reconciliation movement in Canada, universities were among the first public institutions to take action through increased policy efforts, which I refer to in the present study as Indigenizing policy work. In this chapter, I strive to answer the following, overarching research question: What challenges do Indigenous women administrators face when enacting Indigenizing policies within Canadian universities? The study has yielded three main findings related broadly to Indigenizing policy enactments in Canadian universities:

1. Indigenizing policy enactments are shaped by institutional speech acts.
2. Indigenizing policy enactments are messy and contested processes in practice.
3. Indigenizing policies are constrained by ongoing structures of patriarchal white sovereignty within universities.

In this chapter, I draw on the embodied experiences of the participants—Indigenous women administrators who have been hired to champion the implementation of Indigenizing policies in Canadian universities. Through their stories, I assert that Indigenizing policies have inadequately accounted for the complexities of "policy enactments"—that is, the unavoidably political and inherently unpredictable ways that policies are taken up in practice (Ball et al., 2012) within ongoing structures of settler colonialism, hetero-patriarchy, and global capitalism (Grande, 2015). Moreover, I assert that Indigenizing policies are tricky to enact as they are inevitably taken up through "possessive logics of patriarchal white sovereignty" (Moreton-Robinson, 2015), which in turn prevent "decolonial-Indigenization"—the transformative process of moving universities from conventional hierarchies of governance and knowledge production toward realizing Indigenous resurgence and sovereignty (Gaudry & Lorenz, 2018b). Torres Strait scholar Aileen Moreton-Robinson (2015) puts forth the notion of possessive logics of patriarchal white sovereignty as tied to white settler state laws and their institutional practices, and as often functioning through everyday inter-subjectivities that reinforce and reproduce white settler ownership and control over Indigenous lives and lands. In this chapter, I show how possessive logics emerge and operate through university administrative structures and policy practices in ways that subvert Indigenous people's educational sovereignty.

To demonstrate the challenges of policy enactment, I work with Māori scholar Linda Tuhiwai Smith's (2005) notion of trickiness to describe the invisible yet powerful ways in which colonial power is operationalized in academic contexts to benefit certain groups over others, in particular white settlers over Indigenous peoples. While Smith uses the term "trickiness" to describe the ways in which colonial power plays out in Indigenous research practices, between researchers' methodological choices, ethics, and policies, and research subjects, I use the term to examine how white settler academic structures, policy documents and processes, and policy actors' interests converge and diverge in policy enactment practices. Unlike rationalist and instrumentalist approaches to policy that assume policies are apolitical and can be implemented in straightforward, linear, and measurable ways, the trickiness of policy enactment highlights policies as complex, contested, and messy processes, linked to policy actors' positionalities within white settler ongoing structures, inter-subjective assumptions, and biases tied to intersectional forces of power, most notably to patriarchal white sovereignty. Through this critical Indigenous policy lens, Indigenizing policies in Canadian universities can be seen as both a product and an interactive, dynamic, and ongoing political process (Ball, 1990; Taylor et al., 1997; Strakosch, 2015), fundamentally taken up within patriarchal white settler colonial institutions in which Indigenous peoples continue to struggle to assert their Indigenous educational sovereignty.

In examining the trickiness of Indigenizing policy enactments in academic contexts, possessive logics embedded in the patriarchal white sovereignty of the university inevitably creep into policy processes in insidious ways that tend to reproduce settler colonial relations of power;

these in turn create impossible dilemmas and messy divisions that undermine Indigenous sovereignty. Moreover, the trickiness of white possessive logics operates in policy enactment processes in often invisible and common-sensical ways that are connected to a complex regime of power that strives to reproduce settler possession over Indigenous people's educational decision making. Thereby, under white settler colonial gaze and control, Indigenizing policies in universities often become severely limited in practice, strangled by interconnecting systems operating at the intersections of macro, meso, and micro levels of power—that is, at the macro levels of global capitalism, imperial/colonialism, and settler state government and legislation; the meso levels of academic governance systems, policies, and practices embedded in white liberalism; and the micro levels of individual ideological and inter-subjective relations of power.

INSTITUTIONAL SPEECH ACTS

Universities control Indigenizing policy discourses through what Sara Ahmed (2007c) calls "institutional speech acts." Institutional speech acts give the appearance that universities are committed to equity (and reconciliation and Indigenization), but they are non-performative acts, because they do not necessarily accomplish what they claim to commit to or support. Drawing on similar critiques based on "liberal recognition politics" put forth by Dene scholar Glen Coulthard in the context of Canadian government reconciliation policies, I argue that institutional speech acts operate within Indigenizing policies in universities as a politics of recognition, a politics that promotes a psycho-affective attachment that often negates redistribution of power and, in the process, serves to eclipse and displace Indigenous educational sovereignty. For example, new Indigenizing policies in Canadian universities have been heavily scrutinized for their symbolic and tokenistic tendencies (Gaudry & Lorenz, 2018b) and criticized as a "settler spectacle of reconciliation"

(Daigle, 2019). Despite widespread criticisms, however, universities have continued to release a large number of symbolic policy documents, including public apologies, land acknowledgements, public condolences, public letters, memoranda of understanding, and press releases, as outlined in chapter 2.

While public documents are undoubtedly influential in society and a necessary part of institutional policy education and change communication processes, some policy documents, I argue, contribute to greater levels of change than others, especially those policies that are tied to material resources and institutional systems of authority that redistribute power and increase Indigenous collective sovereignty. For example, broad-based Indigenous strategic plans that are tied to institutional budget planning processes and that include the views of Indigenous senior leadership with institutional authority are much stronger than Indigenous action plans within a single unit (such as student affairs) that does not have budget allocation. In my research, I note that such structural and budgetary advances often did not transpire until after the TRC's report was released or universities were publicly criticized. For example, the University of Manitoba underwent a structural shift only after their inaugural vice-provost (Indigenous initiatives) resigned and went public with her negative experiences in 2019. Since then, the University of Manitoba has completed a review of Indigenous policy and senior leadership; the review committee recommended the creation of several associated Indigenous leadership positions along with a budget commensurate to the implementation of the university's Indigenous strategic plan (Indigenous Senior Leadership Advisory Committee, 2019).

Despite the debates surrounding the Indigenizing of policy, many participants in the present study reported some of the troubling ways that Indigenizing policy documents were used symbolically. In particular, participants told of such documents being used in performative ways that gave the appearance that the university was Indigenizing or reconciling when, in reality, Indigenous people continued to experience stark discrepancies between the university's public image and their lived experiences working in the institution. Operating within a white possessive logic, participants often described institutional speech acts as part of deeper neoliberal and neo-colonial economic stories shaped by their universities' desire to improve their competitive brands and to raise their profiles in the neoliberal public domain. One participant said, "It's troublesome for me that universities make public kinds of statements, and we don't back them up with the policies, practices, and resources—all of those things that need to happen to really make meaningful change" (Kaskatinowi-Pisim). This participant challenges the underlying white liberal recognition politics at play in some university statements, because those statements do not always come with the resources needed to drive the changes they promise. Another participant said,

> Indigenizing is being co-opted by a colonial system that is now using the terminology and saying that they're Indigenizing, and all it is is an assimilation project. If anyone wants to Indigenize, then they need to have their Indigenous team making their own decisions and working, operating alongside, and making their own negotiations with equal authority and power within the organization. (Nimitahamowi-Pisim)

In this participant's view, institutional speech acts were at times deceptively tricky, with the university system co-opting the term and twisting the message to serve its institutional needs rather than Indigenous people's needs, thereby reproducing settler colonial relations of power. Several participants reported struggling with the ways that universities used Indigenization as a corporate public affairs opportunity.

One participant described how a public statement made by her university after the trial of the person accused of the murder of a young Cree man, Colten Boushie, in 2016, went wrong:

> Monday comes, and in their scramble to try to get something out, their haste, it was wrong, it was a miscalculation. They said something to the effect of, "The university is proud of our work in Indigenization efforts despite the recent court case"—something like that. Really vague. They didn't even name the family; they didn't send condolences to the Boushie and Baptiste families; they didn't. It was just, "Look at us, we're doing this work, this work, and this work." You know, check, check, check, and it pissed me off. It pissed me off, because I was like, "Uh, I work here. I think everyone's going to say I'm complicit in this erasure." (Niski-Pisim)

This participant questioned the way her university not only used the verdict to make a self-congratulatory claim about its Indigenization efforts but, more troublingly, ended up erasing Indigenous voices and the larger settler colonial problem that shaped the acquittal process. Another participant talked about her work co-authoring an Indigenizing policy at her university and how, in the process, she had to constantly push back against her settler colleagues' desire to paint the university's performance within the public document as positive. When her and her colleagues were writing the report, she explained, "I'd say a lot of the time, I was like, 'No, let's not start off with the [university] is so great; no, we have a lot of work to do.'" Indeed, several participants in the present study found themselves at odds with dominant institutional tendencies toward institutional speech acts as a form of corporate public relations operating within larger global capitalist, neo-colonial, and neoliberal forces. Another participant questioned the growing university practice of publishing press releases including memoranda of understanding (MOUs) to celebrate an institution's steps toward achieving reconciliation. She critiqued this practice by saying,

> Most of the MOUs I see are kind of actionless. They're agreements to work together, basically, but there's no real direct action linked to it

and, as a result, not much has happened in this case anyway. People make a big deal about MOUs, and you see them in the paper all the time. So you find an MOU. But then, like, years later you might go back and start looking at all this and assessing what came out of it. I bet a lot of cases would show you that very little was actually done. (Pimahamowi-Pisim)

In many of their stories, participants underscored the deceptive ways in which settler colonialism operated in Indigenizing policy communication practices—practices that often resulted in institutional speech acts that gave the impression that institutions had changed, while in reality they had not undergone deep levels of decolonial reform.

In scene 8, chapter 7 (p. 141), Weesakechahk enacts a speech act by reciting a university land acknowledgement, a common and highly critiqued policy practice within Canadian universities. In the scene, Weesakechahk enacts a common possessive refrain, wherein a university administrator welcomes the audience (including local Indigenous people) to the university, thereby assuming the role of host. As Sámi scholar Rauna Kuokkanen (2007) argues, the university is based on Western notions of hospitality that reinforce the master host-guest relationship and that merely include Indigenous people as guests. At the same time, the university's welcoming words are deeply scripted (performative) and full of tensions as white settler administrators mispronounce Indigenous names in Indigenous languages and misplace Indigenous people in a guest position on their own land. Heather, the central Indigenous character of this dramatic scene, interrupts the common-sense settler spectacle by reclaiming her place in the university space, speaking out of turn, and finding a voice to tell her story.

Heather's monologue exposes many of the hidden policy truths that surfaced in the present study, truths related to the challenging experiences of Indigenous women administrators enacting Indigenizing policy promises in Canadian universities. Her monologue uncovers the politics behind specific policies, particularly the ways in which federal and provincial governments and jurisdictions interconnect and coalesce—in ways that often structurally limit and marginalize Indigenous people's educational sovereignty. In Heather's monologue, we hear that the TRC has acted as a powerful driving force, compelling the university administration to open up and listen to Indigenous people. While Heather's story highlights how the TRC has contributed to advancing Indigenous people's agency, the story also points to the challenges of mobilizing change without structural reform and within common-sense settler notions of power. Heather's monologue further raises key issues related to the limitations of Indigenizing policy enactments that occur within existing academic structures and that do not take into account the possessive white logics embedded in the academy. The story further sheds light on the complexities of policy enactment experiences among Indigenous people who remain under-represented in the academy. The story shows how policy norms can fall prey to symbolic approaches that do not adequately shift colonial and institutional power structures and dynamics, thereby foreshadowing the troubling ways in which the very policies intended to liberate Indigenous people can end up, paradoxically, exploiting them.

THE MESSY AND CONTESTED NATURE OF POLICY ENACTMENT

In this research, Indigenous women administrators also often described Indigenous policy enactment as messy, contested, and paradoxical in practice—as contradictory—because although policies were claimed to benefit Indigenous people, the lived experiences of many Indigenous people in the enactment process told an opposite story. While participants often talked about Indigenizing policies as advancing institutional change, they also described how such policy sometimes produced unintended consequences that were messy and even contested by Indigenous people within the academy. One participant said,

> It has placed unprecedented demands on Indigenous scholars, staff, students, and leadership. I think a lot of the responsibility is placed on Indigenous peoples to help people interpret the policies and understand the intent and meaning behind them and how they can respectfully be done and not just [treated as items on] a checklist. (Kaskatinowi-Pisim)

Another participant outlined some of the challenges she faced enacting Indigenizing policies within a university system that inherently silenced Indigenous voices, because they were marginalized and under-represented in the academic governance system. "We have this policy called collegial governance or shared governance," she said, which is "where you go out to consult, but [the people we consult are] all non-Indigenous. Our under-representation is the hardest thing. Shared decision making is almost impossible" (Thithikopiwi-Pisim). In their narratives, the participants highlight how patriarchal white sovereignty dominates and reproduces itself through majority rules, thereby often interfering with and obstructing Indigenous people's assertion of their educational sovereignty.

Participants also talked about Indigenizing policies as operating in two contradictory ways—as tools that empower Indigenous people, and as instruments that oppress Indigenous people. Some participants talked explicitly about the strategic use of existing university policies in their leadership (i.e., supporting Indigenous faculty members using existing faculty association policies to make their cases to do Indigenous research in tenure and promotion processes). At the same time, participants also talked about the limits of existing university policies, which are highly Westernized and Eurocentric, and about the need to review and amend those policies to make them more congruent with Indigenous ways of knowing. In some cases, participants talked about developing entirely new, Indigenous-specific policies that privilege Indigenous ways of knowing—smudging policies, for example. Participants also talked about advancing university strategic plans and action plans informed by Indigenous interests, and policies in the areas of Indigenous curriculum and Indigenous faculty hiring. Several participants talked about such policies as their "friends" and as helping them increase Indigenous access to university resources to meet Indigenous needs. One participant described policy use in her leadership in this way:

> We have to have a strong understanding of the policies that are our friends, even though these policies might not look like it; but we have to look at that policy, understand our Indigenous world views, what we're trying to bring forward, and manoeuvre it [accordingly]. I think activism is so linked to policy, and when you're doing activist work and you don't know policy, you're kind of—sometimes trying to advance something that's not going to work. (Ohpahowi-Pisim)

Another participant described her relationship to policy in a university context as "vital"

> because policies help us figure out how to advance Indigenous knowledge within the academy. I think we have to understand the policies, work within the policies that [are] our friends, and then change the policies that are problematic. (Opaskowi-Pisim)

Both participants highlight the utility of existing university policies and the need for Indigenous leaders to have policy literacy in order to interpret and use existing policies to benefit Indigenous people and drive decolonial change. Sara Ahmed (2019), in her book *What's the Use?*, conducts a literature review of the word "use" to examine how it has functioned historically and indeed continues to operate in university policies as a colonial, gendered, and racialized technique for shaping (and disciplining) certain bodies in dominant white spaces. Ahmed argues that utility operates through university policy as a normative technique. She further posits that diversity workers in the United Kingdom use policy as a technique to disrupt normative discourses in universities, which therefore positions policy work as a mode of surviving in the academy, a way of challenging the normative policy functionalism of universities. Similar adoptions of university policies are occurring among Indigenous women administrators in the context of Indigenization policy movements in Canadian universities.

Participants often talked about how Indigenous university policy discourses have dramatically shifted since the TRC, challenging the colonial positioning of Indigenous people as the "Indian problem" in post-secondary educational policy in favour of recognizing the colonial problem embedded within universities. The discourse of the "Indian problem" (Dyck, 1999) has been an enduring colonial narrative in educational policies that has "Othered" Indigenous people and ways of knowing, resulting in them being viewed through a deficit lens and depicted as uncivilized, illiterate, and incapable. The Indigenizing policy movement in Canada has involved pushing back against these colonial narratives. As one participant explained,

> Our students have asked us—and you'll notice in there [*points to the policy document*] that we don't talk much about student support—our students say, "We're not the problem, and we're not sick. And sometimes we get frustrated but sometimes that's from your system. Don't talk about us in the deficit." (Niski-Pisim)

This participant described her university's Indigenous strategic plan as shifting from a focus on changing Indigenous students toward a focus on changing the system. Other participants also highlighted policy shifts that have moved institutions beyond an Indigenous student services model of education that focused on helping Indigenous students to acculturate (i.e., assimilate) into the dominant university system, toward actively changing the university system to be more inclusive of Indigenous people and ways of knowing (Pidgeon, 2016; Rigney, 2017). Another participant explained the change process in this way:

> It's not that we need to help Indigenous people; its more about what Indigenous peoples bring to the academy, how can Indigenous peoples strengthen the academy, and what contributions that they can make. We need to move away from that deficit kind of thinking that the academy is just there to help Indigenous peoples. (Kaskatinowi-Pisim)

While the degree of decolonial change occurring in universities is highly contested and debatable, the calls of the TRC for deeper levels of reform have certainly contributed to shifting conversations on university campuses around who changes, for what purposes, and on what terms. While these shifting policy narratives are important, their goals are taken up in practice—in the policy enactment process—in highly contested ways.

Participants often reported troubling encounters with white settlers in the academy, encounters that silenced their voices. Indigenous people continue to be a minority in academic spaces, which privilege the liberal democratic principles of the individual and the majority. As a result, many Indigenous women administrators found themselves in messy enactment situations in which impossible dilemmas emerged. One participant talked about the challenges she faced trying to hang the flags of local Indigenous Nations on her university campus—because existing university policies limited the types of flags permitted on campus. Only provincial and settler nation-state flags were sanctioned. The privileging of settler flags exemplifies the powerful stranglehold of the doctrine of discovery. These long-standing university policies, steeped in settler colonialism and nationalism, thwarted Indigenous sovereignty and languages and in turn created barriers to enacting Indigenizing policies.

Another participant told of a colonial encounter that emerged in the creation of a smudging policy, which became messy and contested after a settler administrator demonstrated "epistemic ignorance" (Kuokannen, 2007, 2008; Sasakamoose & Pete, 2015), which misrelated smudging practices to the smoking of tobacco. Epistemic ignorance is a violent process of marginalizing, excluding, and discriminating against non-Western epistemic and intellectual traditions, and is based on Eurocentric thought and assumptions (Kuokkanen, 2007). Epistemic ignorance arose in the smudge policy-making process when an individual sanctioned with institutional power enacted and reproduced existing Eurocentric policies. The settler administrator used Eurocentric biases and assumptions about tobacco as a recreational practice to halt the smudge policy-making process. Consequently, the process became so painfully divisive, disrespectful, and undermining of Indigenous ways of knowing and protocols that the Indigenous administrator abruptly ended a meeting to discuss the process. The participant explained how both administrators came back to the process after a first failed attempt:

> So I went back in, and I am meeting with the administrator, and he just said, "I don't want a rehash of last time. I don't want to have to go through that again." He said, "So if we can just take this policy and rip it up." And he ripped it up and put it aside. "Can we just start from scratch?" And I said, "Absolutely." (Ohpahowi-Pisim)

The act of ripping up the old smoke-free policy powerfully illustrates the epistemic dominance of Euro-Western ways of knowing, and the need to disrupt white settler dominance in order to make authentic space for Indigenous ways of knowing to emerge in the academy. Many participants told similar stories about having to challenge and deconstruct the epistemic ignorance that formed the basis of long-standing university policies and practices. Several participants reported that their policy work often involved questioning and deconstructing policies and practices that were taken for granted and normalized through patriarchal white sovereignty. Participants often described their encounters with these embedded epistemic ignorances, however, as deeply challenging.

Several participants reported that the observance of Indigenous ways of knowing and the practising of Indigenous ceremonies such as smudging, feasting, and working with Elders and knowledge carriers often revealed epistemic incongruences. One participant said that many of her policy needs arose out of situations in which Indigenous ways of knowing were being disrespected and often countered by dominant Euro-Western policies and practices on campus:

> So we couldn't have a feast because of the [policy] agreements that are in place with catering and food services companies. So you can't bring your own food on campus, you can't cook your food there, you can't do anything. So that policy urgency arose right away. (Ohpahowi-Pisim)

The food services policy and practices were reported as particularly challenging for the observation of local Indigenous feasting on university campuses. In this and other matters, existing institutional policies, particularly in the areas of human resources and finance, limited the conditions upon which Indigenous participants could respectfully observe Indigenous ways of knowing on campus. Moreover, several of these existing policies were controlled under broader nation-state legislative requirements imposed by settler colonial governments. For example, human resources followed the federal Canada Revenue Agency policy requiring Elders to be paid as non-employees. Indeed, participants' narratives often pointed to larger systemic factors connected to patriarchal white sovereignty, and the ways that meso (university) policies coalesced with macro (global capitalism, imperialism/colonialism, and settler nation-state) systems, which did not benefit Indigenous peoples. As a result, the creation of new Indigenizing policies within universities was severely limited under the settler colonial ethics of incommensurability. Thus, while Indigenizing policies in universities have contributed to institutional change, they, alone, are not a panacea. The Indigenizing policy enactment process within universities often surfaces deeper issues based within ongoing settler colonial and ideological systems.

FOUR RECURRING DILEMMAS

Four recurring dilemmas surfaced in participants' narratives related to constraints on Indigenizing policy enactment within academic structures shaped by patriarchal white sovereignty: (1) increasing Indigenous workloads and Indigenous under-representation; (2) increasing calls for Indigenizing content (curriculum and research) but without Indigenous faculty, knowledge, and experience; (3) institutionalizing Indigeneity and measuring success; and (4) settler moves toward innocence and co-optation.

Increased Workload and Under-Representation

One of the impacts of Indigenizing policy reform that was most talked about among participants was the fact that new policies have placed increasing pressure on the few Indigenous people working in universities. Several participants reported experiencing increasing demands and a growing administrative pressure to take on leadership roles, sometimes earlier than they would have preferred. As one participant attested,

> [The TRC] has placed unprecedented demands on Indigenous scholars, staff, students, and leadership. I think a lot of the responsibility

is placed on Indigenous peoples [to] help people interpret [policies] and understand the intent and meaning behind them and how [that] can...respectfully be done, not just as a checklist. (Kaskatinowi-Pisim)

Many participants also talked about how increased demands often involved them chairing and sitting on new committees as well as educating administration and non-Indigenous people about Indigenous perspectives and needs. According to several participants, these expectations often placed them in vulnerable positions that required them to take on additional emotional and invisible labour, which was not always compensated or recognized, and which created inequitable workloads that sometimes negatively impacted their well-being and their careers (e.g., by affecting their research productivity).

More positively, several Indigenous administrators in this study reported that the TRC and associated Indigenizing policy directives helped them to convince their universities to create more Indigenous-specific staffing positions. While many of these employee advancements were long overdue, the delay being a result of chronic underfunding of Indigenous initiatives overall, several participants reported experiencing challenges filling certain roles because the Indigenous employment market was so competitive, and because there were few Indigenous people available to take on certain positions. This participant described her experience as follows:

When I came into this office, the majority of the staff were term, a number of them were part-time, and we didn't have enough staff. And so, you know, I've really had to push against the system: "You've got a strategic framework and this office is where so much of the support comes from, but the majority of the staff are term and many of them are part-time." Since I've come in, we've been able to get—all of the ones that were term are now base funded. We worked with

human resources, and we went back and re-evaluated every single
job description. We added cultural competencies, so we really fought
hard and we managed to get just about every job in this office to reflect
what people are doing. (Athiki-Pisim)

As part of the shifts in employee relations, participants also reported pushing for an increase in Indigenous faculty cluster hiring—the bringing of several Indigenous faculty members into a university, faculty, or department at one time. While Indigenous faculty cluster hiring was reported by many participants as a common policy initiative, some attested to the challenge of hiring Indigenous staff members as their "number one challenge." One participant said,

We are not aggressively hiring enough Indigenous staff in my view. I
feel like we should almost have an HR person or recruitment person
working with the local reserves, and they're not doing it; they don't
work that way; that's not part of their idea of how things should be
done. You can't really shift the culture of the institution without people,
and we don't have enough people. We need more people. (Kisi-Pisim)

Therefore, while Indigenizing policies have started to shift institutional hiring practices for senior leaders and faculty members and have created some stability in much-needed Indigenous units, they have not necessarily focused enough, according to participants in this study, on hiring more staff members to work in various units across the university.

Indigenizing Content without Knowledge, Experience, or Relationships

Another policy dilemma that surfaced in this study relates to calls to Indigenize curriculum despite a lack of expertise among most faculty members. Indigenizing policies have certainly contributed to some positive preliminary shifts in curriculum in Canadian universities (Gaudry & Lorenz, 2018a), but approaches vary across the sector and within institutions. Curriculum policy approaches included instituting mandatory undergraduate courses on Indigenous topics (Gaudry & Lorenz, 2018a); creating required courses within professional programs such as education, medicine, and law; approving policy directives that require integration of a percentage of Indigenous content into specific programs; incentivized funding envelopes to develop learning opportunities for faculty members; and the hiring of Indigenous curriculum advisers to develop and deliver professional development programs.

Participants in this study corroborated previous research reports that pointed to structural, pedagogical, and ideological challenges that surface when instituting Indigenizing curriculum policies (Gaudry & Lorenz, 2018b). While participants did not dispute the need to bring Indigenous perspectives into university teaching and learning, their concerns arose around policy approaches that focused on Indigenizing for the masses rather than on developing Indigenous community-based programs. Several participants also questioned whether an infusion model for Indigenizing the curriculum across the institution would necessarily positively impact Indigenous academic units such as Indigenous studies. One participant expressed concerns with the hyper-focus on Indigenizing the curriculum for the masses, arguing that it often took attention away from Indigenous students and Indigenous community-based programs, thus re-centring the needs of the dominant white settler group. She said, "I don't want to talk about whether we have an Indigenous content requirement within the curriculum across all the faculties. When we focus on this, we forget about the Indigenous learner. We can't expect everyone to be an expert with Indigenous content, and more harm than good is often the result" (Opaskowi-Pisim). This participant also talked about what she thought Indigenization should focus on:

> We need to focus on Indigenous resurgence, gathering our bundles, gathering our ceremony, gathering our traditions, gathering our languages, the land, the knowledge, and us becoming healthier. I want to focus on having Indigenous people be successful within these colonial walls, so we focus on supporting Indigenous peoples. (Opaskowi-Pisim)

She raised questions about broad-based Indigenizing curriculum policy approaches that often, in her opinion, lost sight of Indigenous students and community needs, and ended up centring too much on dominant white settler needs.

Another participant reported that her university's curriculum policy approach—which required all undergraduate programs within two years to develop, at a minimum, one Indigenous course equivalent—ended up placing a lot of demands on her small Indigenous team. The participant reported that many faculties at her university were slow to get started on the Indigenous curriculum planning process, and that their lack of understanding of Indigenous matters and their initial inaction wreaked havoc in her office as faculty members scrambled at the last minute for support. She said,

> Our office has developed a suite of resources for faculty to refer to. We hired a graduate student who spent months resourcing texts and readings so that people in all disciplines can turn to this and say, "Oh, wow, there's Indigenous-authored work in my field." But they have to do the work; I can't do it for them and obviously just spoon-feed them. (Niski-Pisim)

Institutionalizing Indigeneity and Measuring Success

In response to increasing calls to Indigenize the academy, participants in the present study reported a growing administrative desire to track and measure Indigenization efforts. This administrative work often involved tracking Indigenous students and members of the workforce, as well as defining how the success of the Indigenizing process is to be measured. Part of the process inevitably involved tracking Indigenous bodies, and thereby institutionalizing Indigeneity—an already highly contested process tied to politics of evidence and regimes of surveillance that have not historically served Indigenous people (Walter & Anderson, 2013). While Lynn Lavallee (2020) agrees that metrics attached to reconciliation are needed, she argues that the most important metric should be university budgets. Nonetheless, several participants in this study reported an increasing administrative pressure for them not only to track and report Indigenization outcomes, but also to verify Indigenous people's ancestry claims. These concerns stemmed from cases of ethnic fraud (Flaherty, 2015; Lawford & Coburn, 2019) in which some faculty and staff members falsely claimed Indigenous ancestry to gain access to academic and leadership positions intended for Indigenous people (Sterrit, 2019). Valid community concerns regarding appropriative issues of ethnic fraud have placed increasing pressure on participants to develop new policies and practices that verify applicants' claims of Indigeneity and connections to community in order to safeguard against identify fraud (NIUSLA, 2022).

While Indigenous identity- and ancestry-verification practices for hiring Indigenous people or awarding Indigenous students scholarships varied across (and even within) universities, they often precipitated debates around authenticity and community belonging. The comments of some participants suggest that certain ancestry-verification processes capitulated to colonial definitions that relied on government authentication processes (e.g., Indian Status). While some universities went beyond settler colonial definitions by requiring letters from First Nations, Métis, Inuit, and urban Indigenous organizations to confirm authenticity, asking applicants to make positionality statements, and/or involving Indigenous people in the hiring processes, many participants attested to the struggles of their universities to define consistent institutional verification processes. One participant described the challenges of authenticating community connections by saying that the process

> calls into question what are you calling "the community"? Are the only communities the reserves? That's the only valid Indigenous community? What about all the non-status communities, which are legitimate places? They exist in reality all over the country. It's more complicated than any of us are wanting to talk about. (Kisi-Pisim)

Beyond tensions related to defining and authenticating Indigenous community in faculty and leadership hiring processes, several participants identified escalating calls for the tracking and reporting of Indigenous people, and the evaluation of Indigenous initiatives overall. The administrative desire to track, count, surveil, and report on Indigenous people in order to be accountable brings forth administrative power relations and historical and ongoing processes that have defined and controlled Indigenous people in troubling ways. One participant shared the administrative challenge she faced when instituting an Indigenous student self-identification process at her university:

> I got right on board with the [student] self-identification process, because I wanted the data to build my case, but it was one of the most challenging things I've ever done. I should have realized because I have lived experience and know how contentious identity and policy are. It kept me up many nights, I'll tell you, because there is no agreement; there were people that really didn't agree that self-identification was the best route. (Thithikopiwi-Pisim)

This participant disclosed her own administrative desire to track Indigenous students in order to build a stronger case to obtain more institutional resources to serve growing Indigenous needs. She also described the Indigenous community's concerns around colonial surveillance that surfaced in the Indigenous student self-identification policy development process, concerns that contributed to several Indigenous people disputing and not participating in the process altogether. Her dilemma revealed how a government bill to gather personal information from institutions raised new Indigenous community concerns that interfered with the participation process.

Other participants expressed concerns with how emerging faculty ancestry-verification processes differed from Indigenous student self-identification processes. Many Indigenous student processes rely on self-declaration, whereas emerging staff- and faculty-verification processes are more comprehensive, requiring applicants to provide positionality statements and, sometimes, support documents. One participant questioned the inconsistencies between these different approaches and worried that some institutions were narrowly relying on documents that might exclude vulnerable and disenfranchised Indigenous populations. She argued,

> You can't draw those hard-and-fast lines between faculty, staff, and students when you start talking about self-identification or ancestry. In the end, you are going to involve the students in that. Some of us are saying, "Well, we're only talking about keeping frauds out of the job." What I'm most concerned about, actually, is the injustice I can see happening out of trying to create a rigid...line about this stuff. (Opawahcikanasis)

This participant underscores the unintended and negative consequences of institutionalizing policies around Indigeneity in ways that may not critically interrogate colonial definitions, and that may have unintended oppressive impacts. Expanding on what she meant by "injustice," she added:

There are thousands and thousands of Indigenous adoptees out there, or if they weren't adopted, they went to the foster child system. They truly don't know anything, and they're the first to admit that. Many have no way of reconnecting even with their own family. They might want to reconnect to a community, and they may not be able to. (Kisi-Pisim)

This participant highlighted the violent lineage of colonial Indian policies in Canada—such as the Sixties Scoop—and how the consequences continue to linger and impact Indigenous people's sense of Indigeneity as well as their connections to and disconnections from Indigenous communities. She also underscored the ways that Indigenous people have been disenfranchised from community, land, and place intergenerationally, and how many Indigenous people are only now reconnecting. She further questioned how institutionalizing Indigeneity too narrowly within the university can inadvertently reproduce patriarchal white sovereignty, ideologies, and racial constructs that reproduce settler colonial systems of power, and negatively impact more vulnerable segments of the Indigenous population such as disenfranchised Indigenous people. Thus, normative administrative policies that measure institutional success using evidence-based approaches emerge as a tension, which in turn points to deeper questions around measuring success in ethical and culturally relevant ways that observe Indigenous data sovereignty.

SETTLER MOVES TO INNOCENCE AND DESIRES TO CO-OPT

On the opposite end of the spectrum, many Indigenizing policy enactments were criticized by participants in this study for being too broad and, thereby, open to settler co-optation. Arguably, the axiom "nothing about us without us" emerged out of the Indigenous pushback against the rise of settler colonial co-optation in the reconciliation movement in Canada. Several participants talked candidly about witnessing Indigenizing policies in their universities being taken up problematically by self-proclaimed non-Indigenous allies who did not have the knowledge, expertise, or networks to enact Indigenizing policy work. They often shared examples of ways in which Indigenous people were prevented from directing Indigenizing policy solutions, yet they were still often turned to by non-Indigenous policy actors to help implement predetermined and often short-sighted policy initiatives. Some participants attested to an observed influx of non-Indigenous people requesting institutional resources to advance their careers under the semblance of Indigenization and reconciliation. This type of co-optation was a prickly point for many participants, because the favoured policy approaches often infringed on Indigenous educational sovereignty and obstructed the placement of Indigenous people in decision-making positions. Participants reported that these co-optative tendencies sometimes resulted from universities advancing Indigenizing policies without establishing strong systems and structures to place Indigenous units and leaders in positions of power, a move that could prevent settler co-optation. The reported rise of settler co-optation of Indigenizing policies in universities created deep frustration among some Indigenous participants in this study, and a feeling that Indigenizing policies were being taken advantage of and were not necessarily used to benefit the Indigenous people they were meant to serve.

Some participants shared their views on the inequitable power dynamics that emerge when Indigenization policies are taken up without Indigenous people in positions of power, or by non-Indigenous people who lack the cultural knowledge, networks, credibility, and expertise to lead and effectively implement policy aims. One participant described her office being cut out of an initiative when she questioned the good intentions of a colleague. The incident resulted in a problematic settler co-optation:

How much experience do they [non-Indigenous peoples] have to have when working with Indigenous peoples? And there's never any clear guidelines about what constitutes that work that they can do on their own. So I'll give you an example. An equity project was being led by a white woman, and so she did all the planning with a small group of people—invited students, faculty—and decided among that small group. I was never consulted, and it was supposed to be [a matter of equity]. So I wrote and asked them, "Where's the Indigenous piece?"...But they contacted some Indigenous students and slid it past my office, with a view that they felt that I'm always burdened by all these requests, so they thought they'd just do it themselves. That creates this kind of, oh, so you want them [non-Indigenous peoples] to do that work, but at the same time we tell them that's not okay. You still need to let me know what you're doing because I'm still the senior Indigenous lead and this office is trying to coordinate all these things, right? Do you see? So it's kind of like they still are able to control, they're still controlling the talk that happens by excluding some key people and using the people that are more vulnerable and who don't have much power in the system to say anything. They excluded myself and my office, who are in a much better position to kind of stand up and resist stuff. (Opawahcikanasis)

This participant points out a lack of policy guidelines that could have helped mitigate settler co-optation in Indigenizing policy enactment processes. She also pointed to the powerful role of policy actors' positionalities in policy enactment processes, and further made important distinctions between Indigenous and non-Indigenous policy actors' power and privilege, and even between different types of positions that Indigenous policy actors may hold. She distinguished power relations between an Indigenous academic administrator, for example, and an Indigenous student. From her perspective, policy actors' positionalities in relation to settler colonial and institutional power need to be reflected upon in nuanced and ongoing ways.

Another participant shared an experience of working with a "well-intentioned" non-Indigenous colleague who ended up creating a lot of extra work for her:

> So, someone who knows a little bit about Indigenous issues and people and has a genuine interest in the area and sees the need and gaps and wants to do something—so, he sends me an email with this idea and wants to gather all of the people of the university working on anything. Sounds great, right? [*Laughter.*] However, it's not quite as easy as it sounds. First of all, [Indigenous people] didn't like that it was a non-Indigenous person directing the enterprise. He dropped the whole idea after two quite acrimonious meetings with them. So, let's just pop out and do this and that, it's just a lot of well-meaning people who are trying to make a difference and to support Indigenous projects and just ends up making a lot of work for us. (Kisi-Pisim)

This story highlights the troubling ways that some Indigenous women administrators became engrossed in settler colonial desires to move toward resettlement and to reconcile settler guilt and complicity rather than attend to Indigenous educational sovereignty. These moves were often led by well-intentioned non-Indigenous people in ways that advanced a "politics of distraction" (G. Smith, 2003)—a colonizing process that involves the colonizer keeping Indigenous people busy with trivial things that end up reproducing settler privilege and not serving Indigenous educational needs. While this non-Indigenous policy actor may not have been fully aware of how he was resettling settler colonialism and contributing to a politics of distraction, the Indigenous administrator was nevertheless pulled into the messy policy-enactment process.

In this case, good intentions were riddled with the trickiness of settler colonial power relations that kept settlers in power and reproduced dynamics that placed Indigenous people in subordinate positions. These policy-related consequences place extra demands on Indigenous administrators in the academy and take their limited time and attention away from leading more strategic and proactive work based in Indigenous community needs.

GOVERNING LIMITS OF POLICY ENACTMENT

Participants in this study often talked about the inhibitive nature of enacting Indigenizing policy within existing academic systems, including governance structures. One of the most pervasive structures limiting Indigenous educational sovereignty in decision making is the complex and decentralized bicameral governance system of the university, along with its ties to the nation-state. While there have been calls for decolonial-Indigenization in the area of university governance (Gaudry & Lorenz, 2018b; Lavallee, 2019; Staples et al., 2021), including calls to increase Indigenous participation on, for example, student councils, university senates, and boards of governors, participants reported that universities were slow to make structural changes. The unwillingness to create Indigenous seats on boards of governors had in some cases been justified because of a reluctance to open up the *University Act* (a unique piece of provincial legislation that grants universities the power to operate as both a public institution that receives government funding and as a corporate enterprise that may generate funding). While many new senior Indigenous administrators had gained membership on their university senates, they were generally non-voting members, a status that was criticized as tokenistic and insufficient (Lavallee, 2019). Thus, under the current academic structure, Indigenous people continued to lack decision-making capacity in academic matters.

A related barrier that participants reported as limiting Indigenous participation in decision making was the creation of an increasing number of Indigenous advisory councils, including short-term committees put in place to support the implementation of TRC's Calls to Action. In many cases, participants recognized the increase in Indigenous advisory councils as a positive development, because those committees often engaged local Indigenous communities in university affairs. While such groups were recognized for bringing new and diverse perspectives to the table, participants also observed that these committees relied heavily on university leadership to ensure meaningful engagement. Many stressed that advisory committees lacked decision-making authority. As one participant said, Indigenous advisory councils "don't have the authority to really change any of the systems or any of the policies or any of the practices. They're just advising you as to what's going on across the country" (Pimahamowi-Pisim). Several participants agreed that while universities have been slowly opening up and shifting their practices to become more engaged and answerable to Indigenous communities, Indigenous advisory councils were still seen as limited in their decision-making capacities and not necessarily respected in leadership circles.

Several participants questioned Indigenous senior leadership roles and, more specifically, where those roles were located in the university hierarchy. Several participants talked candidly about how organizational structures, and their individual positions within them, mattered and impacted their abilities to enact Indigenizing policies. While participants' titles, positions in the academic hierarchy, and experiences varied, they often spoke about the complexities of driving decolonial-Indigenization within existing academic settings. They talked about how administrative roles were highly structured and how the organizational hierarchy impacted their credibility and experiences navigating the academy. Several participants talked about the challenges they faced as Indigenous staff administrators (e.g., as executive directors and vice-presidents) trying to enact academic-related policies and strategies when they did not have academic credentials or research experience. Some participants who were academics expressed concerns around Indigenous staff-administrative appointments, because they felt that the staff administrators did not have the same security and protection as academic administrators with tenured faculty appointments (e.g., vice-provosts, associate vice-provosts). Finally, several participants questioned the unique challenges and viability of special advisers and lead positions in universities. One participant spoke about her experiences as a special adviser: "I'm seeing the limitations of the adviser role because I'm not included in the senior meetings. The reason they are saying is [that] I'm not in a permanent position. I am being blocked from certain discussions" (Thithikopiwi-Pisim). This participant underscores the tricky space of navigating a temporary position as a special adviser, being sometimes excluded from senior meetings and not always accepted by other administrators as "the leader" because she occupied an interim role.

Beyond straddling complex geographic and epistemic borderlands between universities and Indigenous communities, women in this book often underscored the limits of the academic governance system and its ties to the settler colonial nation-state as an ongoing invasive structure. For example, the liberal bicameral academic governance system, and Indigenous people's challenges in terms of penetrating this system as a minority population with little power, underscored academia's tendency to reproduce white liberal settler colonial dynamics of power.

The themes presented in this chapter demonstrate how underlying academic structures continue to constrain the ways in which Indigenizing policies are enacted within current academic systems. That system is fundamentally a Euro-Westernized structure of disciplines and policies that are taken for granted and invisibilized, but which privilege white settler colonial ideologies that often leave Indigenous women's voices on the margins of the decision-making process. While some Indigenous people—some individual administrators and some faculty members—may be gaining access to these spaces, this is not the norm, and access is arguably limited as they continue to struggle to find voice, legitimacy, and credibility. The enactment of Indigenizing policies, therefore, is severely limited within the existing university governance system, where structures continue to obstruct Indigenous people in their attempts to assert Indigenous educational sovereignty.

Recognizing the powerful role of policy in universities, Indigenous women demonstrate how they strategically worked as a collective to claim policies as tools to Indigenize the academy and pursue a decolonial reform movement in higher education. At the same time, however, women commonly attested to the ongoing challenges they face in putting Indigenizing policy into practice. They attested to institutional tendencies toward tokenistic approaches, misinterpretation, and the fact that policy implementation was often messy, contested, and political in practice. While women commonly described Indigenizing policies as useful tools in asserting decolonial aims, they simultaneously highlighted, throughout their stories, the limits of Indigenizing policies as they were often taken up in tricky fields of practice where white possessive logics ensued and crept around many corners. Women also shared common experiences that resulted in policy dilemmas for Indigenous people, such as increased workloads and Indigenous under-representation, calls to Indigenize curriculum without Indigenous people and expertise, and greater pressure to institutionalize Indigeneity and measure success under colonial administrative conditions. The limitations of Indigenizing policy enactment often pointed back to incommensurabilities when it comes to achieving Indigenous educational sovereignty. Indigenizing policies, therefore, are not a panacea. While such policies may be a useful tool in shifting toward decolonial aims, Indigenous people continue to struggle in advancing their collectivist values and autonomous decision making within the white liberal settler colonial academy.

CHAPTER 10

REFUSALS *as* PART *of an* INDIGENOUS LEADERSHIP PRAXIS

Appearing in the interstices, Weesakechahk defies binaries and the colonial boundaries of institutionally demarcated space and power. An infamous mischievous misfit, a willful subject, a truth teller, and a colonial rule bender who disrupts settler colonial common sense and structure, interrupts taken-for-granted truths, and brings old and new ways of thinking into everyday consciousness and practice, Weesakechahk continues to be one of the greatest teachers.

Two overarching research questions remain to be answered: How do Indigenous women administrators encounter the settler colonial academy? And how can Indigenous women administrators contest and resist settler colonialism in their educational leadership and policy work? The concept of "Indigenous refusal" (Grande, 2018a, 2018b; A. Simpson, 2014; Tuck, 2018) is used in this chapter to explain the limits of the settler colonial academy, and the needs of Indigenous women administrators in asserting boundaries that advance Indigenous educational sovereignty in higher education.

The literature indicates that Indigenous people working to change the university operate on a "shaky bridge" (Bunda et al., 2012). Several participants in the present study shared accounts of the dangers of working on a bridge as a borderland between the settler colonial academy and Indigenous communities. Indigenous women administrators in this study operated on a borderland facing dangerous working conditions shaped by the triple bind of settler colonialism, patriarchy, and borderland work; these conditions meet and intersect, often placing Indigenous women administrators in challenging positions that forced them to resist their own oppression. This resistance often took the form of "Indigenous refusal" (Grande, 2018a, 2018b; A. Simpson, 2014; Tuck & Yang, 2019), a concept that helps explain Indigenous resistance to the settler colonial academy. The need to resist calls upon Weesakechahk, Trickster consciousness. Fictionalized stories inspired by the participants' experiences (chapter 7) illustrate some of these refusals. In scene 7 in that chapter (p. 136), Heather gets embroiled in an administrative hiring fiasco that results in university administrators expecting her to help manage Indigenous political unrest (another Indigenous refusal). The situation forces Heather to stand up against the administration's settler colonial nature and refuse to participate in the management of "Indian problems." In these scenes, Weesakechahk helps to speak Heather's inner voice and explicate the dominant Euro-Western norms placed upon her, showing her how these tendencies not only place her in a difficult intermediary position, but also obstruct Indigenous educational sovereignty. The dramatic scenes in chapter 7 are intended to illustrate the resonant experiences several participants in this study shared, experiences related to leading Indigenizing policy work within a white settler colonial space—a space that has historically displaced, erased, and strived to eliminate Indigenous people and ways of knowing, replacing those ways of knowing with an imposed settler colonial architecture and intellectual border. Heather's mere presence in this administrative space interrupts the settler colonial status quo. As the first Indigenous vice-provost of her university, she is figuratively situated on the borderland between Indigenous communities and Euro-Western university communities. In other dramatic scenes, characters like Maria are also situated here, celebrated as beacons of their university's ability to achieve reconciliation. Yet participants commonly testified, as Heather did, to being painfully marked and troubled as out of place, strangers in academic administrative spaces. Heather's experiences are accentuated by the ominous physicality of the university campus and of Convocation Hall, which appears like an invasive structure, a physical as well as an intellectual structure that erases Indigenous women's voices and presence and aims to thwart Indigenous resistance through management logics. Weesakechahk appears in the space between, in goose form, foreshadowing a looming Indigenous student protest on the administration's hands—a collective enactment of Indigenous refusal to be silent and accept the denial of Indigenous voice and agency in educational decision-making processes. Indeed, Indigenous refusals figured prominently in participants' stories in multiple and complex thematic ways, including (1) refusing settler reconciliation discourses; (2) refusing settler notions of leadership; (3) refusing settler co-optation, tokenism, and politics of distraction; and (4) refusing performative approaches.

REFUSING SETTLER RECONCILIATION DISCOURSES

Several participants in this study reported negotiating complex institutional discourses in their leadership, especially around their use of key concepts such as reconciliation, Indigenization, decolonization, and resurgence. Several participants outright refused to use the word "reconciliation" in their leadership communications. For many, "reconciliation" has, like the word "decolonization," become so metaphorized, abstracted, and co-opted by settler colonial "moves toward innocence" (Tuck & Yang, 2012) that it effectively dodges the messy and uncomfortable conversations around power, colonialism, and racism that they argue are necessary to enact "decolonial-Indigenization" (Gaudry & Lorenz, 2018b). Co-optation is a colonizing trick that, Tuck and Yang (2012) have suggested, is used to evade decolonial possibilities and alleviate settler guilt and complicity with ongoing settler colonialism systems. As one participant described it,

> I question [my use of the term "reconciliation"] because reconciliation is not my work as I've come to understand it. Reconciliation is the work of settlers. My work is the work of resurgence. Resurgence is raising up our ways of knowing and being, our languages, our culture, our traditions, our spirituality, our governance—that's always been what informs everything I am and everything I do. And in between here, that's where Indigenization happens in the university; but I also think that's where decolonization happens. Indigenization cannot happen without decolonization. (Mikisiwi-Pisim)

While the use of reconciliation discourse was critiqued by many participants, some confessed to strategically employing it when driving institutional change processes with non-Indigenous settlers in the academy. One participant attested,

> There's lots of critiques of reconciliation at the theoretical level and also at the practice level. But in my own experience of working in the university, reconciliation has opened up spaces, conversations, and opportunities in ways that other discourses and frameworks and processes of decolonization have not. My feelings are that reconciliation has been able to mobilize in ways that decolonization has not in the past. (Kaskatinowi-Pisim)

This participant highlights the powerful nature of reconciliation discourses in inciting individual and some institutional changes, especially when universities are dominated by white settlers. In the same conversation, however, this participant recognized the pitfalls and limits of reconciliation discourses:

> So [reconciliation] could also be a problematic space that some people are coming into and feeling good about themselves, because they can support this, because it's about reconciliation. So if I invite people into a space of reconciliation, people can come. But when I start to do it through a decolonization framework, and I say you are complicit in the theft of land and colonialism, and I bring that into it, immediately then you can start to see a backing away of people. So I think about these processes of reconciliation, decolonization, and Indigenization as related. They can occur together and in different ways and at different times. (Kaskatinowi-Pisim)

She points to the strategic utility of the word "reconciliation" for getting settlers to the table, even though she later says that she often pivoted her approach to introducing decolonial understandings. Several participants attested to using the rhetoric of reconciliation to obtain financial support from institutions. While reconciliation discourses were deliberately used by several Indigenous leaders, many participants still felt ambivalent about using the word, as it had become increasingly critiqued and dangerously co-opted by many non-Indigenous settlers. As one participant said,

> I don't want to talk about reconciliation. Like, reconciliation is not possible for me. Reconciliation has become a distraction, and it's become a bureaucracy within the academy, kind of like within the government. So, reconciliation is becoming a checkbox. Indigenization is

a checkbox. So, I think using the terminology Indigenization, reconciliation, and decolonization is a distraction. Indigenous resurgence is about us gathering our bundles, gathering our ceremony, gathering our traditions, gathering our languages, the land and becoming healthier. (Opaskowi-Pisim)

Sara Ahmed's (2012) critique of the language of diversity in the context of universities in the United Kingdom can be applied to the discourses of reconciliation, Indigenization, and decolonization in Canadian universities. In this context, these ubiquitous terms have been reduced to discursive moves and techniques used by institutions to institute speech acts and manage Indigenous difference. Several participants talked about their refusal to engage with such discourses, and even to use the word "reconciliation" to describe their approach and institutional work. One talked about the need for more nuanced understandings of terms based on one's positionality:

> I have nothing invested in Indigenizing the academy. I have everything invested in decolonizing the university, and I have everything invested in Indigenizing my classroom, and the spaces that I work in, because I don't think that everyone can Indigenize, but I think everyone can decolonize. I think only Indigenous people can truly Indigenize, and so I struggle a bit with the language, but it's not a hill I'm going to die on. (Athiki-Pisim)

This participant not only underscores the complicated nature of language and concepts and their lineages and discursive uses, she also shows how these terms are understood differently at personal and organizational levels, and how one's positionality dramatically shapes one's orientation. She recognizes the limitations to the university Indigenizing at an organizational level.

REFUSING SETTLER NOTIONS OF LEADERSHIP

While Indigenous women administrators described refusing to use certain terminology in their leadership, they also described refusing to succumb to white settler desires for neutrality in their leadership. One participant said,

> I feel more like some administrators are not happy when I am not supporting the ivory tower. But once you are in that role, they have their own club, and all of a sudden it's assumed that your sole allegiance is actually to move their collective agenda forward versus moving an Indigenous agenda forward. They get upset because most of us aren't operating that way, and they feel we're traitors. (Nimitahamowi-Pisim)

This participant talked about the unspoken expectation of some senior administrators in the academy that Indigenous leaders should advance the overall mission of the university and succumb to the dominant institutional project. Arguably, this norm in leadership emanates from a genealogy in administrative science whereby structural functionalist and interpretivist epistemologies in leadership and organizational change are understood as dominant in institutions.

Another participant shared a story about being challenged for being too political in her leadership:

> So I go into the [senior leadership meeting] and I read off [the Indigenous plan] very slowly and very softly because I already know that as a brown woman I am threatening as hell, and I have to curb that as much as I can, otherwise I won't get buy-in. So I spoke sweetly. So one of my colleagues said, "Don't you think you would have greater buy-in if you didn't use such political language?" And I said, "Excuse me, sir, but we are talking about colonialism and oppression and

domination and white supremacy. All of these terms are political. There is no nice way to talk about them." (Ohpahowi-Pisim)

Later, this participant called the desire to depoliticize policy language a form of "whitewashing":

No matter how we code terms to talk with them—and before we say anything in reference to their questions, we have already decoded it five different ways—we have watered it down. We have softened it up. We have taken the "aggression" out. By the time it comes out, it's been whitewashed. I find this frustrating 'cause no matter how much you've whitewashed it, they still come back and say you are so aggressive. (Ohpahowi-Pisim)

She points out that the intersectional power of colonialism, gender, and racism shapes the ways she is often heard by other administrators, and she disclosed that she adjusts her communications by speaking softly to avoid being perceived as aggressive. At the same time, when a senior leader questions a policy's "political language," she refuses to change certain words, such as "racism" and "colonialism," to something less threatening, because to do so would be to accommodate white dominance. Ahmed (2012) has noted that the politics of language often play out in diversity policy work in universities because certain words are more acceptable than others—the word "diversity," for example, is much less threatening than "racism" or "anti-racism." Ahmed (2007c) argues that institutions use the language of diversity over the language of anti-racism to conceal structurally embedded inequities and evade action as a useful neoliberal technique of government. Similarly, participants in the present study attested to preferences in administration for the word "reconciliation" over "decolonization." The term "reconciliation" is a common institutional buzzword, whereas "decolonization" is often questioned by university administration as potentially divisive.

While the participant quoted above modified some of her communication to appease a common-sense desire among settlers to be happy and celebratory in leadership, she still confronted attempts to further neutralize policy language. Scenes 6 and 7 in chapter 7 (pp. 134–140) illustrate another issue whereby the perceived threat of an Indigenous student protest gets the administration's attention and brings particular administrators to the table to manage the situation. The discourse around the table, however, quickly turns to an age-old administrative desire to manage the "Indian problem," and surfaces troubling colonial and racial ideologies associated with the perceived primitive edge of protest and its misperception of disruption within a white settler lens. The response to a protest as an Indian problem to be managed reflects an administrative tendency to control the situation in order to maintain institutional power, a response in which Heather becomes complexly entangled. Behind closed doors, Heather is expected to advise on how to control Indigenous refusals as problems—how to control the public narrative and defuse and redirect disruption, and to be the token spokesperson vis-à-vis the media. At the same time, however, Indigenous students and communities turn to Heather to advocate for Indigenous voices and needs. These conflicting expectations place Heather, in different ways, on tricky ground. The tensions created by differing expectations accentuate colonial power and epistemic distances between Indigenous and Westernized worlds; they leave Heather ready to implode, until she stands up, draws a line, and speaks her truth.

These institutional tendencies are tied to underlying assumptions based in structural functionalist and interpretivist epistemologies prevalent in university administration, assumptions that power is evenly distributed within white liberal meritocratic systems rather than structured according to systemic inequities (Capper, 2019). White settler uneasiness with naming the colonial problem in educational systems, and the politics of disciplinary structures, policies, and norms, create roadblocks for Indigenous leaders trying to change the university system to be more inclusive of Indigenous peoples and ways of knowing.

Similarly, under such structural functionalist and interpretivist frames, the goal of Indigenizing policy is not to change the system and the underlying ideologies that shape it, but rather to include Indigenous peoples superficially and reproduce apolitical notions of education that maintain Euro-Western dominance. Such a goal to improve the existing educational system's image and its efficiencies and effectiveness might include Indigenous peoples at a representational level, but only based on conditional forms of inclusion. These hegemonic administrative norms place Indigenous women administrators who refuse them on dangerous ground. Under such colonial conditions, Indigenous women administrators who push back against norms become problematic—"they become a problem when they name and resist the [colonial] problem" (Ahmed, 2017, p. 39). "They become labeled the Indian problem."

REFUSING SETTLER CO-OPTATION

Indigenous women administrators in this study described white settlers co-opting Indigenizing policies in ways that did not advance Indigenous educational sovereignty or benefit Indigenous people. Through such co-optation, some white settlers, without working alongside Indigenous communities, subsume Indigenizing policy interests into their own work agendas. According to several participants, white settler co-optation was most pervasive in the area of research and curriculum. Many new researchers do not understand their ethical responsibilities to Indigenous communities. These non-Indigenous scholars, while often well-intentioned, underestimated the deep epistemological shifts and relationship building needed before moving into collaborative partnerships with Indigenous communities. In the context of research, one participant reported that she was expected by other leaders to automatically open up her networks to help non-Indigenous researchers gain access to Indigenous communities for their own research purposes. She drew on chapter 9 of the *Tri-Council Policy Statement 2* to assert boundaries as an Indigenous refusal:

> The community engagement of chapter 9 is there for a reason. I say, "If you don't have the connections, don't do the work." I refuse to do that engagement for somebody and help non-Indigenous peoples get money for their research. (Opaskowi-Pisim)

Similarly, several participants spoke of times in their careers and in their administrative roles when they felt used by non-Indigenous researchers who invited them to be involved in research in tokenistic ways. They described becoming much warier of getting involved in preplanned research projects led by some non-Indigenous scholars who did not have long-standing records or previous working relationships with Indigenous people.

In more nuanced ways, some participants described settler co-optation as an inner struggle to not be overtaken by a "politics of distraction" (G. Smith, 2003) within their leadership. Participants expressed fears that ongoing colonial desires in education could condition them and invade their administrative priorities. For example, some participants reported struggling with a fear of being co-opted under settler colonial institutional tendencies. Their concerns emanated from pressures arising from the academic system itself as well as from non-Indigenous colleagues who pressured them to conform (code-switch) to hegemonic ways of leading. One participant attested,

> You have to learn how to talk. If we go into a university and say, "We want to change the whole system to accommodate us," they're going to say, "No." Because it's not our system, it's theirs. And so that's the

big argument we're involved in right now....Where's the line? So you know, the Western administration, the white administration will put forward a line and say, "This is as far as we are willing to go." But maybe our line is another couple leagues past that. We're like, "Well, actually, we would really like to go here." But they [say], "Let's get to this line first, and then we'll pitch the rest." Because we can't, you know, just say, "No, okay fine, I'm not doing it." (Pimahamowi-Pisim)

This participant likens her efforts to Indigenize the university to a ball game—a progression of negotiations and compromises within a system that is not hers and in which she acknowledges she is not in a position of power. Several participants described their leadership as "playing the game"—as sometimes involving what Graham Hingangaroa Smith would describe in his conversation with Margaret Kovach as "strategic concessions" (Kovach, 2009). A strategic concession may be finding room to advance Indigenous priorities in the university by fitting into government reconciliation agendas. Under such pretenses, Indigenous women administrators found themselves facing the common "interest convergence dilemma"* (Bell, 1980) in which white settler interests still controlled and negated Indigenous initiatives. While fruitful synergisms between Indigenous and university initiatives were sometimes generated, the act of trying to fit Indigenous work into pre-established academic structures and priorities pointed to some of the troubling ways in which Indigenous initiatives were limited, thus reinforcing problematic and conditional forms of inclusion. One participant described the issue as follows:

---

* Black legal scholar and critical race theorist Derrick Bell first coined the concept "interest convergence" to demonstrate that it was only when white and Black interests converged that the civil rights of Black people in the United States were recognized in law. I suggest that similar dynamics of interest convergence play out in reconciliation policies between settlers and Indigenous peoples in Canada in the context of Indigenous rights.

> Personally, I think a lot of our [Indigenous] students are being lost within the reconciliation movement, because we are not attending to their needs and aspirations. You know, we are not creating a safe learning environment. Consider mandatory courses: we don't have enough Indigenous people to teach the courses. If we place an Indigenous person in the course, they are going to experience violence, and possibly be traumatized. But if we place a non-Indigenous person, and they don't critically take up their positionality, that can create all sorts of power dynamics in the classroom. (Kaskatinowi-Pisim)

The struggle of aligning Indigenous initiatives also often pointed to deeper epistemic tensions and structural inequities that exist for Indigenous people operating within the settler colonial university. For example, predetermined priority areas were often rooted in Euro-Western thought, positivistic, evidence-based regimes, and neoliberal forces that were not only incongruent with Indigenous ways of knowing, but that placed them in asymmetrical power relations. Simply fitting Indigenous initiatives into existing academic structures was not necessarily conducive to achieving Indigenous decolonial aims and advancing Indigenous educational sovereignty. Enacting refusal meant that Indigenous leaders needed to be aware of settler ideologies and tendencies and to be willing to avoid getting caught up in settler desires when they did not serve Indigenous futurities.

Several participants talked about large-scale institutional strategies for Indigenizing the academy that often catered to the dominant white settler masses rather than to Indigenous students and community needs. One participant explained,

> When we think about the settler focus that reconciliation has taken, in ways that have shifted the focus away from Indigenous students—I'm going to use teacher education and our required [Indigenous] course

as an example, which is really about shifting attitudes and the knowledge of largely settler-dominant classrooms....We need to be thinking about the journey and furthering the journey of our Indigenous students. And furthering that journey is their own resurgence, their own reclamation and self-determination. Their journey for themselves and their communities. (Kaskatinowi-Pisim)

Another example was shared by a participant who talked about the resistance she faced from a non-Indigenous administrator concerning an Indigenous project the participant was leading. A dean at this participant's university challenged her Indigenous research strategy, because, the dean felt, it "silenced non-Indigenous faculty members doing Indigenous research." The Indigenous leader pushed back against the dean's framing of the issue by deconstructing the ways in which the Euro-Western university automatically silences and marginalizes Indigenous researchers and Indigenous ways of knowing, and through these structures of inequity disadvantages Indigenous researchers, thus reinforcing the need for some strategies to focus on Indigenous researchers. This example demonstrates that the systemic nature of settler colonialism in the academy remains invisible, that settlers aim to re-centre white settler majoritarian needs, and that these issues in turn can quickly undermine the effort to privilege the needs of Indigenous scholars. Indigenous refusals thereby involved Indigenous leaders making visible otherwise invisible settler assumptions.

REFUSING SETTLER COLONIAL TOKENISM

Several participants in this study reported openly refusing to participate in certain university activities that undermined Indigenous voices and agency. In one example, a participant described being invited to join a committee. Upon arriving at the first meeting, she realized that the committee was led by a corporate industrial entity that had troubling relations with First Nations communities. It appeared to her that the senior leader who had invited her to join the committee was motivated by tokenism. After realizing this, and sensing the decolonial limits of the committee itself, she excused herself, and refused to be part of a photograph intended for the media. She described the experience as a classic example of colonial tokenism—the desire for Indigenous representation, but only in the form of a single, marginalized voice with little power. Another participant talked about resisting becoming a token because it would be tantamount to becoming a manipulative prop for her supervisor, a senior leader who constantly sought the participant's advice but never acted on it, yet still presented decisions in a way that left people with the impression that the Indigenous leader supported such actions. As a way to refuse this problematic positioning and tokenism, the participant explained to everyone in one meeting that she was not in agreement with the direction taken by the senior administrator. After she did this, the administrator's "jaw kind of dropped," she said, "and that was actually when [my supervisor] stopped talking to me" (Nimitahamowi-Pisim).

Other participants shared similar stories about how they resisted setter colonial tokenism by refusing to be involved in or support problematic research guided by scholars who did not properly educate themselves about, or work authentically to serve and build partnerships with, Indigenous communities. In these cases, participants simply refused to collaborate or actively support these research projects.

REFUSING PERFORMATIVE APPROACHES

Several participants in this study talked about refusing to participate in symbolic approaches to Indigenization that were often nested within problematic neoliberal and neo-colonial university practices. At least three participants talked explicitly about actively refusing "business as usual" communications approaches related to Indigenization. One participant acknowledged that her "talking to the media made [administration] nervous. I let [senior administration] know, and they wanted me to have my messaging vetted through the [president's office], and I didn't do that. There was this unwritten rule, and I was not playing" (Athiki-Pisim). Another participant said she disliked the ways in which her university's public affairs office operated, explaining that she tried working with the office to push back against their problematic practices. She explained, "[I said to them] these types [of communication changes] need to happen, and, no, we're not going to praise ourselves, no, we're not going to say we're reconciling because that's impossible until justice can overturn itself from the inside" (Niski-Pisim). Another participant recognized the tricky space within which she operated when she talked to the media:

> The media contacted me, and all of a sudden I started talking about my work, but I was talking to the media and I was very aware of how I could be framed, and how my voice was suddenly speaking from this role, and I felt like I was in the twilight zone because I realized that I can't say the same things, or at least I felt like I couldn't say the same things. I had to tone it down a little. (Thithikopiwi-Pisim)

This participant highlighted the challenges of navigating her administrative leadership position when talking to the public, and of managing and anticipating potential media misrepresentations. She also touched upon the delicate balance of having to both represent the university and maintain her own independent voice as an Indigenous woman and scholar. Several participants shared stories about continuing to assert their own voices as Indigenous leaders by participating in collective public letter writing, policy development, and using their political voices to advocate for broader systemic change.

REFUSING STRATEGICALLY

Indigenous refusals sometimes took on subtler forms that would avoid the negative colonial, gendered, and racialized stereotypes and discrediting that often accompanied Indigenous women leaders' work. Because the ground of the borderland is so contentious (Ottmann, 2009), several participants described negotiating their refusals in nuanced ways, an often unseen and underestimated dimension of their leadership work. As part of this negotiation, they carefully and critically assessed each situation and each potential refusal as an infraction with implications, weighing out risks and benefits, and considering whether the issue was a "hill worth dying on" (Athiki-Pisim). As one participant said,

> Initially, I would be offended that I wasn't drawn into a conversation that I thought was important or had some relevance to me or my work or my staff. But eventually I just thought—how much fighting should I...I mean, I'm not afraid of a good fight, if it's necessary. But, I mean, assessing things became a natural response. So on a scale of 1 to 10, how significant is this particular issue? Should I say something, or hold my peace? (Opawahcikanasis)

Another participant said, "So you have to pick your battles: okay I'll let that one go, this one, I'm going to stand. You have to be conscious all the time" (Pimahamowi-Pisim). While this participant underscores the need to strategically assessing whether a refusal is necessary, examples of discreet Indigenous refusals commonly involved ignoring bad advice from senior colleagues, participating in social action but not necessarily taking the lead position, sharing non-confidential information with appropriate people, and giving advice to Indigenous and allied groups who were on the front line of resistance work. One participant shared a story about being discouraged by a senior administrative colleague from proceeding with an Indigenous strategy. He encouraged her to focus on one or two smaller objectives within her "overly ambitious" plan. To justify not taking his advice, the participant talked about her refusal as simply carrying on with her work with the support of the Indigenous Education Council:

> So that's how I pushed back; I just carried on. Sometimes you get advice from senior people above you, and you have to make a decision whether you are going to change the plan and only focus on one or two [aspects of that plan], or carry on, and so sometimes you just carry on because that's what the council wants. (Opawahcikanasis)

Another way in which participants enacted more discreet Indigenous refusals was by finding good allies who supported their efforts and were willing to refuse alongside them; refusing collectively was stronger and less risky than refusing individually, and Indigenous women recognized how sometimes settlers were more likely to be heard than Indigenous leaders. A more subtle form of refusal involved mentoring Indigenous people and offering them advice about how to navigate their own refusal processes. One participant described this type of work as "softly supporting the fight" (Opiniyawiwi-Pisim). A final example of an implicit type of Indigenous refusal involved strategically inviting outside Indigenous scholars or leaders to the university to give advice on a project and encouraging them to say the difficult things administrators at their university needed to hear. In these instances, participants drew on the collective power of Indigenous voices in the larger movement, including the voices of students, faculty members, and community partners, to work together strategically to refuse and call on the university to change. These nuanced understandings of resistance operated at collective levels; as such, they started to shift conventional understandings of leadership away from individualized and positional conceptions (e.g., that one Indigenous administrator should be responsible for leading and refusing the system alone) toward collective Indigenous conceptions of leadership.

Refusal as Opting Out of Administration

In some cases, Indigenous women administrators refused the university by relinquishing their administrative appointments altogether. These cases were often linked to particularly toxic environments where leaders felt they had no other choice. Indeed, one-third of the participants in this study left their administrative positions at some point. While some of these participants stayed in academe, and even at their own universities as faculty members, others moved to other institutions or left the academy altogether.

Several participants referred to two prominent cases in Canada in which two Indigenous women senior administrators left their universities and went public with their experiences (Alex, 2018; UofM, 2018; Prokopchuk, 2018). One participant said,

> Those resignations are happening because people are going into an institution with certain expectations. If you look at a [university's] strategic plan, you think, "Wow, there must be some great non-Indigenous people there driving that." But you [get there and realize] you can't be a token. (Opaskowi-Pisim)

This participant pointed to discrepancies between what her university displayed in their policy and public affairs statements and what she experienced in her own life as an Indigenous leader at the university. She argued that incongruences between institutional speech acts and Indigenous experiences contributed to her resignation, and she suspected that this same dynamic likely contributed to the resignations of other women at other universities. Another participant described her decision to resign from her administrative appointment in this way:

> I'm okay with walking away from these things, and I think they were stunned. Why would you walk away from this super-duper fancy club because this is the best thing since sliced bread? It's like, no, it's not. I think it's partly because at the end of the day I go home. At the end of the day, we go home and there is no difference [in Indigenous communities]. (Nimitahamowi-Pisim)

This particular participant's narrative demonstrates that some Indigenous leaders struggled with the divergence and inequities between Indigenous communities and Westernized university contexts. Another participant insisted that she experienced such a stark contrast between these two worlds that she needed to walk away from her university role altogether. This participant talked similarly about her decision to leave her administrative appointment and return to her First Nations community and lend her leadership to do land-based resurgence work:

> I think it was just [that] I had enough. I was ready for a change. I think that was the biggest reason. I just wanted some openness to do something different. I don't think my heart was in it anymore. I didn't want to be in an admin role, so I left on a high note. (Opiniyawiwi-Pisim)

Most participants who left university administration described their decision to leave as based on an incongruence between their Indigenous values or Indigenous community expectations and the institutional culture that reigns in universities. For example, a couple of participants described how some institutional approaches to Indigenous curriculum centred non-Indigenous programs and student needs, whereas some Indigenous community members wanted to see the university invest more in Indigenous community-based programming. For example, one participant said,

> The expectations of [the Indigenous] community and the expectations of the institution [are not aligned]. I think if the institution was in more alignment [it would have helped me], because I can't choose to stand with the institution and stand against community. Sometimes those are decisions that you're forced to make—well, I'm being forced to make. I'm going to go stand with community. I don't even want to talk about being a sellout; it's being authentic to who I am. I think that, in these positions, institutions do not want a social activist. But that's sometimes what they need to get things done in order for change to occur. (Opaskowi-Pisim)

In this account, the participant described a misalignment in goals that contributed to her decision to depart university administration. In each departure story, Indigenous women administrators attested that their decisions to leave were not made lightly. Moreover, it is important not to confuse Indigenous women's departures with an absolutist sense of Indigenous refusal. After all, most of the participants in this study continued to work in the university in different ways.

Most participants talked about the dangers and consequences they faced in enacting explicit Indigenous refusals in the academy. Indigenous refusals were rife with politics that surfaced the risk of being problematized as unruly, oppositional, and disruptive to the administrative status quo. Participants often saw acts of Indigenous refusal as having the possibility to negatively impact their credibility, professional reputation in the university, and even, in extreme cases, contributing to a justification of their dismissal or the choice not to reappoint them. Therefore, enacting explicit Indigenous refusals placed Indigenous women administrators on dangerous ground, requiring them to negotiate carefully and at times be discreet.

ENACTING INDIGENOUS REFUSAL AS A DECOLONIAL INTERVENTION

When operating within dominant epistemic leadership frameworks—structuralism, functionalism, instrumentalism, interpretivism—Indigenous leaders are expected to fit into the system and to assimilate into Euro-Western ways of administering education; when they do not, Indigenous leaders are labelled as problems—they are cast out and de-legitimized. When women challenged dominant, taken-for-granted epistemologies in leadership, they were often positioned in the classic colonial way as "the Indian problem." When they did not adhere to dominant epistemologies in leadership, they were negatively stereotyped and discredited as "too political," "divisive," and even "ineffective" in their leadership. As a result, many women, when they confronted the hegemony of the institution, were seen to be a threat to the dominant white settler liberal democratic order.

Lynn Lavallee (2020) recounts being "unwittingly put in the position of Indian agent controlling Indian problems" in her leadership role at the University of Manitoba. As such, Lavallee argues that "efforts to decolonize academic institutions that are funded by government are futile but we can bring awareness and transparency to the colonial curtain" (2020, p. 30). She points to the role of Indigenous administrators in *calling out* colonial norms in the academy. Her unwillingness to adopt colonial administrative expectations and remain silent about the colonial nature of academic administration at her university compelled the institution, after her premature departure, to complete a review of Indigenous senior leadership. The review committee recommended several deeper structural changes, including the development of several leadership positions and the provision of adequate levels of funding (Indigenous Senior Leadership Advisory Committee, 2019).

Indigenous refusals as an act of resistance and regeneration emerged as a prominent theme in this research. Indigenous women commonly testified that, as part of their leadership, they needed to contest the taken-for-granted settler colonial hegemonies and the dominant educational leadership norms and ideologies pervasive in the academy. Indeed, one's willingness to enact refusals has emerged as a necessary disposition for Indigenous administrators who strive to advance Indigenous educational aims and priorities. In enacting such refusals, however, Indigenous women administrators were not necessarily unproductive, adversarial, or out on the picket lines protesting explicitly, although these types of activism do occur, are worthwhile, and are often necessary. Instead, women recounted confronting institutional hegemony through various forms of action, such as not lending their labour to certain projects, proactively creating and changing policies, and addressing colonial assumptions as they arose in their day-to-day encounters.

Women's stories reaffirmed the overwhelmingly unsafe nature of the academic environment within which they operated. To combat normative Euro-Western approaches to leadership, they described enacting Indigenous refusals as part of their agency and resistance to ongoing settler colonial dynamics. Their refusals were seen, however, as a contentious aspect of Indigenous leadership and policy work. In response to the ongoing threat of racialized, gendered, and colonial stereotypes placed on them for being too political when refusing, some participants drew on more nuanced and subtler forms of refusal as a survival mechanism. These different types of refusals were enacted in multiple ways—explicitly, discreetly, and strategically—demonstrating that resistance mechanisms can be complex and nuanced. Indeed, women shared many stories of struggle, resistance, and strategic astuteness in the face of ongoing colonial pressures.

Women in this book also commonly described a need to engage in ongoing critical self-reflexivity around their use of Indigenous refusals. They described their desire to examine and evaluate, on an ongoing, case-by-case basis, the implications of enacting Indigenous refusal. They also identified a need to reflect on their own intersectional positionalities and relational dynamics, and to examine the ethical implications of their leadership practices and decision making in relation to their reconciliation efforts and attempts to elevate Indigenous voices in education. Their insights offer critical direction for educational leadership training in the context of reconciliation movements in the future.

Further nuances surrounding leadership agency and conceptions emerged from women's notions that Indigenous leadership was a collective political process whereby Indigenous peoples worked in relationship—with Indigenous faculty members, with local Indigenous community members, with Elders, with Indigenous students, and with settler allies—and in different roles with different responsibilities to influence systemic change. In these cases, leadership was portrayed as complex, collective, strategic, and political. At the same time, women commonly reported that dominant leadership roles and power were often conceived and reinforced in universities at both the individual and hierarchal levels. They were earned through liberal meritocratic and hierarchal authority systems (Foster, 1986; Mallot, 2010) that often marginalized Indigenous people and Indigenous conceptions of leadership that rely more heavily on critical, collectivist, and relational paradigms.

CHAPTER 11

CONCLUDING THOUGHTS

Throughout my study, Indigenous women pointed to an emerging decolonial educational leadership praxis at play within their Indigenization leadership and policy work, a praxis that called on them to work with Indigenous peoples collectively and at times contest and resist settler colonial assumptions and structures embedded in the Westernized academy. Indigenous women's leadership work was further characterized as intensely laborious, isolating, and even dangerous because it sometimes involved leaders challenging the very foundations of the modern academy. Given that Indigenous women featured prominently in university administration, and that academic leadership is a professional environment dominated by masculinist norms, Indigenous women's Indigenization work was gendered.

RETURNING TO INDIGENOUS UNDERSTANDINGS OF THE BUFFALO

Cree-Saulteaux scholar Blair Stonechild, in a seminal piece on Indigenous post-secondary education titled *The New Buffalo: The Struggle for*

Aboriginal Post-Secondary Education in Canada (2006), documented First Nations' evolving relationship with post-secondary education, describing both its origins as a tool of colonial assimilation and its growing possibilities as an instrument of empowerment among First Nations. Stonechild drew on the words of Plains Elders to position post-secondary education as "the new buffalo"—a way for Indigenous peoples to survive in the modern world. Since its publication, scholars and leaders have adopted the buffalo metaphor to help promote university education within Indigenous communities.

While Stonechild's work was not premised on advancing Western colonial educational agendas, some scholars have warned against using the buffalo in education as a metaphor that falls prey to uncritical and manipulative Western trappings (Hubbard, 2009). Tuck and Yang (2012) have warned scholars that "when metaphors invade decolonization, it kills the very possibility of decolonization; it recenters whiteness, it resettles theory, it extends innocence to the settler, it entertains a settler future" (p. 3). This criticism points to the ways that settler colonial power is lurking around every corner of Indigenization policies and leadership practices, waiting to invade, co-opt, and manipulate Indigenous understandings of education to serve its own aims. The mischievous nature of settler colonialism reminds me of Cree Weesakechahk teachings. In similar ways, Anishnawbe storyteller and scholar Leanne Betasamosake Simpson, in her Anishnawbe story "Please Be Careful when You're Getting Smart" (2013a), reminds Indigenous learners of the tricky dynamics of colonialism in educational settings. Simpson draws on the Anishnawbe storytellers Nokomis and Nanaboozoo to enact an Indigenous pedagogy of the land that reinforces critical Indigenous thinking in the university. Inspired by Simpson's story and praxis, I argue that Indigenous peoples must be critical when engaging with the trickiness of Indigenizing policies and administrative practices in the academy; we must proceed with caution, and, more importantly, avoid automatically positioning Western approaches as the new buffalo.

CONCLUDING THOUGHTS

The experiences of Indigenous women administrators without doubt support the notion that settler colonialism permeates Canadian university structures and infiltrates Indigenizing policy practices. I am thereby compelled, as are other scholars (Andreotti et al., 2015; Gaudry & Lorenz, 2018b; Grande, 2019a, 2019b; Lavallee, 2020; Tuck, 2019), to question whether Indigenizing policies on their own can accomplish the radical decolonial change needed to advance Indigenous sovereignty in Canadian university education.

Within numerous debates on decolonizing the Westernized university, many critical decolonial scholars argue that the academy is beyond reform (Andreotti et al., 2015), that it is unsalvageable and is instead in need of hospicing (Grande, 2018a, 2018b; Machado de Oliveira, 2021; Tuck, 2019). Some Indigenous peoples argue that we need to create our own universities or Indigenous educational institutes founded on Indigenous ways of knowing. The idea of hospicing the Westernized university involves an education around death. For me, this type of learning is deeply spiritual since it forces us to examine the very meaning of life. Some educational scholars who promote the idea of hospicing the university advance different experimental projects in education, projects that no longer waste precious time trying to reform a broken system, but that instead refocus themselves on using the institution to reorient humans to learn to sit with uncomfortable truths and face our humanity. In Indigenous societies, a teaching about death is a teaching about life; it's connected to our Original Laws and Creation Stories, which orient humans around a relational and ethical way of life with all living beings. Perhaps, Indigenous knowledges can support us in hospicing the modern university.

Yet the promise of a higher education is still too often positioned to Indigenous peoples under the seductive assurance that our increased access and attainment within the existing model will give us the social mobility and social capital needed to survive in a modern world, and to solve complex colonial and intergenerational problems that structure our reality. Yet in fact, the education system continues to reproduce harmful systems of thinking and doing that reinforce ways of life that serve to disconnect humans from relational connections between humans, non-humans, and the planet. In fact, our human species is moving in such a consumerist and destructive direction at such a rapid rate that we are facing an undeniable climate crisis, which may very well lead to our own demise if we do not dramatically reorient ourselves. I believe part of the solution rests in shifting our educational system, its aims and priorities, to more relational ways of life. This shift calls on those in power to unsettle everyday common-sense assumptions aimed at feeding a human-centred society that supports unlimited accumulation of wealth at the expense of a relational intergenerational and holistic understanding. We need an education system that disrupts normative notions of progress, knowledge, and ethics; we need to move toward deeper, more sustainable ways of knowing and being. For me, decolonizing and Indigenizing higher education has the potential to contribute to this shift in consciousness as it can align with the philosophies of Indigenous peoples and our connections to the land and non-humans. Like the Plains peoples and their connection to the buffalo, this educational work can nurture intergenerational knowledges and interconnections. *I hear an echo.*

WORKING ON TRICKY GROUND

Yet Indigenous women working in existing academic administrative structures find themselves operating in contexts that continue to be dominated by institutional norms and structures of indifference; they find themselves working on tricky ground. During my study, trickiness emerged strongly in the in-between spaces and in the messiness of leadership and policy enactments; in the paradoxes and complexities of leaders navigating tensions and debates around key concepts and discourses; in the

CONCLUDING THOUGHTS

difficulties of putting policy promises into practice; in the divide between rhetoric and experience; in the contradictions according to which leaders are seen simultaneously as a symbol of the solution and the problem; in the tensions between the liberal academy's favouring of individualism and Indigenous communities' embrace of collectivism; in the ambivalence that results from being the target of policy and media attention and experiencing structural marginalization; and in the disjuncture stemming from being the subject of public celebration and being overly scrutinized by colonial surveillance. In reflecting on the trickiness of practice, one is struck by the paradoxically messy, violent, and political nature of being an Indigenous women and leading Indigenous education and policy practices in universities, and by the elusive nature of settler colonialism.

Highlighting the trickiness of practice requires attending to the ways in which Weesakechahk appears as a transformer and truth teller. Trickster stories such as Weesakechahk stories are useful in destabilizing simplistic binary thinking, colonizing norms, and static claims to knowing and being that are embedded in Euro-Western ideologies, modernistic thinking, and university systems. Despite the fact that my study is focused on the settler colonial academy—an inherently Euro-Western intellectual and physical environment and architecture—I found myself continuously pulled to draw upon Indigenous stories as theory. Trickster stories offer a criticism of unequal power and colonial ways of knowing and doing. This calling to draw on Weesakechahk was fuelled by an inner insistence that Weesakechahk could help me understand and explain Indigenous women's experiences. From this Cree centre of knowing, I sat with and reflected deeply and seriously on the Weesakechahk opening story. My commitment to privileging Indigenous story as theory is unapologetically rooted in my own positionality as a mixed Cree woman striving to reclaim my Indigenous ways of knowing and foster authentic intellectual space for Indigenous (Cree) thought in academic, leadership, and policy research and practice. In the dramatic script (chapter 7), Weesakechahk's humour-laced approach to storytelling helped to convey the difficult and violent embodied experiences of Indigenous women, disrupt hierarchy, and question authority while simultaneously pointing to the deceptive nature of settler colonial power in policy rhetoric and practice.

A BUFFALO JUMP CLIFF?

Trickiness also emerged in the analysis of Indigenous women's dangerous and vulnerable positions in university leadership contexts. In one interview, a participant and I discussed the phenomena of the "glass cliff" (Ryan & Haslam, 2004) experienced by some Indigenous women administrators. The "glass cliff" was first identified during workplace feminization in Britain in the 1990s, when scholars observed that women (predominantly white women) were being appointed to leadership roles during highly turbulent times, and that they often failed—as though falling off a cliff because of the harsh environment into which they had been placed. In the corporate context, the glass cliff metaphor was an extension of the earlier feminist concept of the glass ceiling, which focused on the invisible barriers that prohibited many women from moving up the corporate leadership hierarchy. The glass cliff phenomenon involves an opening up of leadership roles for women, but only during risky and stressful periods when men are less likely to take on leadership roles. The glass cliff phenomenon places women in vulnerable and dangerous positions where they are often scapegoated because organizational conditions are beyond their control. The concept of the glass cliff has also been associated with Indigenous women administrators working in public institutions, particularly universities, since the TRC (EagleWoman, 2019). Angelique EagleWoman, a Dakota leader and scholar and the first Indigenous dean of law at Lakehead University in Ontario, Canada, resigned from her academic administrative post and went public with her experiences on the glass cliff in 2018. Both enacting agency and refusing to participate in the problematic administrative approaches occurring at her university, EagleWoman resigned after only two years in her decanal role and went so far as to file a civil suit against Lakehead University in November 2018 ("Lakehead settles discrimination suit," 2021). EagleWoman has argued that the glass cliff can easily become a reality in universities where Indigenous women can become "characterized as incompetent or as not exhibiting a proper leadership style which shifts the blame to the woman who dared to step into her power and lead from and Indigenous perspective" (EagleWoman, 2019).

In one interview, a participant and I considered that another type of cliff—perhaps a buffalo jump cliff—could be used to describe the treacherous colonial terrain of academic administration among Indigenous women. The buffalo jump is an ancient herd-hunting technique, commonly used by Indigenous Plains hunters, in which buffalo are herded off a high cliff to their deaths. The buffalo jump is a perilous formation that may describe the nature of settler colonialism in academic administration and university policy work among Indigenous women. We might ask: Are Indigenous women administrators being misled by the trickiness of settler colonialism in universities, similar to the way the buffalo were misled when they were herded off a cliff? While the experience of Indigenous women in administrative roles in the academy is different from those of white women who experienced the feminization of the corporate workplace during the 1990s, one wonders if duplicitous colonial promises have led some universities to place Indigenous women in a metaphorical buffalo jump.

The inclusion of Indigenous women in academic administrative roles, however, cannot be tied to Indigenous men not wanting to take on leadership, as was the issue among white women and men during the corporate feminization period. Indigenous men are not featured strongly in universities, either as students or as university leaders. Nonetheless, Indigenizing work in the academy has certainly been found, both in the present study and in other literature, to be dangerous, and to place all Indigenous people on contentious ground (Ottmann, 2009). Yet in this study, Indigenization work was found to be quite gendered, and to operate on tricky ground that is arguably tantamount to a buffalo jump—a glass cliff or, to add yet another metaphor, a shaky bridge (Bunda et al., 2012).

Perhaps the goals that animate the policy work of Indigenizing the academy are so seductive in terms of their promissory nature that they lure some Indigenous leaders into believing that they are achievable, when in actuality "decolonization is a messy, dynamic, and contradictory process" (Sium et al., 2012). As a result of the inherently Euro-Westernized nature of the administrative academy, coloniality is deeply embedded, constantly shifting and morphing like a Trickster, often leaving Indigenous administrators vulnerable and Indigenous projects in unsustainable positions in which they are susceptible to eradication and co-optation. More troublingly, Indigenous women administrators who dare to work in the academy inherit and struggle within a structural incommensurability that makes achieving Indigenous educational sovereignty or "decolonial-Indigenization" (Gaudry & Lorenz, 2018b) arguably—though one hesitates to say it—impossible.

LOOKING BACK, INSTITUTIONAL-INDIGENIZATION WORK IS NOT FUTILE

Despite the undeniable challenges and tensions experienced by Indigenous women leaders who contributed to my study, I do not want to leave readers thinking that Indigenizing policy work in universities is not worthwhile or that positive institutional changes that benefit Indigenous peoples have not materialized over the last seven years. Indigenizing policies have certainly shifted many aspects of academia. In a short time, Indigenizing policies have opened up new spaces and conversations across the university sector. While there is still a lot to do, universities

CONCLUDING THOUGHTS

have created new offices of Indigenous initiatives, instituted new senior leadership positions, implemented mandatory courses in some areas, created smudging and feasting policies, hired more Indigenous staff and faculty members, and created new Indigenous learning spaces—actions that, while long overdue, have nonetheless taken place under a reconciliation policy directive. Certainly, Indigenous peoples would argue that the fight for recognition and resources long predates the age of the TRC. While the degree, speed, and sustainability of institutional change is debatable, Indigenizing policies have indeed acted as powerful transformative tools, and Indigenous leadership has assisted in mobilizing their uses.

More relevant to the discussion here is the fact that leading institutional-Indigenization work has been deeply racialized, colonial, and gendered work. The embodied and holistic (intellectual, emotional, physical, and spiritual) consequences experienced by Indigenous people—notably Indigenous women leaders—working in academic administrative spaces, however, has so far been left unexamined and underappreciated in research and public discourse. Moreover, the consequences of Indigenizing the academy have been challenging for many Indigenous women administrators operating within ongoing structures of colonialism. My enduring hope is that my study and the discussion here will help amplify Indigenous women's voices and experiences, and more importantly, centre Indigenous communities' visions for a different kind of education system—one that has yet to be co-created.

At the same time, policies continue to have immense currency in this movement; they are the language of institutions, and they continue to effect/affect nearly every facet of Indigenous people's lives. Therefore, understanding how policies are made, and how they are used in universities and society in general, continues to be useful work for Indigenous peoples. The degree of agency Indigenous peoples possess in terms of enacting policies in university structures relative to settler colonial power, however, raises ongoing critical questions about how much the

Euro-Western academic system continues to control Indigenous agency. As Graham Hingangaroa Smith asserts,

> developing sovereignty and self-determination in an institution where we do not have power just doesn't ring true. We need to know the terrain on which we are struggling. We need to know the limits and capacities of what can be achieved in particular sites. I think we need to make strategic concessions to win what we can, but the critical understanding is that this is only one site of struggle—we ought to be developing transformation in many sites. (Smith quoted in Kovach, 2009, p. 90)

Smith's words reflect the importance of transformative work in multiple sites, including within the university system, but also from outside—from within settler colonial governments, industries, Indigenous communities, on the land, and in ourselves in ways that sustain and nurture Indigenous ways of knowing and being. Indigenous people seduced by policy promises and who labour inside the academy, as I do, must, however, do so cautiously, remaining vigilant of the tricky ways in which settler colonial power dynamics play out in the academy, and simultaneously look elsewhere for multiple solutions to complex colonial problems. This is a difficult balance indeed. Moreover, Indigenous people working within the administrative academy must be willing and able to strategically enact Indigenous refusals. Despite such acts of refusal being cast as threats, we must rise above these misinterpretations and demonstrate how Indigenous refusals are not necessarily violent or destructive, but rather generative—an assertion of Indigenous agency and a move toward Indigenous educational sovereignty. Indigenous refusals are often necessary and can be inherently purposeful.

Going back to the teaching of "education is the new buffalo," this has me reflecting on two questions in particular: What does higher education

CONCLUDING THOUGHTS

as the new buffalo mean within an Indigenous ontological paradigm? And how can Indigenous leaders ensure that this notion is not misinterpreting Elders' teachings from the perspective of a Euro-Western ontological paradigm? Fully comprehending the meaning of the words and the teaching requires an understanding of what a profound relationship with the buffalo means to many Indigenous peoples.

Dr. Leroy Little Bear, renowned Blackfoot scholar and Elder, reminds us that the buffalo have acted as a keystone in Indigenous life for as long as the Blackfoot can remember (University of Lethbridge UNews, 2017). Providing all the necessities for survival, the buffalo continue to be highly revered and respected among many Indigenous peoples. Highly interdependent upon the buffalo, Plains Indigenous societies were careful not to disrespect these animals since they helped them sustain a complex balance in their ecosystem and their ontological relationship with the land and cosmos. Buffalo hunters did not over-hunt or disrespect the buffalo. Beyond providing vital sustenance to the collective, every part of the buffalo was used to maintain Indigenous life. During the 1800s, however, settler colonists, recognizing the sacred, symbiotic, interdependent buffalo-human relationship, used the buffalo against Plains Indigenous peoples, attempting to kill off the population and, in turn, starve and eliminate "Indians" and get rid of the so-called Indian problem. In devastating settler colonial attempts to disappear Indigenous peoples, or at least coerce them into complying with government assimilationist policies, settlers intentionally over-hunted the buffalo. The Canadian settler government used the killing of the buffalo to pressure Indigenous peoples to comply with land-settlement processes (Canadian Geographic, 2018). The buffalo was co-opted, misused, and deeply disrespected by colonizers. Consequently, buffalo herds estimated to be in the millions at the start of the nineteenth century were decimated throughout Turtle Island. Today, only a few small herds of buffalo survive. Much like Indigenous women and Indigenous peoples generally, however, the buffalo are resilient. And Plains Indigenous peoples are working within their values and ontological relationships to revitalize and restore the herds. The buffalo continue to be honoured in Indigenous ceremonies such as the Sun Dance, in the telling of buffalo stories, and in art and creative expression (Hubbard, 2009).

Returning to the deeper meaning of the buffalo means moving beyond a metaphor—being vigilant against settler metaphorization in education, and reminding ourselves about how "the buffalo embody the struggle against forces of colonialism, colonialism's subsequent failure to eradicate and erase Indigenous presence from the land, and the return of both Indigenous presence and creative consciousness" (Hubbard, 2009, p. 78). This thought compels me to ask another question: How can Indigenous ontological relationships with the land and non-humans like the buffalo better guide the aims of Indigenous higher education, policy directions, and leadership approaches? The buffalo are powerful teachers. "The buffalo are coming back," says Dr. Leroy Little Bear ("Little Bear," 2017).

NOW WHAT?

I hope this research offers some insights and possibilities for Indigenous educational policy and leadership practice. Because of the unique dimensions that characterize institutional-Indigenizing work within universities, many participants in my study underscored the urgent need for Indigenous leadership development and training for the current and next generation of Indigenous leaders engaged in universities. The importance of such development and training was emphasized by several women who remarked on their sense of isolation and the lack of formal networks they experienced while working in predominantly white settler colonial environments. Several women also reported that existing leadership programs did not address their unique leadership-training needs from Indigenous epistemological perspectives. While this book focuses on Indigenous women working in the university, much of its content is relevant to Indigenous and non-Indigenous people across a wide array of sectors, including anyone working in public policy, such as educators, leaders, and students, as it speaks to the complex processes of reconciliation, Indigenization, and decolonization, which are timely and cross-sectional.

With these training needs in mind, I call on future Indigenous leadership training and development programs to include critical Indigenous decolonial theory and praxis, and a background in Indigenous educational policy and practice, as key ingredients. This type of leadership training would significantly challenge existing leadership programs, "as most system-wide training tends to be about finances; risk and image management; curriculum and policy implementation; buildings and grounds; community liaison; marketing and entrepreneurship; health and wellbeing and stress management" (Blackmore, 2010, p. 55). I argue that these normative approaches to leadership training are biased, based as they are in white liberal and colonial notions of change and administration. New Indigenous leadership training programs for Indigenous peoples working to transform mainstream spaces are needed. These programs should be grounded in transformative decolonial approaches and should include Indigenous-led instruction that takes up specific examples of the politics of distraction (G. Smith, 2003) and of Indigenous refusals in practice, and that supports ongoing, critical self-reflectivity in relation to settler co-optation, misappropriation of Indigenous knowledge, Indigenous leaders' intersectional Indigeneity, and Indigenous ethics in leadership practice. Further, the university sector must advance and support the construction of a national Indigenous leadership network coalition—a network that is adequately funded and governed by Indigenous leaders, not white settlers and their institutions. Since completing my doctoral research in 2021, the National Indigenous University Senior Leaders' Association was co-founded by Dr. Jacqueline Ottmann and Dr. Michael Hart. The purpose of this network is to bring together leaders to engage in constructive dialogue and actions that pertain to academic university leadership contexts.

To support the work of Indigenous leaders and policy actors in the academy, I conclude by offering critical decolonial questions (see table 2) for leadership and policy practitioners to consider as part of their pedagogical practice. While the questions extend beyond the scope of my research, they offer some possibilities for future research and practice. The questions are centred on Māori scholars and leaders Linda Tuhiwai Smith and Graham Hingangaroa Smith's (2018) five tests for veracity.

Table 2. Critical Questions for Veracity

Tests for Veracity	Critical Decolonial Questions
Positionality	• Who is leading Indigenous policy initiatives? • Where do policy actors locate themselves intersectionally and in relation to the Indigenous land upon which the university is geographically located? • Who are Indigenous peoples on and off campus? What representation and diversity exists? • How are all leaders encouraged to reflect on their complex positionalities in relation to settler colonialism and to advance critical decoloniality in their leadership and policy praxis?
Criticality	• How do Indigenous educational needs drive policy visions and goals? • What underlying assumptions underpin policy problems and solutions? • Are Indigenous peoples and/or Indigenous knowledges portrayed in deficit ways as problems in policy discourse? • How do settler colonial authorities, structures, norms, and power dynamics shape Indigenous policy visions, interpretations, enactments, and decision-making processes?

CONCLUDING THOUGHTS

Criticality	• Are there structures to elevate Indigenous agency in the policy enactment processes? • Do Indigenous policies in practice inadvertently reproduce white settler colonial institutional interests, needs, and desires over Indigenous interests, needs, and desires? • Do Indigenous policy enactments give opportunities for white settlers to uncritically co-opt, appropriate, and commodify Indigenous policy goals? • Do Indigenous policy enactments reproduce unequal dynamics between settlers and Indigenous peoples?
Structuralist & culturalist considerations	*Structuralist* • How is Indigenous educational sovereignty advanced in academic governance, leadership, and accountability structures in the university? • What structural systems of governance, leadership, and accountability are in place for universities to be answerable to Indigenous communities in their various forms? • What institutional mechanisms are in place to critically challenge settler colonial assumptions, biases, and dominances in policy enactment processes? *Culturalist* • How do Indigenous policies and practices advance and protect Indigenous educational and intellectual sovereignty? • How do Indigenous policies and practices advance Indigenous theorizing, epistemologies, methodologies, and languages? • What are the unintentional consequences of Indigenous policy enactments for the survivance of Indigenous research, Indigenous ways of knowing, and languages in education?
Praxicality	• How are critical Indigenous theories and Indigenous knowledges contributing to new ways of leading, governing, and achieving academic excellence and change?

Praxicality	• How are Indigenous leaders supported in advancing Indigenous decolonial approaches to leadership in the academy? • How are all leaders taught about the histories and ongoing nature of settler colonialism in the academy and its relationship to Indigenous peoples and ways of knowing?
Transformability	• What changes are advanced because of Indigenous policy work? • How do such changes support Indigenous futures and desires in education? • What are some unintended consequences of Indigenizing policy work? • Who benefits from Indigenous policies, and how do you know they are benefiting? • How do universities measure Indigenous institutional change in holistic, respectful, and culturally relevant ways that balance quantitative and qualitative approaches? • How does the university observe Indigenous data and intellectual sovereignty in the collection, analysis, and reporting of research and institutional measures relating to Indigenous policies?

FUTURE RESEARCH

The present findings point to the need for further research on Indigenous educational leadership and policy that focuses on the experiences of Indigenous men, Indigenous Two Spirit people, and Indigenous staff members from Indigenous epistemological perspectives. I call on future scholars to engage in deeper and more nuanced explorations of Indigenous educational leadership as it occurs inside, outside, and on the borderland of the academy, in between Euro-Western institutions and Indigenous communities, and at various levels including intersectional micro levels, institutional meso levels, and national/global macro levels. Potential research questions to be explored include: (1) How can leaders advance decolonial-Indigenization approaches inside and outside the settler colonial academy? (2) What shapes Indigenous educational leadership ethics? (3) What existing educational leadership approaches and methods are useful and can be Indigenized to advance decolonial reform within academic settings? (4) How are Indigenous leaders shaping new conceptions of educational leadership grounded in Indigenous epistemologies including Indigenous stories? And (5) how do Indigenous leaders (broadly) approach Indigenizing their leadership from within their own Indigeneity and through Indigenous pedagogies?

These research findings further suggest new questions for policy researchers, including the following: (1) What underlying epistemologies underpin existing university governance structures, dominant university policy approaches and assumptions, and conventional ways of measuring policy success? (2) What are the limitations of the current academic administrative system in terms of advancing decolonial-Indigenization and asserting Indigenous educational sovereignty? And (3) how can universities transform their governance and organizational structures to advance Indigenous educational sovereignty in the areas of governance, leadership and policy enactment, student affairs, teaching and learning, and faculty relations?

EPILOGUE

Indigenous ways of knowing and Indigenous storytelling respect the integrity of learners and their ability to make their own meaning of stories by drawing on them as teachers. Within this orientation to teaching and learning, I can only internalize the opening Weesakechahk story and answer the role of this story for myself; I cannot make meaning for others, as this could violate a central ethic in Indigenous life.

Nevertheless, the opening Weesakechahk story has acted for me as a grounding anchor re-membering me in relationship to Cree ways of knowing and being, embedded within my own personal relationships to family, community, Nation, Territory, and cosmos. The story has brought me back into the circle over and over again, and at times has kept me from flying away on my own, out of collective formation. The story has helped me to reflect on my own internalized colonial patterns and complicities, to which I—like all of us—am not immune. Through naming and showing the contradictory and slippery nature of settler colonial power relations pervasive in Euro-Western ideologies, institutions, and administration, Weesakeechahk has helped me to honour my own embodied and paradoxically messy desires and experiences trying to lead in a complicated colonial world.

This book would be incomplete without inviting readers to reflect on the role of Indigenous theories and stories in Indigenous leadership and education for themselves. Throughout these pages, I have drawn on one Weesakechahk story as theory to challenge dominant Euro-Western conceptions of leadership and policy. To conclude, I leave readers to reflect on some related questions:

How can Indigenous theories and stories inform Indigenous leadership and policy frameworks in higher education?

What are some lessons you can learn from Weesakechahk's story in relation to leadership and policy?

What principles of leadership can be drawn from the Weesakechahk story and the experiences of Indigenous women administrators shared in this book?

Can other Indigenous theories and stories offer new frameworks for thinking, organizing, and practising educational governance, leadership, and policy?

REFERENCES

Absolon, K. (2011). *Kaandossiwin: How we come to know*. Fernwood Publishing.

Absolon, K., & Willett, C. (2005). Putting ourselves forward: Location in Aboriginal research. In L. Brown & S. Strega (Eds.), *Research as resistance: Critical, Indigenous & anti-oppressive approaches* (pp. 97–126). Canadian Scholars' Press.

Academic Women's Association [University of Alberta]. (2019). *The diversity gap in 2019* [Infographic series with the following subtitles: *Canadian universities – U15 presidents' leadership teams or cabinets; Leadership diversity: U15 deans; Canadian universities – U15 leadership pipeline; Canadian U15 universities – Leadership pipeline by position*]. Retrieved June 12, 2023, from https://uofaawa.wordpress.com/awa-diversity-gap-campaign/

AC-EDID (Advisory Committee on Equity, Diversity, Inclusion, and Decolonization). (2021, March 8). *Igniting change: Final report and recommendations*. Advisory Committee on Equity, Diversity, Inclusion and Decolonization. https://www.federationhss.ca/sites/default/files/2021-10/Igniting-Change-Final-Report-and-Recommendations-en.pdf

Acker, S. (2012). Chairing and caring: Gendered dimensions of leadership in academe. *Gender and Education*, 24(4), 411–28. https://doi.org/10.1080/09540253.2011.628927

Acoose, J. (1995). *Iskwewak: Kah' Ki Yaw Ni Wahkomakanak. Neither Indian princesses nor easy squaws*. Women's Press.

Aguiar, M., Calliste, A., & Dei, G. (Eds.) (2000). *Power, knowledge and anti-racism education: A critical reader*. Fernwood Publishing.

Aguilera-Black Bear, D., & Tippeconnic III, J.W. (2015). *Voices of resistance and renewal: Indigenous leadership in education.* University of Oklahoma Press.

Ahmed, S. (2000). *Strange encounters: Embodied others in post-coloniality.* Routledge.

Ahmed, S. (2006a). The non-performativity of anti-racism. *Borderlands,* 5(3). *Gale Academic OneFile.* https://link.gale.com/apps/doc/A169508887/AONE?u=lond95336&sid=bookmark-AONE&xid=349a8ad8

Ahmed, S. (2006b). The nonperformativity of antiracism. *Meridians,* 7(1), 104–26.

Ahmed, S. (2007a). The language of diversity. *Ethnic and Racial Studies,* 30(2), 235–56. https://doi.org/10.1080/01419870601143927

Ahmed, S. (2007b). A phenomenology of whiteness. *Feminist Theory,* 8(2), 149–68. https://doi.org/10.1177/1464700107078139

Ahmed, S. (2007c). "You end up doing the document rather than doing the doing": Diversity, race equality and the politics of documentation. *Ethnic and Racial Studies,* 30(4), 590–609. https://doi.org/10.1080/01419870701356015

Ahmed, S. (2009). Embodying diversity: Problems and paradoxes for Black feminists. *Race, Ethnicity and Education,* 12(1), 41–52. https://doi.org/10.1080/13613320802650931

Ahmed, S. (2012). *On being included: Racism and diversity in institutional life.* Duke University Press.

Ahmed, S. (2014). *Willful subjects.* Duke University Press.

Ahmed, S. (2017). *Living a feminist life.* Duke University Press.

Ahmed, S. (2018). Rocking the boat: Women of colour as diversity workers. In J. Arday & H. Mirza (Eds.), *Dismantling race in higher education: Racism, whiteness and decolonising the academy* (pp. 331–48). Palgrave Macmillan. https://doi.org/10.1007/978-3-319-60261-5

Ahmed, S. (2019). *What's the use? On the uses of use.* Duke University Press.

Ahmed, S., & Swan, E. (2006). Doing diversity. *Policy Futures in Education,* 4(2), 96–100. https://doi.org/10.2304/pfie.2006.4.2.96

Ah Nee-Benham, M.K.P., & Cooper, J.E. (1998). *Let my spirit soar! Narratives of diverse women in school leadership.* Corwin Press.

Ah Nee-Benham, M.K.P., & Murakami-Ramalho, E. (2010). Engaging in educational leadership: The generosity of spirit. *International*

Journal of Leadership in Education, 13(1), 77–91. https://doi.org/10.1080/13603120903242899

Ahtone, T., & Lee, R. (2021). Looking forward from land-grab universities. NAIS: *Journal of the Native American and Indigenous Studies Association*, 8(1), 176–82. https://doi.org/10.1353/nai.2021.a784832

Aldama, F., & González, C. (2018). *Latinx studies: The key concepts*. Routledge.

Almeida, D. (2015). Standing on my head spitting (Indian Head) nickels: Racial battle fatigue as it relates to Native Americans in predominantly white institutions of higher education. In K. Fasching-Varner, K. Mitchell, & A. Chaunda (Eds.), *Racial battle fatigue in higher education: Exposing the myth of post-racial America* (pp. 157–78). Rowman & Littlefield.

Ambler, M. (1992). Women leaders in Indian Education: More women are running tribal colleges. What does this mean for the future of Native American Societies? *Tribal College Journal*, 3(4), 10–14.

Andersen, C., & O'Brien, J. (2017). Introduction: Indigenous studies: An appeal for methodological promiscuity. In C. Andersen & J. O'Brien (Eds.), *Sources and methods in Indigenous studies* (pp. 1–12). Routledge. https://doi.org/10.4324/9781315528854

Anderson, K. (2000). *A recognition of being: Reconstructing Native womanhood* (2nd ed.). Women's Press.

Anderson, K. (2009). Leading by action: Female Chiefs and the political landscape. In G.G. Valaskakis, M. Dion Stout, and E. Guimond (Eds.), *Restoring the balance: First Nations women, community and culture* (pp. 99–103). University of Manitoba Press.

Anderson, K. (2010). Affirmations of an Indigenous feminist. In C. Suzack, S. Huhndorf, J. Perreault, and J. Barman (Eds.), *Indigenous women and feminism: Politics, activism, culture* (pp. 81–91). University of British Columbia Press.

Anderson, K. (2016). *A recognition of being: Reconstructing Native womanhood* (2nd ed.). Women's Press.

Anderson, K., Ruiz-Flores, E., Stewart, G.T., Tlostanova, M. (2019). Symposium: What can Indigenous feminist knowledge and practices bring to "Indigenizing" the academy? *Journal of World Philosophies*, 4(1), 121–55. https://scholarworks.iu.edu/iupjournals/index.php/jwp/article/view/2646/217

Andreotti, V.D.O., Stein, S., Ahenakew, C., & Hunt, D. (2015). Mapping interpretations of decolonization in the context of higher education. *Decolonization: Indigeneity, Education & Society* 4(1), 21–40.

Anzaldúa, G. (2012). *Borderlands/La frontera: The new Mestiza.* Aunt Lute Books.

Anzaldúa, G. (2009). *The Gloria Anzaldúa reader.* Duke University Press.

Apple, M. (2001). Comparing neo-liberal projects and inequality in education. *Comparative Education,* 37(4), 409–23.

Archibald, J. (2008a). An Indigenous storywork methodology. In J.G. Knowles & A. Cole (Eds.), *Handbook of the arts in qualitative research: Perspectives, methodologies, examples and issues* (pp. 371–84). Sage Publications.

Archibald, J. (2008b). *Indigenous storywork: Educating the heart, mind, body, and spirit.* University of British Columbia Press.

Archibald, J. (2009). Creating an Indigenous intellectual movement at Canadian universities: The stories of five First Nations female academics. In G. Valaskakis, E. Guimond, & M.D. Stout (Eds.), *Restoring the balance: First Nations women, community, and culture* (pp. 125–48). University of Manitoba Press.

Archibald, J., Lundy, J., Reynolds, C., Williams, L. (2010). *ACDE accord on Indigenous education.* Association of Canadian Deans of Education. http://csse-scee.ca/acde/wp-content/uploads/sites/7/2017/08/Accord-on-Indigenous-Education.pdf

Archibald, J., Pidgeon, M., & Hawkey, C. (2010). *Aboriginal transitions: Undergraduate to graduate. Phase I final report.* Indigenous Education Institute of Canada, University of British Columbia. http://aboriginallearning.ca/wp-content/uploads/2015/02/ubc-Aboriginal-Transitions.pdf

Arvin, M., Tuck, E., & Morrill A. (2013). Decolonizing feminism: Challenging connections between settler colonialism and heteropatriarchy. *Feminist Formations,* 25(1), 8–34.

Asch, M., Borrows, J., & Tully, J. (2018). *Resurgence and reconciliation: Indigenous-settler relations and earth teachings.* University of Toronto Press.

Ashcraft, K., & Mumby, D. (2004). *Reworking gender: A feminist communicology of organization.* Sage Publications.

Axworthy, L., De Riviere, L., & Moore-Rattray, J. (2016). Community learning and university policy: An inner-city university goes back to school. *International Indigenous Policy Journal,* 7(2), 1–13.

REFERENCES

Backhouse, C., Milton, C., Kovach, M., & Perry, A. (Eds.). (2021). *Royally wronged: The Royal Society of Canada's role in the marginalization of Indigenous knowledge.* McGill-Queen's University Press.

Baldy, C.R. (2015). Coyote is not a metaphor: On decolonizing, (re)claiming and (re)naming "Coyote." *Decolonization: Indigeneity, Education & Society* 4(1), 1–20. https://jps.library.utoronto.ca/index.php/des/article/view/22155/18469

Ball, S.J. (1990). *Politics and policy making in education: Explorations in policy sociology.* Routledge.

Ball, S.J., Maguire, M., & Braun, A. (2012). *How schools do policy: Policy enactments in secondary schools.* Routledge.

Barkdull, C. (2009). Exploring intersections of identity with Native American women leaders. *Affilia,* 24(2), 120–36. https://doi.org/10.1177/0886109909331700

Barker, J. (2008). Gender, sovereignty, rights: Native women's activism against social inequality and violence in Canada. *American Quarterly,* 60(2), 259–66.

Barker, J. (Ed.) (2017). *Critically sovereign: Indigenous gender, sexuality, and feminist studies.* Duke University Press.

Barnard, D.T. (2015, June 8). *The role of Canada's universities in reconciliation.* Universities Canada. http://www.univcan.ca/media-room/media-releases/david-t-barnard-the-role-of-canadas-universities-in-reconciliation/

Battiste, M. (1986). Micmac literacy and cognitive assimilation. In J. Barman, Y. Hébert, & D. McCaskill (Eds.), *Indian education in Canada, Volume 1: The legacy* (pp. 23–44). University of British Columbia Press.

Battiste, M. (1998). Enabling the autumn seed: Toward a decolonized approach to Aboriginal knowledge, language, and education. *Canadian Journal of Native Education,* 22(1), 16–27.

Battiste, M. (Ed.) (2000). *Reclaiming Indigenous voice and vision.* University of British Columbia Press.

Battiste, M. (2013). *Decolonizing education: Nourishing the learning spirit.* Purich Publishing.

Battiste, M. (2013, April). *You can't be the doctor if you're the disease: Eurocentrism and Indigenous renaissance.* Distinguished Academic Lecture presented to the Council of Academic University Teachers, Ottawa, ON.

Battiste, M. (Ed.) (2016). *Visioning a Mi'kmaw humanities: Indigenizing the academy*. Cape Breton University Press.

Battiste, M. (2017). Foreword. In F. Pirbhai-Illich, S. Pete, & F. Martin, (Eds.), *Culturally responsive pedagogy: Working toward decolonization, Indigeneity, and inter-culturalism* (pp. vii–xi). Palgrave Macmillan.

Battiste, M. (2018). Reconciling Indigenous knowledge in education: Promises, possibilities, and imperatives. In M. Spooner & J. McNinch (Eds.), *Dissident knowledge in higher education* (pp. 123–48). University of Regina Press.

Battiste, M., Bell, L., & Findlay, L.M. (2002). Decolonizing education in Canadian universities: An interdisciplinary, international, Indigenous research project. *Canadian Journal of Native Education*, 26(2), 82–95.

Battiste, M., & Youngblood Henderson, J. (2009). Naturalizing Indigenous knowledge in Eurocentric education. *Canadian Journal of Native Education*, 32(1), 5–18.

Bedard, R.E.M. (2018). "Indian in the cupboard": Lateral violence and Indigenization of the academy. In C.L. Cho, J.K. Corkett, and A. Steele (Eds.), *Exploring the toxicity of lateral violence and microaggressions: Poison in the water cooler* (pp. 75–101). Springer International.

Bell, D. (1980). *Brown v. Board of Education* and the interest-convergence dilemma. *Harvard Law Review*, 93(3), 518–33.

Benham, M.K.P. (2007). Moʻōlelo: On culturally relevant story making from an Indigenous perspective. In D.J. Clandinin (Ed.), Handbook of narrative inquiry: Mapping a methodology (pp. 512–34). Sage Publications.

Bhambra, G.K., Gebrial, D., & Nişancıoğlu, K. (2018). *Decolonising the university*. Pluto Press.

Bird, L. (2005). *Telling our stories: Omushkego legends and histories from Hudson Bay*. Broadview Press.

Bird, L. (2007). *The spirit lives in the mind: Omushkego stories, lives and dreams*. McGill-Queen's University Press.

Bird, C.P., Lee, T., & Lopez, N. (2013). Leadership and accountability in American Indian education: Voices from New Mexico. *American Journal of Education*, 119(4), 539–63.

Bishop, R. (1999). Collaborative storytelling: Meeting Indigenous peoples' desires for self-determination in research. In *Indigenous education around the world: Workshop papers from the World Indigenous People's

REFERENCES

Conference: Education (Albuquerque, New Mexico, June 15–22, 1996). ERIC Clearinghouse. https://files.eric.ed.gov/fulltext/ED467396.pdf

Blackmore, J. (1999). *Troubling women: Feminism, leadership and educational change.* Open University Press.

Blackmore, J. (2010). "The other within": Race/gender disruptions to the professional learning of white educational leaders. *International Journal Leadership in Education,* 13(1), 45–61.

Blackmore, J., & Sachs, J. (2007). *Performing and reforming leaders: Gender, educational restructuring, and organizational change.* State University of New York Press.

Blakesley, S. (2008). Remote and unresearched: Educational leadership in Canada's Yukon Territory. *Compare: A Journal of Comparative and International Education,* 38(4), 441–54.

Bopp, M., Brown, L., & Robb, J. (2017). *Reconciliation within the academy: Why is Indigenization so difficult?* Four Worlds Centre for Development Learning. http://www.fourworlds.ca/pdf_downloads/Reconciliation_within_the_Academy_Final.pdf

Borrows, J. (2013). Maajitaadaa: Nanaboozhoo and the flood, part 2. In J. Doerkfler, N.J. Sinclair, & H.K. Stark, (Eds.), *Centering Anishinaabeg studies: Understanding the world through stories* (pp. ix–xiv). University of Manitoba Press.

Brayboy, B.M.J. (2004). Hiding in the ivy: American Indian students and visibility in elite educational settings. *Harvard Educational Review,* 74(2), 125–52.

Brayboy, B.M.J. (2005). Transformational resistance and social justice: American Indians in Ivy League universities. *Anthropology and Education Quarterly,* 36(3), 193–211.

Brayboy, B.M.J., & Solyom, J.A. (2017). *A study of Indigenous boys and men.* RISE for Boys and Men of Color. http://www.equalmeasure.org/wp-content/uploads/2017/08/A-Study-of-Indigenous-Boys.pdf

Brayboy, B.M.J., Solyom, J.A., & Castagno, A. (2015). Indigenous peoples in higher education. *Journal of American Indian Education,* 54(1), 154–86.

Broadhead, L.-A., & Howard, S. (2021). Confronting the contradictions between Western and Indigenous science: A critical perspective on *Two-Eyed Seeing. AlterNative: An International Journal of Indigenous Peoples,* 17(1), 111–19. https://doi.org/10.1177/1177180121996326

Brower, P. (2016). *Tumitchiat: Iñuqqaat Aullarrisiatun Iḷisaġviit, a new pathway: Indigenous leadership in higher education* [Unpublished doctoral dissertation]. University of Alaska Fairbanks.

Brunette, C., & Richmond, C. (2018). *Guide for working with Indigenous students.* Western University. https://teaching.uwo.ca/pdf/teaching/Guide-for-Working-with-Indigenous-Students.pdf

Brunette-Debassige, C., Wakeham, P., Smithers-Graeme, C., Haque, A., & Chitty, S.M. (2022). Mapping approaches to decolonizing and Indigenizing the curriculum at Canadian universities: Critical reflections on current practices, challenges, and possibilities. *International Indigenous Policy Journal,* 13(3). https://doi.org/10.18584/iipj.2022.13.3.14109

Bryant, M.T. (1998). Cross-cultural understandings of leadership: Themes from Native American interviews. *Educational Management & Administration,* 26(1), 7–20.

Bunda, T., Zipin, L., & Brennan, M. (2012). Negotiating university "equity" from Indigenous standpoints: A shaky bridge. *International Journal of Inclusive Education,* 16(9), 941–57.

Butler, J. (1988). Performative acts and gender constitution: An essay in phenomenology and feminist theory. *Theatre Journal,* 40(4), 519–31. https://doi.org/10.2307/3207893

Butler, J. (1993). *Bodies that matter: On the discursive limits of "sex."* Routledge.

Cajete, G. (2016). Indigenous education and the development of Indigenous community leaders. *Leadership,* 12(3), 364–76.

Campbell, L. (2021). Indigeneity Indigenous feminisms and Indigenization. In J. Evans & E. Lee (Eds.), *Indigenous women's voices: 20 years on from Linda Tuhiwai Smith's* Decolonizing Methodologies (pp. 123–35). Zed Books.

Canadian Geographic. (2018). *Indigenous Peoples atlas of Canada* (1st ed.). Royal Canadian Geographical Society.

Canadian Institutes of Health Research, Natural Sciences and Engineering Research Council of Canada, and Social Sciences and Humanities Research Council of Canada. (2014). *Tri-council policy statement: Ethical conduct for research involving humans.* https://www.cmcc.ca/Tri-Council%20Policy%20Statement.pdf

Canadian Institutes of Health Research, Natural Sciences and Engineering Research Council of Canada, and Social Sciences and Humanities

REFERENCES

Research Council of Canada. (2018). *Tri-council policy statement: Ethical conduct for research involving humans.* https://ethics.gc.ca/eng/policy-politique_tcps2-eptc2_2018.html

Capper, C. (2019). *Organizational theory for equity and diversity: Leading integrated, socially just education.* Routledge.

CAUT (Canadian Association of University Teachers). (n.d.). *Recognition of increased workload of academic staff members in equity seeking groups.* https://www.caut.ca/about-us/caut-policy/lists/caut-policy-statements/recognition-of-increased-workload-of-academic-staff-members-in-equity-seeking-groups-in-a-minority-context

CAUT (Canadian Association of University Teachers). (2016a). *Guide to acknowledging First Peoples & traditional territory.* https://www.caut.ca/content/guide-acknowledging-first-peoples-traditional-territory

CAUT (Canadian Association of University Teachers). (2016b). *Indigenizing the academy.* https://www.caut.ca/about-us/caut-policy/lists/caut-policy-statements/indigenizing-the-academy

CAUT (Canadian Association of University Teachers). (2018). *Underrepresented & underpaid: Diversity & equity among Canada's post-secondary education teachers.* Canadian Association of University Teachers. https://www.caut.ca/sites/default/files/caut_equity_report_2018-04final.pdf

CAUT (Canadian Association of University Teachers). (2020). *Bargaining for Indigenization of the academy.* Canadian Association of University Teachers. https://www.caut.ca/sites/default/files/caut-bargaining-advisory-bargaining-for-indigenization-of-the-academy_2020-01.pdf

Champagne, D. (2007). In search of theory and method in American Indian studies. *American Indian Quarterly,* 31(3), 353–72.

Chavez, A.F., & Sanlo, R. (2013). *Identity and leadership: Informing our lives, informing our practice.* National Association of Student Personnel Administrators.

Cherubini, L. (2012). Postsecondary Aboriginal educational policy in Ontario: Policy and practical implications. *Aboriginal Policy Studies,* 2(1), 42–55. https://doi.org/10.5663/aps.v2i1.12371

Cherubini, L., Hodson, J., Manley-Casimir, M., & Muir, C. (2010). "Closing the gap" at the peril of widening the void: Implications of the Ontario Ministry of Education's policy for Aboriginal education. *Canadian Journal of Education,* 33(2), 329–55.

Chiefs of Ontario (2017). *First Nations post-secondary education: Rights, responsibilities, and recommendations* [Post-secondary position paper]. https://education.chiefs-of-ontario.org/education/download/fn-pse-rights-2017/?wpdmdl=1363&masterkey=5fdbad0581a44

Chilisa, B. (2012). *Indigenous research methodologies.* Sage Publications.

Cho, C.L., Corkett, J.K., & Steele, A. (2018). Introduction. In C.L. Cho, J.K. Corkett, & A. Steele (Eds.), *Exploring the toxicity of lateral violence and microaggressions: Poison in the water cooler* (pp. 1–9). Springer International. https://doi.org/10.1007/978-3-319-74760-6

Chua, A. (2023, January). How dispossessed Indigenous lands financed UofT's development. The Varsity. Retrieved online. https://thevarsity.ca/2023/1/30/how-dispossessed-indigenous-lands-financed-u-of-ts-development/

Clandinin, D.J., & Connelly, F.M. (2000). *Narrative inquiry: Experience and story in qualitative research.* Jossey-Bass.

Clark, D.A., Kleiman, S., Spanierman, L.B., Isaac, P., & Poolokasingham, G. (2014). "Do you live in a teepee?" Aboriginal students' experiences with racial microaggressions in Canada. *Journal of Diversity in Higher Education, 7*(2), 112–25.

Clark, N. (2016). Red intersectionality and violence-informed witnessing praxis with Indigenous girls. *Girlhood Studies, 9*(2), 46–64. https://doi.org/10.3167/ghs.2016.090205

Collins, P.H. (1986). Learning from the outsider within: The sociological significance of Black feminist thought. *Social Problems, 33*(6), S14–S32. https://doi.org/10.1525/sp.1986.33.6.03a00020

Connelly, F.M., & Clandinin, D.J. (1990). Stories of experience and narrative inquiry. *Educational Researcher, 19*(5) 2–14.

Connelly, F.M., & Clandinin, D.J. (1999). *Shaping a professional identity: Stories of educational practice.* Teachers College Press.

Cook-Lynn, E. (1999). American Indian studies: An overview. Keynote address at the Native Studies Conferences, Yale University, February 5, 1998. *Wicazo Sa Review, 14*(2), 14–24.

Corntassel, J. (2011, January 12). Indigenizing the academy: Insurgent education and the roles of Indigenous intellectuals [Blog post]. *Federation for the Humanities and Social Sciences.* https://www.federationhss.ca/en/blog/indigenizing-academy-insurgent-education-and-roles-indigenous-intellectuals

REFERENCES

Corntassel, J. (2012). Re-envisioning resurgence: Indigenous pathways to decolonization and sustainable self-determination. *Decolonization: Indigeneity, Education & Society*, 1(1), 86–101.

Cote-Meek, S. (2014). *Colonized classrooms: Racism, trauma and resistance in post-secondary education*. Fernwood Publishing.

Cote-Meek, S. (2018a, November 6). From the admin chair: Making a long-term commitment to Indigenous education. *University Affairs*. https://www.universityaffairs.ca/opinion/from-the-admin-chair/making-a-long-term-commitment-to-indigenous-education/

Cote-Meek, S. (2018b, August 23). From the admin chair: What we can learn from great leaders. *University Affairs*. https://www.universityaffairs.ca/opinion/from-the-admin-chair/what-we-can-learn-from-great-leaders/

Cote-Meek, S. (2019, September 17). From the admin chair: Four questions to ask yourself when considering a move within senior academic administration. *University Affairs*. https://www.universityaffairs.ca/opinion/from-the-admin-chair/four-questions-to-ask-yourself-when-considering-a-move-within-senior-academic-administration

Cote-Meek, S. (2020). Intergenerational Indigenous resilience and navigating academic administration. In T. Moeke-Pickering, S. Cote-Meek & A. Pegoraro (Eds.), *Critical reflections and politics on advancing women in the academy* (pp. 151–65). IGI Global Publishing.

Coulthard, G. (2014). *Red skins, white masks: Rejecting the colonial politics of recognition*. University of Minnesota Press.

Crazy Bull, C., Lindquist, C., & Gipp, D.M. (2015). An act of sovereignty: Governing tribal higher education. *Tribal College Journal*, 26(4), 18–22.

Crenshaw, K. (1995). Mapping the margins: Intersectionality, identity politics, and violence against women of color. In Crenshaw, K., Gotanda, N.T., Peller, G., & Thomas, K. (Eds.), *Critical race theory: The key writings that formed the movement* (pp. 357–83). New Press.

Creswell, J. (2014). *Research design: Qualitative, quantitative and mixed methods approaches*. Sage Publications.

Cross, N., & Peace, T. (2021). "My own old English friends": Networking Anglican settler colonialism at the Shingwauk Home, Huron College, and Western University. *Historical Studies in Education*, 33(1). https://doi.org/10.32316/hse-rhe.v33i1.4891

Cupples, J., & Grosfoguel, R. (2018). *Unsettling Eurocentrism in the Westernized university*. Routledge. https://doi.org/10.4324/9781315162126

CUSC (Canadian University Survey Consortium). (2017). *2017 middle-years university student survey*. Canadian University Survey Consortium. http://www.cusc-ccreu.ca/publications/CUSC_2017%20Middle-Year%20Student%20Survey_Master%20Report%20(English)_FINAL.pdf

Daigle, M. (2019). The spectacle of reconciliation: On (the) unsettling responsibilities to Indigenous peoples in the academy. *Environment and Planning D: Society & Space*, 37(4), 703–21. https://doi.org/10.1177/0263775818824342

Davidson, P., & Jamieson, R. (2018, November 19). Advancing reconciliation through postsecondary education. *Policy Options*. https://policyoptions.irpp.org/magazines/november-2018/advancing-reconciliation-through-post-secondary-education/

Debassige, A., & Brunette-Debassige, C. (2019). Indigenizing work as "willful work": Toward Indigenous transgressive leadership in Canadian universities. *Cultural and Pedagogical Inquiry*, 10(2) 119–38. https://journals.library.ualberta.ca/cpi/index.php/cpi/article/view/29449/21460

Deer, F. (2015). Indigenous rights in Canada: Implications for leadership in education. *Antistasis*, 5(1), 37–40.

Deer, F. (2020). The Indigenous achievement agenda and identity politics in university administration: Navigating faculty recruitment in an era of institutional change. In E. Samier & P. Milley (Eds.), *Educational administration and leadership identity formation: International theories, problems and challenges* (pp. 103–16). Routledge.

de Leeuw, S., Lindsay, N., Greenwood, M. (2013). Troubling good intentions. *Settler Colonial Studies*, 3(3–4), 381–94. https://doi.org/10.1080/2201473X.2013.810694

Denzin, N.K. (2018). Performing ethnography: Staging resistance. *Cultural Studies*, 18(6), 453–62. https://doi.org/10.1177/1532708618787460

Denzin, N.K., Lincoln, Y.S., & Smith, L.T. (2008). *Handbook of critical and Indigenous methodologies*. Sage Publications.

Dyck, N. (1991). *What is the Indian "problem"? Tutelage and resistance in Canadian Indian administration*. Institute of Social and Economic Research, Memorial University of Newfoundland.

REFERENCES

EagleWoman, A. (2019, June 12). Falling over glass cliff: Meaningful reconciliation to support leadership of Indigenous women. *Lawyer's Daily.* https://www.angeliqueeaglewoman.com/_files/ugd/d039dc_467233c3721e48d69d2bad2358ebf8a5.pdf

Eastman, J., Jones, G.A., Trottier, C., & Bégin-Caouette, O. (2022). *University governance in Canada: Navigating complexity* (1st ed.). McGill-Queen's University Press.

Ellis, C.D. (Ed.) (1995). *âtalôhkâna nesta tipâcimôwina: Cree legends and narratives from the West Coast of James Bay.* Publications of the Algonquian Text Society. University of Manitoba Press.

Elson, P.H. (2019, November). A journey into university-Indigenous relations: Proposed policy framework provides new insights. *Martlet: University of Victoria's Independent Newspaper.* https://www.martlet.ca/a-journey-into-university-indigenous-relations/

Episkenew, J. (2009). *Taking back our spirits: Indigenous literature, public policy, and healing.* University of Manitoba Press.

Fagan, K. (2010). What's the trouble with the Trickster? An introduction. In D. Reder and L.M. Morra (Eds.), *Troubling Tricksters: Revisioning critical conversations* (pp. 3–20). Wilfrid Laurier University Press.

Faircloth, S. (2017). Reflections on the concept of authentic leadership: From an Indigenous scholar/leader perspective. *Advances in Developing Human Resources,* 19(4), 407–19. https://doi.org/10.1177/1523422317728935

Faircloth, S., & Tippeconnic, J. (2013). Leadership in Indigenous education: Challenges and opportunities for change. *American Journal of Education,* 119(4), 481–6. https://doi.org/10.1086/671017

Fallon, G., & Paquette, J. (2014). Rethinking conceptions of educational leadership within a First Nations settings in Canada. *Journal of Educational Administration,* 52(2), 193–209.

Fitzgerald, T. (2003a). Changing the deafening silence of Indigenous women's voices in educational leadership. *Journal of Educational Administration,* 41(1), 9–23. https://doi.org/10.1108/09578230310457402

Fitzgerald, T. (2003b). Interrogating orthodox voices: Gender, ethnicity and educational leadership. *School Leadership & Management,* 23(4), 431–44. https://doi.org/10.1080/1363243032000150962

Fitzgerald, T. (2004). Powerful voices and powerful stories: Reflections on the challenges and dynamics of intercultural research. *Journal of Intercultural Studies,* 25(3), 233–45.

Fitzgerald, T. (2006). Walking between two worlds: Indigenous women and educational leadership. *Educational Management Administration & Leadership*, 34(2), 201-13. https://doi.org/10.1177/1741143206062494

Fitzgerald, T. (2010). Spaces in-between: Indigenous women leaders speak back to dominant discourses and practices in educational leadership. *International Journal of Leadership in Education: Disrupting Notions of Leadership from Feminist Post-Colonial Positions*, 13(1), 93-105. https://doi.org/10.1080/13603120903242923

Fitzgerald, T. (2014). *Women leaders in higher education: Shattering the myths*. Routledge.

FitzMaurice, K. (2011). Transgressing the boundaries of Native studies: Traces of White Paper policy in academic patterns of Indigenization. *Canadian Journal of Native Studies*, 31(2), 63-76.

FNIGC (First Nations Information Governance Centre). (2014, May 23). *Ownership, control, access and possession: The path to First Nations information governance*. First Nations Information Governance Centre. https://achh.ca/wp-content/uploads/2018/07/OCAP_FNIGC.pdf

Ford, L., Guthadjaka, K., Daymangu, J., Danganbar, B., Baker, C., Ford, C., Ford, E., Thompson, N., Ford, M., Wallace, R., St. Clair, M., & Murtagh, D. (2018). Re-imaging Aboriginal leadership in higher education: A new Indigenous research paradigm. *Australian Journal of Education*, 62(3), 276-88. https://doi.org/10.1177/0004944118808364

Former law school dean sues Thunder Bay's Lakehead University for "racial discrimination." (2018, November 21). *CBC News*. www.cbc.ca/news/canada/thunder-bay/eaglewoman-suing-lakehead-university-1.4914462

Gallop, C., & Bastien, N. (2016). Supporting success: Aboriginal students in higher education. *Canadian Journal of Higher Education*, 46(2), 206-24.

Garneau, D. (2016). Imaginary spaces of conciliation and reconciliation: Art, curations and healing. In D. Robinson and K. Martin (Eds.), *Arts of engagement: Taking aesthetic action in and beyond the Truth and Reconciliation Commission of Canada* (pp. 21-42). Wilfrid Laurier University Press.

Gaudry, A. (2016, January). Paved with good intentions: Simply requiring Indigenous content is not enough [Blog post]. *Active History*. http://activehistory.ca/2016/01/paved-with-good-intentions-simply-requiring-indigenous-content-is-not-enough/

REFERENCES

Gaudry, A., & Lorenz, D. (2018a). Decolonization for the masses? Grappling with Indigenous content requirements in the changing Canadian post-secondary environment. In E. Tuck & W. Yang (Eds.), *Indigenous and decolonizing studies in education: Mapping the long view* (pp. 159–74). Routledge.

Gaudry, A., & Lorenz, D. (2018b). Indigenization as inclusion, reconciliation, and decolonization: Navigating the different visions for Indigenizing the Canadian academy. *AlterNative: An International Journal of Indigenous Peoples*, 14(3), 218–27.

Giroux. H.A. (2014). Austerity and the poison of neoliberal miseducation. *Symploke*, 22(1–2), 9–21. https://doi.org/10.5250/symploke.22.1-2.0009

Goddard, J.T., & Foster, R.Y. (2002). Where cultures collide: Educational issues in northern Alberta. *Canadian Journal of Education*, 27(1), 1–20.

Goeman, M.R. (2009). Notes toward a Native feminism's spatial practice. *Wicazo Sa Review*, 24(2), 169–87. https://doi.org/10.1353/wic.0.0040

Goeman, M.R. (2013). *Mark my words: Native women mapping our Nations.* University of Minnesota Press.

Goeman, M.R., & Nez Denetdale, J. (2009). Native feminisms: Legacies, interventions, and Indigenous sovereignties. *Wicazo Sa Review*, 24(2), 9–13. https://doi.org/10.1353/wic.0.0035

Gomes, F.M.K. (2016). *Paths to leadership of Native Hawaiian women administrators in Hawaii's higher education system: A qualitative study* [Unpublished doctoral dissertation]. University of Nebraska.

Grafton, E., & Melançon, J. (2020). The dynamics of decolonization and Indigenization in an era of academic "reconciliation." In S. Cote-Meek & T. Moeke-Pickering (Eds.), *Decolonizing and Indigenizing education in Canada* (pp. 135–53). Canadian Scholars Press.

Grande, S. (2003). Whitestream feminism and the colonialist project: A review of contemporary feminist pedagogy and praxis. *Educational Theory*, 53(3), 329–46.

Grande, S. (2015). *Red pedagogy: Native American social and political thought*. Rowman & Littlefield.

Grande, S. (2018a). Refusing the settler society of the spectacle. In E.A. McKinley & L.T. Smith (Eds.), *Handbook of Indigenous education* (pp. 1013–1029). Springer. https://www.springer.com/gp/book/9789811038983

Grande, S. (2018b). Refusing the university. In M. Spooner & J. McNinch (Eds.), *Dissident knowledge in higher education* (pp. 168–85). University of Regina Press.

Green, J. (Ed.) (2017). *Making room for Indigenous feminism* (2nd ed.). Fernwood Publishing.

Green, R. (1975). The Pocahontas perplex: The image of Indian women in American culture. *Massachusetts Review*, 16(4), 698–714.

Greenwood, M., de Leeuw, S., Fraser, T.N. (2008). When the politics of inclusivity become exploitative: A reflective commentary on Indigenous peoples, Indigeneity, and the academy. *Canadian Journal of Native Education*, 31(1), 198–207.

Grosfoguel, R. (2016). The dilemmas of ethnic studies in the United States. In R. Grosfoguel, R. Hernández, & E. Rosen Velásquez (Eds.), *Decolonizing the Westernized university: Interventions in philosophy of education from within and without* (pp. 27–38). Lexington Books.

Gunstone, A. (2013). Indigenous leadership and governance in Australian universities. *International Journal of Critical Indigenous Studies*, 6(1), 1–11.

Gunter, H. (2001). Critical approaches to leadership in education. *Journal of Educational Enquiry*, 2(2), 94–108.

Hall, B. (2018). Beyond epistemicide: Knowledge democracy and higher education. In M. Spooner & J. McNinch (Eds.), *Dissident knowledge in higher education* (pp. 65–84). University of Regina Press.

Hallinger, P., & Leithwood, K. (1996). Culture and educational administration: A case of finding out what you don't know you don't know. *Journal of Educational Administration*, 34(5), 98–116. https://doi.org/10.1108/09578239610148296

Hardison-Stevens, D. (2014). *Knowing the Indigenous leadership journey: Indigenous people need the academic system as much as the academic system needs Indigenous people* [Unpublished doctoral dissertation]. Antioch University.

Harvey, C.P.A. (unpublished). *Bricks and mortarboards: University-building in the settlement empire 1840-1920*. Doctoral dissertation. Princeton University.

Harvey, C.P.A. (2021). The wealth of knowledge: Land-grab universities in a British imperial and global context. *NAIS: Journal of the Native American and Indigenous Studies Association*, 8(1), 97–105. https://doi.org/10.5749/natiindistudj.8.1.0097

REFERENCES

Henry, F. (2012). Indigenous faculty at Canadian universities: Their stories. *Canadian Ethnic Studies Journal*, 44(2), 101–32.

Henry, F., Dua, E., James, C.E., Kobayashi, A., Li, P., Ramos, H., & Smith, M. (2017). *The equity myth: Racialization and Indigeneity at Canadian universities.* University of British Columbia Press.

Henry, F., & Tator, C. (2009). *Racism in the Canadian university: Demanding social justice, inclusion, and equity.* University of Toronto Press.

Highway, T. (2003). *Comparing mythologies.* Charles R. Bronfman Lecture in Canadian Studies. University of Ottawa Press.

Hochschild, A. (1983). *The managed heart: Commercialization of human feeling.* University of California Press.

Hopeha (Ngāpuhi), M.K. (2013). Educational leadership and Indigeneity: Doing things the same, differently. *American Journal of Education*, 119(4), 617–31.

Hubbard, T. (2009). "The buffaloes are gone" or "return: buffalo"? The relationship of the buffalo to Indigenous creative expression. *Canadian Journal of Native Studies*, 29(1–2), 65–85.

Hunt, S. (2013). Ontologies of Indigeneity: The politics of embodying a concept. *Cultural Geographies*, 21(1), 27–32. https://doi.org/10.1177/1474474013500226

Indigenous Senior Leadership Advisory Committee. (2019, August 31). *University of Manitoba Indigenous senior leadership: Report and recommendations to the provost and vice president (academic).* University of Manitoba. https://umanitoba.ca/sites/default/files/2020-06/isl_report_final.pdf

Innes, R.A. (2010). Introduction: Native Studies and Native cultural preservation, revitalization, and persistence. *American Indian Culture and Research Journal* 34(2), 1-9.

Innes, R.A. (2013). *Elder brother and the law of the people: Contemporary kinship and Cowessess First Nation.* University of Manitoba Press.

Innes, R.A. (2017). Elder brother as theoretical framework. In C. Andersen & J.M. O'Brien (Eds.), *Sources and methods in Indigenous studies* (pp. 135–42). Routledge.

Irwin, N.J. (1992). *Native Indian leadership from within* [Unpublished master's thesis]. University of Alberta.

Jewell, E., & Mosby, I. (2020). *Calls to action accountability: A 2020 status update on reconciliation.* Yellowhead Institute. https://

yellowheadinstitute.org/wp-content/uploads/2020/12/yi-trc-calls-to-action-update-full-report-2020.pdf

Johnson, S. (2016). Indigenizing higher education and the calls to action: Awakening to personal, political, and academic responsibilities. *Canadian Social Work Review*, 33(1), 133-9. https://doi.org/10.7202/1037096ar

Johnson, V.J. (1997). *Weavers of change: Portraits of Native American women educational leaders* [Unpublished doctoral dissertation]. Michigan State University.

Johnson, V.J., Benham, M.K.P., & VanAlstine, M.J. (2003). *Native leadership: Advocacy for transformation, culture, community and sovereignty.* In M.K.P. Benham & W.J. Stein (Eds.), *The renaissance of American Indian higher education: Capturing the dream.* Lawrence Erlbaum Associates Publishers.

Jones, G., Shanahan, T., & Goyan, P. (2001) University governance in Canadian higher education. *Tertiary Education and Management*, 7(2), 135-48.

Joseph, B. (2019). *Indigenous relations: Insights, tips and suggestions to make reconciliation a reality.* Indigenous Relations Press.

Jules, F. (1999). Native Indian leadership. *Canadian Journal of Native Education*, 23(1), 40-56.

Justice, D.H. (2004). Seeing (and reading) red: Indian outlaws in the ivory tower. In D.A. Mehesuah and A.C. Wilson (Eds.), *Indigenizing the academy: Transforming scholarship and empowering communities* (pp. 100-23). University of Nebraska Press.

Kelley, R. (2016). Black study, black struggle. *Boston Review*, 41(2), 1-15.

Kenny, C., & Fraser, T.N. (2012). *Living Indigenous leadership: Native narratives on building strong communities.* University of British Columbia Press.

Khalifa, M., Khalil, D., Marsh, T., & Halloran, C. (2019). Toward an Indigenous, decolonizing school leadership: A literature review. *Educational Administration Quarterly*, 55(4), 571-614. https://doi.org/10.1177/0013161X18809348

Kidwell, C.S. (2009). American Indian studies: Intellectual navel gazing or academic discipline? *American Indian Quarterly*, 33(1), 1-17.

Kim, J. (2017). *Understanding narrative inquiry: The crafting and analysis of stories as research.* Sage Publications.

REFERENCES

King, T. (2008). *The art of Indigenous knowledge: A million porcupines crying in the dark.* In J.G. Knowles & A. Cole (Eds.), *Handbook of the arts in qualitative research: Perspectives, methodologies, examples and issues* (pp. 13–25). Sage Publications.

Kirkness, V.J., & Barnhardt, R. (1991). First Nations and higher education: The four R's—respect, relevance, reciprocity, responsibility. *Journal of American Indian Education*, 30(3), 1–15.

Klikauer, T. (2013). *Managerialism: A critique of an ideology.* Palgrave Macmillan.

Knowles, J.G., & Cole, A. (Eds.) (2008). *Handbook of the arts in qualitative research: Perspectives, methodologies, examples and issues.* Sage Publications.

Kovach, M. (2009). *Indigenous methodologies: Characteristics, conversations, and contexts* (1st ed.). University of Toronto Press.

Kovach, M. (2010). Conversational method in Indigenous research. *First Peoples Child & Family Review*, 5(1), 40–8.

Krumm, B., & Johnson, W. (2011). Tribal colleges: Cultural support for women campus presidencies. In *Women of color in higher education: Turbulent past, promising future* (pp. 263–89). https://doi.org/10.1108/S1479-3644(2011)0000009017

Kuokkanen, R. (2007). *Reshaping the university: Responsibility, Indigenous epistemes, and the logic of the gift.* University of British Columbia Press.

Kuokkanen, R. (2008). What is hospitality in the academy? Epistemic ignorance and the (im)possible gift. *Review of Education, Pedagogy, and Cultural Studies*, 30(1), 60–82. https://doi.org/10.1080/10714410701821297

Lajimodiere, D.K. (2011). Ogimah Ikwe: Native women and their path to leadership. *Wicazo Sa Review*, 26(2), 57–82.

Lajimodiere, D.K. (2013). American Indian females and stereotypes: Warriors, leaders, healers, feminists; not drudges, princesses, prostitutes. *Multicultural Perspectives*, 15(2), 104–9. https://doi.org/10.1080/15210960.2013.781391

Lakehead settles discrimination suit with former law dean. (2021, February 8). *TBNews Watch*. https://www.tbnewswatch.com/local-news/lakehead-settles-discrimination-suit-with-former-law-dean-3361814

Lavallee, L. (2019, January 3). Recommendations and thoughts regarding Indigenous governance and matters in academia and UofM [Blog post]. *Indigenous Resurgence and Insurgence.* https://lynnflavallee.home.blog/2019/01/03/recommendations-and-thoughts-regarding-indigenious-governance-and-matters-in-academia-and-uofm

Lavallee, L. (2020). Resisting exotic puppetry: Experiences of Indigenous women leadership in the academy. In T. Moeke-Pickering, S. Cote-Meek, & A. Pegoraro (Eds.), *Critical reflections and politics on advancing women in the academy* (pp. 21–32). IGI Global Publishing.

Lawrence, B., & Anderson, K. (Eds.). (2003). *Strong women stories: Native vision and community survival.* Sumach Press.

Lincoln, Y.S. (2018). A dangerous accountability: Neoliberalism's veer toward accountancy in higher education. In M. Spooner & J. McNinch (Eds.), *Dissident knowledge in higher education* (pp. 3–20). University of Regina Press.

Lindberg, D., Asch, J., & Sellar, Y. (2016). *Gender inside Indigenous law toolkit.* Indigenous Law Research Unit, Faculty of Law, University of Victoria. https://www.cerp.gouv.qc.ca/fileadmin/Fichiers_clients/Documents_deposes_a_la_Commission/P-288.pdf

Little Bear plays role in bringing bison back to Banff. (2017, March 6). *UNews,* University of Lethbridge. https://www.ulethbridge.ca/unews/article/little-bear-plays-role-bringing-bison-back-banff

Louie, D. (2019). Aligning universities' recruitment of Indigenous academics with the tools used to evaluate scholarly performance and grant tenure and promotion. *Canadian Journal of Education, 42*(3), 791–815.

Macdonald, M. (2016, April 6). Indigenizing the academy: What some universities are doing to weave Indigenous peoples, cultures and knowledge into the fabric of their campuses. *University Affairs.* https://www.universityaffairs.ca/features/feature-article/indigenizing-the-academy/

Machado de Oliveira, V. (2021). *Hospicing modernity: Facing humanity's wrongs and the implications for social activism.* North Atlantic Books.

Maddison, S. (2019). *The colonial fantasy: Why white Australia can't solve black problems.* Allen & Unwin.

Malatest, R.A., & Associates Ltd. (2004). *Aboriginal peoples and post-secondary education: What educators have learned.* Canada Millennium Scholarship Foundation. https://www.kpu.ca/sites/default/files/downloads/Aboriginal_Peoples_PostSecondary6358.pdf

REFERENCES

Malott, C. (2010). *Policy and research in education: A critical pedagogy for educational leadership*. Peter Lang.

Maracle, L. (1996). *I am woman: A Native perspective on sociology and feminism*. Press Gang Publishers.

Maracle, S., Bergier, A., Anderson, K., & Neepin, R. (2020). "The work of a leader is to carry the bones of the people": Exploring female-led articulation of Indigenous knowledge in an urban setting. *AlterNative: An International Journal of Indigenous Peoples*, 16(4), 281–9. https://doi.org/10.1177/1177180120954441

Marker, M. (2015). Geographies of Indigenous leaders: Landscapes and mindscapes in the Pacific Northwest. *Harvard Educational Review*, 85(2), 229–53. https://doi.org/10.17763/0017-8055.85.2.229

Marker, M. (2017). Indigenous knowledges, universities, and alluvial zones of paradigm change. *Discourse: Studies in the Cultural Politics of Education*, 40(4), 500–13. https://doi.org/10.1080/01596306.2017.1393398

Marshall, A., Bartlett, C., & Iwama, M. (2006, November 6). *Two-eyed seeing: Seeing with the strengths of bringing together Indigenous & Western scientific knowledges*. Science Café, Acadia University. www.integrativescience.ca/uploads/articles/2006November-Bartlett-Iwama-Integrative-Science-Two-Eyed-Seeing-Aboriginal-knowledge-science-cafe-Acadia.pdf

Mawhiney, A.-M. (2018, March 21). Reaching true reconciliation at our universities. *Policy Options*. http://policyoptions.irpp.org/magazines/march-2018/reaching-true-reconciliation-at-our-universities/

Maxwell, J., Lowe, K., & Salter, P. (2018). The re-creation and resolution of the "problem" of Indigenous education in the Aboriginal and Torres Strait Islander cross-curriculum priority. *Australian Educational Researcher*, 45(2), 161–77. https://doi.org/10.1007/s13384-017-0254-7

Mayes, C. (2007). *No higher priority: Aboriginal post-secondary education in Canada*. Report of the Standing Committee on Aboriginal Affairs and Northern Development, February 2007, 39th Parliament, 1st Session. https://www.ourcommons.ca/Content/Committee/391/AANO/Reports/RP2683969/aanorp02/aanorp02-e.pdf

McCue, H.A. (2011, June 6; updated April 17, 2023). Indigenous peoples in Canada. *Canadian Encyclopedia*. https://www.thecanadianencyclopedia.ca/en/article/aboriginal-people-education

McLeod, N. (2007). *Cree narrative memory: From treaties to contemporary times*. Purich Publishing.
Mendelson, M. (2006, July). *Aboriginal peoples and postsecondary education in Canada*. Caledon Institute of Social Policy. http://www.caledoninst.org/Publications/PDF/595ENG
Merriam, S.B. (1998). *Qualitative research and case study applications in education*. Jossey-Bass.
Merriam, S.B. (2009). *Qualitative research: A guide to design and implementation*. John Wiley & Sons.
Mignolo, W. (2000). Local histories/global designs : coloniality, subaltern knowledges, and border thinking. Princeton University Press.
Mignolo, W. (2007). Delinking: The Rhetoric of Modernity, the Logic of Coloniality and the Grammar of De-Coloniality. *Cultural Studies* 21(2-3), 449–514. https://doi.org/10.1080/09502380601162647
Mignolo, W. (2010). Epistemic disobedience, independent thought and decolonial freedom. *Theory, Culture & Society*, 26(7–8), 159–81. https://doi.org/10.1177/0263276409349275
Mihesuah, D.A. (2003). *Indigenous American women: Decolonization, empowerment, activism*. University of Nebraska Press.
Mihesuah, D.A., & Wilson, A.C. (2004). *Indigenizing the academy: Transforming scholarship and empowering communities*. University of Nebraska Press.
Minthorn, R., & Chavez, A.F. (2015). *Indigenous leadership in higher education*. Routledge.
Moeke-Pickering, T. (2020). Women in academia matter: Indigenous worldviews and women movements activism. In T. Moeke-Pickering, S. Cote-Meek, and A. Pegoraro (Eds.), *Critical reflections and politics on advancing women in the academy* (pp. 1–20). IGI Global Publishing.
Mohamed, T., & Beagan, B. (2019). "Strange faces" in the academy: Experiences of racialized and Indigenous faculty in Canadian universities. *Race, Ethnicity and Education*, 22(3), 338–54. https://doi.org/10.1080/13613324.2018.1511532
Monture, P. (2009). "Doing academia differently": Confronting "whiteness" in the university. In F. Henry & C. Tator (Eds.), *Racism in the Canadian university: Demanding social justice, inclusion and equity* (pp. 76–105). University of Toronto Press.

REFERENCES

Moran, R. (2016). Truth, sharing and hearing: The Canadian Truth and Reconciliation Commission and the challenge of civic engagement. In S. Maddison, T. Clark, & R. de Costa (Eds.), *The limits of settler colonial reconciliation: Non-Indigenous peoples and the responsibility to engage* (pp. 177–91). Springer.

Moreton-Robinson, A. (2000). *Talkin' up to the white woman: Indigenous women and feminism*. University of Queensland Press.

Moreton-Robinson, A. (2013). Towards an Australian Indigenous women's standpoint theory: A methodological tool. *Australian Feminist Studies*, 28(78), 331–47. https://doi.org/10.1080/08164649.2013.876664

Moreton-Robinson, A. (2015). *The white possessive: Property, power and Indigenous sovereignty*. University of Minnesota Press.

MTCU (Ministry of Training, Colleges and Universities). (2015). *Achieving results through partnership: First progress report on the implementation of the Ontario Aboriginal Postsecondary Education and Training Policy Framework*. Ministry of Training, Colleges and Universities. https://www.tcu.gov.on.ca/pepg/publications/APSET2015Progress Report.pdf

Muller, H.J. (1998). American Indian women managers: Living in two worlds. *Journal of Management Inquiry*, 7(1) 4–28.

Nakata, M. (2002). Indigenous knowledge and the cultural interface. In A. Hickling-Hudson, J. Matthews, & A. Woods (Eds.), *Disrupting preconceptions: Postcolonialism and education* (pp. 19–38). Post Pressed.

Nakata, M., Nakata, V., Keech, S., & Bolt, R. (2012). Decolonial goals and pedagogies for Indigenous studies. *Decolonization: Indigeneity, Education & Society*, 1(1), 120–40.

Nash, M.A. (2019). Entangled pasts: Land-grant colleges and American Indian dispossession. *History of Education Quarterly*, 59(4), 437–67. https://doi.org/10.1017/heq.2019.31

NASSA (National Aboriginal Student Services Association). (n.d.) *Home* [Facebook page]. Facebook. Retrieved June 17, 2023, from https://www.facebook.com/p/National-Aboriginal-Student-Services-Association-NASSA-100054207850288/

Newhouse, D. (2016). The meaning of Indigenization in our universities. *CAUT Bulletin*, 63(6). https://bulletin-archives.caut.ca/bulletin/articles/2016/06/the-meaning-of-indigenization-in-our-universities

Ngunjiri, F.W., & Gardiner, R.A. (2017). Future strategies for developing women as leaders. In S.R. Madsen (Ed.), *Handbook of research on gender and leadership* (pp. 423–37). Edward Elgar Publishing.

Niemann, Y., Gutiérrez y Muhs, G., & Gonzalez, C. (2020). *Presumed incompetent II: Race, class, power, and resistance of women in academia.* Utah State University Press.

NIMMIWG (National Inquiry into Missing and Murdered Indigenous Women and Girls). (2019). *Reclaiming power and place: Executive summary of the final report.* National Inquiry into Missing and Murdered Indigenous Women and Girls. https://www.mmiwg-ffada.ca/wp-content/uploads/2019/06/Executive_Summary.pdf

National Indigenous University Senior Leaders' Association (NIUSLA). (2022). Indigenous Voices on Indigenous Identity: What Was Heard Report. First Nations University of Canada. https://www.fnuniv.ca/wp-content/uploads/Indigenous-Voices-on-Indigenous-Identity_National-Indigenous-Identity-Forum_Report_March-22_June-22-final.pdf

Ortega, M. (2016). *In-between: Latina feminist phenomenology, multiplicity, and the self.* State University of New York Press.

Ottmann, J. (2005). *First Nations leadership development within a Saskatchewan context* [Unpublished doctoral dissertation]. University of Saskatchewan.

Ottmann, J. (2009). Leadership for social justice: A Canadian perspective. *Journal of Research on Leadership Education*, 4(1), 1–9. https://doi.org/10.1177/194277510900400105

Ottmann, J. (2013). Indigenizing the academy: Confronting "contentious ground." In K. Anderson & M. Hanrahan, (Eds.), *Morning watch* [special 40th anniversary edition]. http://www.mun.ca/educ/faculty/mwatch/vol40/winter2013/indigenizingAcademy.pdf

Ottmann, J. (2017). Canada's Indigenous peoples' access to post-secondary education: The spirit of the "new buffalo." In J. Frawley, S. Larkin, & J.A. Smith (Eds.), *Indigenous pathways, transitions and participation in higher education: From policy to practice* (pp. 95–117). Springer.

Ottmann, J., White, N., & Fasoli, L. (2010). Notes from the editors: An institutional leadership paradigm: Transferring practices, structures and conditions in Indigenous higher education. *Ngoonjook: Batchelor Journal of Aboriginal Education: Special Edition* 34, 5–12.

REFERENCES

Palmater, P. (2014, November 26). Stephen Harper and the myth of the crooked Indian. *Rabble.ca*. https://rabble.ca/blogs/bloggers/pamela-palmater/2014/11/stephen-harper-and-myth-crooked-indian

Paquette, J., & Fallon, G. (2010). *First Nations education policy in Canada: Progress or gridlock?* University of Toronto Press.

Paquette, J., & Fallon, G. (2014). In quest of Indigeneity, quality and credibility in Aboriginal post-secondary education in Canada: Problematic, contexts, and potential ways forward. *Canadian Journal of Educational Administration and Policy (CJEAP)*, 165(10), 1–35.

Patton, M. (2015). *Qualitative research & evaluation methods: Integrating theory and practice* (4th ed.). Sage Publications.

Peace, T. (2016, January 25). Indigenous Peoples: A starting place for the history of higher education in Canada. *Active History*. https://activehistory.ca/2016/01/rethinking-higher-education-colonialism-and-indigenous-peoples/

Pete, S. (2016). 100 ways: Indigenizing & decolonizing academic programs. *Aboriginal Policy Studies*, 6(1), 81–9. https://journals.library.ualberta.ca/aps/index.php/aps/article/view/27455

Pete, S. (2018). Meschachakanis, a coyote narrative: Decolonising higher education. In G.K. Bhambra, D. Gebrial, & K. Nişancıoğlu (Eds.), *Decolonising the university* (pp. 173–89). Pluto Press.

Pete-Willett, S. (2001). *Kiskinawacihcikana: Aboriginal women faculty experiences in the academy* [Unpublished doctoral dissertation]. University of Arizona.

Phillips, L., & Bunda, T. (2018). Sharing through storying. In *Research through, with and as storying* (1st ed.). Routledge. https://doi.org/10.4324/9781315109190-5

Pidgeon, M. (2001). *Looking forward…A national perspective on Aboriginal student services in Canadian universities* [Unpublished master's thesis]. Memorial University of Newfoundland. https://research.library.mun.ca/9258/1/Pidgeon_Michelle.pdf

Pidgeon, M. (2008). *It takes more than good intentions: Institutional accountability and responsibility to Indigenous higher education* [Unpublished doctoral dissertation]. University of British Columbia. https://open.library.ubc.ca/cIRcle/collections/ubctheses/24/items/1.0066636

Pidgeon, M. (2012). Transforming and Indigenous interconnections: Indigeneity, leadership and higher education. In C. Kenny & T.N. Fraser (Eds.), *Living Indigenous leadership: Native narratives on building strong communities* (pp. 137–49). University of British Columbia Press.

Pidgeon, M. (2014). Relationships matter: Supporting Aboriginal graduate students in British Columbia. *Canadian Journal of Higher Education*, 44(1), 1–21.

Pidgeon, M. (2016). More than a checklist: Meaningful inclusion in higher education. *Social Inclusion*, 4(1), 77–91.

Prokopchuk, M. (2018, April 24). Indigenous leaders call for "immediate change" in the wake of Ontario law school dean's resignation. *CBC News.* https://www.cbc.ca/news/canada/thunder-bay/aboriginal-law-dean-no-support-1.4632680

Puwar, N. (2004). *Space invaders: Race, gender and bodies out of place.* Berg.

Raffoul, J., Ward, J., Calvez, S., Kartolo, A., Haque, A., Holmes, T., Attas, R., Kechego, J., Kustra, E., & Mooney, J. (2022). Institutional structures and individual stories: Experiences from the front lines of Indigenous educational development in higher education. *AlterNative : an International Journal of Indigenous Peoples*, 18(1), 163–172. https://doi.org/10.1177/11771801211062617

Ray, L. (2016). "Beading becomes a part of your life": Transforming the academy through the use of beading as a method of inquiry. *International Review of Qualitative Research*, 9(3), 363–78.

RCAP (Royal Commission on Aboriginal Peoples). (1996). *Report of the Royal Commission on Aboriginal Peoples.* Canada Communication Group.

Reder, D., & Morra, L. (2010). *Troubling Tricksters: Revisioning critical conversations.* Wilfrid Laurier University Press.

Restoule, J., Mashford-Pringle, A., Chacaby, M., Smillie, C., Brunette, C., & Russel, G., (2013). Supporting successful transitions to postsecondary education for Indigenous students: Lessons from an institutional ethnography in Ontario, Canada. *International Indigenous Policy Journal*, 4(4). https://doi.org/10.18584/iipj.2013.4.4.4

Riessman, C. (1993). *Narrative analysis.* Sage Publications.

Riessman, C. (2002). Analysis of personal narratives. In J.F. Gubrium, J.A. Holstein, A.B. Marvasti, & K.D. McKinney (Eds.), *The Sage handbook of interview research: The complexity of the craft* (pp. 367–80). Sage Publications.

REFERENCES

Rigney, L. (2017). A design and evaluation framework for Indigenisation of Australian universities. In J. Frawley, S. Larkin, & J.A. Smith (Eds.), *Indigenous pathways, transitions and participation in higher education: From policy to practice* (pp. 45–68). Springer.

Robinson, I., White, D., & Robinson, D. (2019). Indigenous women in educational leadership: Identifying supportive contexts in Mi'kmaw Kina'matnewey. *International Journal of Leadership in Education*, 23(6), 1–21. https://doi.org/10.1080/13603124.2018.1562103

Said, E. (1978). *Orientalism*. Routledge & Kegan Paul.

Saldana, J. (2011). *Ethnotheatre: Research from page to stage*. Taylor & Francis.

Samier, E., & Milley, P. (Eds.) (2021). *Educational administration and leadership identity formation: International theories, problems and challenges*. Routledge.

Santamaría, L.J. (2013). *Indigenous women's leadership: "We are the ones we have been waiting for."* Retrieved August 18, 2023, from https://lorrijsantamaria.academia.edu/research#papers

Santamaría, L.J., & Jean-Marie, G. (2014). Cross-cultural dimensions of applied, critical, and transformational leadership: Women principals advancing social justice and educational equity. *Cambridge Journal of Education*, 44(3), 333–60. https://doi.org/10.1080/0305764X.2014.904276

Santamaría, L.J., & Santamaría, A.P. (2012). *Applied critical leadership in education: Choosing change*. Routledge.

Sasakamoose, J., & Pete, S. (2015). Toward Indigenizing university policy: Kakwe-iyiniwasta kihci-kiskinwahamâtowikamikohk wiyasiwâcikanisa. *Education Matters*, 3(1). https://journalhosting.ucalgary.ca/index.php/em/article/view/62922/46909

School of Policy Studies [Queen's University] & National Centre for Truth and Reconciliation [University of Manitoba]. (2016, November). *Sharing the land, sharing a future: Report on a national forum on reconciliation—marking the 20th anniversary of the Royal Commission on Aboriginal Peoples*. https://www.queensu.ca/sps/events/conferences-and-workshops/rcap-20th-anniversary-conference

Sensoy, O., Diangelo, R. (2017). "We are all for diversity but...": How faculty hiring committees reproduce whiteness and practical suggestions for how they can change. *Harvard Educational Review*, 87(4), 77–91.

Shanahan, T.G. (2019). Good governance and Canadian universities: Fiduciary duties of university governing boards and their implications for shared collegial governance. *International Journal of Education Policy and Leadership*, 14(8). https://doi.org/10.22230/ijepl.2019v14n8a861

Shore, C., Wright, S., & Pero, D. (2011). *Policy worlds: Anthropology and the analysis of contemporary power*. Berghahn Books.

Shotton, H., Lowe, S., & Waterman, S. (2013). *Beyond the asterisk: Understanding Native students in higher education*. Stylus.

Simpson, A. (2014). *Mohawk interruptus: Political life across the borders of settler states*. Duke University Press.

Simpson, A. (2016). The state is a man: Theresa Spence, Loretta Saunders and the gender of settler sovereignty. *Theory & Event*, 19(4). https://www.muse.jhu.edu/article/633280

Simpson, L.B. (2013a). *The gift is in the making: Anishinaabeg stories, retold by Leanne Simpson*. Highwater Press.

Simpson, L.B. (2013b). Theorizing resurgence from within Nishnaabeg thought. In J. Doerfler, N.J. Sinclair, & H.K. Stark (Eds.), *Centring Anishinaabeg studies: Understanding the world through stories* (pp. 279–93). University of Manitoba Press.

Simpson, L.B. (2014). Land as pedagogy: Nishnaabeg intelligence and rebellious transformation. *Decolonization: Indigeneity, Education & Society*, 3(3), 1–25.

Simpson, L.B. (2016). Indigenous resurgence and co-resistance. *Critical Ethnic Studies*, 2(2), 19–34. https://www.jstor.org/stable/10.5749/jcritethnstud.2.2.0019

Simpson, L.B. (2017). *As we have always done: Indigenous freedom through radical resistance*. University of Minnesota Press.

Sinclair, N.J. (2010). Trickster reflections: Part I. In D. Reder & L. Morra (Eds.), *Troubling Tricksters: Revisioning critical conversations* (pp. 21–58). Wilfrid Laurier University Press.

Sium, A., Desai, C., & Ritskes, E. (2012). Toward the "tangible unknown": Decolonization and the Indigenous future. *Decolonization: Indigeneity, Education & Society*, 1(1), i–xii.

Six years' summary of the proceedings of the New England Company for the civilization and conversion of Indians, blacks, and pagans in the Dominion of Canada and the West Indies, 1873–1878. (1879). Gilbert and Rivington.

REFERENCES

Smith, D.W. (2017) Reconciliation and the academy: Experience at a small institution in northern Manitoba. *Canadian Journal of Educational Administration and Policy*, 183, 61–81.

Smith, G.H. (2003, October). *Indigenous struggle for the transformation of education and schooling* [Keynote address]. Alaskan Federation of Natives Convention, Anchorage, Alaska. http://www.ankn.uaf.edu/curriculum/Articles/GrahamSmith/

Smith, G.H. (2005, May). *Notes on the problematic of "Indigenous theorizing": A critical reflection* [Paper presentation]. University of Washington Native Graduate seminar series, Seattle, Washington.

Smith, J. (2018, June). *Strengthening evaluation in Indigenous higher education contexts in Australia: Equity Fellowship report*. National Centre for Student Equity in Higher Education. https://www.ncsehe.edu.au/wp-content/uploads/2018/06/JamesSmith_FellowshipReport_final_accessible.pdf

Smith, L.T. (1999). *Decolonizing methodologies: Research and Indigenous peoples* (2nd ed.). Zed Books.

Smith, L.T. (2005). On tricky ground: Researching the Native in the age of uncertainty. In N.K. Denzin & Y.S. Lincoln (Eds.), *The Sage handbook of qualitative research* (pp. 85–107). Sage Publications.

Smith, L.T. (2018). The art of the impossible: Defining and measuring Indigenous research? In M. Spooner & J. McNinch (Eds.), *Dissident knowledge in higher education* (pp. 21–40). University of Regina Press.

Smith, L.T., & Smith, G.H. (2018). Doing Indigenous work: Decolonizing and transforming the academy. In E.A. McKinley & L.T. Smith (Eds.), *Handbook of Indigenous education* (pp. 1075–1101). Springer. https://www.springer.com/gp/book/9789811038983

Snyder, E., Napoleon, V., & Borrows, J. (2015). Gender and violence: Drawing on Indigenous legal resources. *University of British Columbia Law Review*, 48(2), 624–54.

Spivak, G. (1998). Can the subaltern speak? In P. Williams and L. Chrisman (Eds.), *Colonial discourse and post-colonial theory* (pp. 66–111). Columbia University Press.

Spooner, M., & McNinch, J. (Eds.). (2018). *Dissident knowledge in higher education*. University of Regina Press.

St. Denis, V. (2007). Feminism is for everybody: Aboriginal women, feminism and diversity. In J. Green (Ed.), *Making space for Indigenous feminism* (pp. 33–51). Fernwood Publishing.

Staples, K., Klein, R., Southwick, T., Kinnear, L., Geddes, C., & Gingell, J. (2021). Indigenization and university governance: Reflections from the transition to Yukon University. *Tertiary Education and Management*, 27, 209–25.

Statistics Canada. (2022, November 30). *Highest level of education by major field of study and Indigenous identity: Canada, provinces and territories, census metropolitan areas and census agglomerations with parts*. https://doi.org/10.25318/9810041401-eng

Stein, S. (2019). Navigating different theories of change for higher education in volatile times. *Educational Studies: A Journal of the American Educational Studies Association*, 55(6), 667–88. https://doi.org/10.1080/00131946.2019.1666717

Stein, S. (2020). A colonial history of the higher education present: Rethinking land-grant institutions through processes of accumulation and relations of conquest. *Critical Studies in Education*, 61(2), 212–28. https://doi.org/10.1080/17508487.2017.1409646

Stein, S. (2023). *Unsettling the university: Confronting the colonial foundations of US higher education*. Hopkins Press.

Steinhauer, P. (2001). Situating myself in research. *Canadian Journal of Native Education*, 25(2), 183–7.

Steinman, E.W. (2015). Decolonization not inclusion: Indigenous resistance to American settler colonialism. *Sociology of Race and Ethnicity*, 2(2), 219–36. https://doi.org/10.1177/2332649215615889

Sterritt, A. (2019, May 8). Rush for Indigenous hires at universities opens door to failure, impostors, say academics. *CBC News*. https://www.cbc.ca/news/canada/british-columbia/rush-for-indigenous-hires-opens-door-to-failure-impostors-1.5128015

Stiegman, M.L., & Castleden, H. (2015). Leashes and lies: Navigating the colonial tensions of institutional ethics of research involving Indigenous peoples in Canada. *International Indigenous Policy Journal*, 6(3), 1–27.

Stinson, J. (2018). *How does intersectionality relate to Indigenous and Western linking frameworks*. Canadian Research Institute for the Advancement of Women (CRIAW). https://www.criaw-icref.ca/wp-content/uploads/2021/04/Fact-Sheet-3-en-final_Accessible.pdf

Stonechild, B. (2006). *The new buffalo: The struggle for Aboriginal postsecondary education in Canada*. University of Manitoba Press.

Strauss, A., & Corbin, J. (1990). *Basics of qualitative research*. Sage Publications.

REFERENCES

Styres, S., & Kempf, A. (Eds.). (2022). *Troubling truth and reconciliation in Canadian education: Critical perspectives* (1st ed.). University of Alberta Press.

Sue, D.W., Capodilupo, C.M., Torino, G.C., Bucceri, J.M., Holder, A.M.B., Nadal, K.L., & Esquilin, M. (2007). Racial microaggressions in everyday life: Implications for clinical practice. *American Psychologist*, 62(4), 271–86. https://doi.org/10.1037/0003-066X.62.4.271

Sunseri, L. (2010). *Being again of one mind: Oneida women and the struggle for decolonization.* University of British Columbia Press.

Suzack, C. (2015). Indigenous feminisms in Canada. *Nordic Journal of Feminist and Gender Research*, 23(4), 261–74.

Suzack, C., Huhndorf, S.M., Perrault, J., & Barman, J. (2010). *Indigenous women and feminism: Politics, activism, culture.* University of British Columbia Press.

Tanchuk, N., Kruse, M., McDonough, K. (2018). Indigenous course requirements: A liberal-democratic justification. *Philosophical Inquiry in Education*, 25(2), 135–53.

Taner, S. (1999). The evolution of Native studies in Canada: Descending from the ivory tower. *Canadian Journal of Native Studies*, 19(2), 289–319.

Taylor, S., Rizvi, F.A., & Henry, M. (1997). *Educational policy and the politics of change.* Routledge.

Thomas, R. (2018). *Protecting the sacred cycle: Indigenous women and leadership.* J. Charlton Publishing.

Thorp, S. (2014). *Aboriginal postsecondary education in Canada and the Standing Committee on Aboriginal Affairs and Northern Development: A critical policy analysis* [Unpublished master's thesis]. University of Western Ontario.

Tippeconnic, J. (2006). Identity-based and reputational leadership: An American Indian approach to leadership. *Journal of Research on Leadership Education*, 1(1), 1–3.

Tippeconnic-Fox, M.J., Luna-Firebaugh, E.M., & Williams, C. (2015). American Indian female leadership. *Wicazo Sa Review*, 30(1), 82–99.

TRC (Truth and Reconciliation Commission of Canada). (2015). *Honouring the truth, reconciling for the future: Summary of the final report of the truth and reconciliation commission of Canada.* Truth and Reconciliation Commission of Canada. https://ehprnh2mwo3.exactdn

com/wp-content/uploads/2021/01/Executive_Summary_English_Web.pdf

Tuck, E. (2018). Biting the university that feeds us. In M. Spooner & J. McNinch (Eds.), *Dissident knowledge in higher education* (pp. 149–68). University of Regina Press.

Tuck E., & Yang, K.W. (2012). Decolonization is not a metaphor. *Decolonization: Indigeneity, Education & Society*, 1(1), 1–40.

Tuck, E., & Yang, K.W. (2014a). R-words: Refusing research. In D. Paris and M.T. Winn (Eds.), *Humanizing research: Decolonizing qualitative inquiry with youth and communities* (pp. 223–47). Sage Publications.

Tuck, E., & Yang, K.W. (2014b). Unbecoming claims: Pedagogies of refusal in qualitative research. *Qualitative Inquiry*, 20(6), 811–18.

Turner, D., & Simpson, A. (2008, May). *Indigenous leadership in a flat world* [Research paper]. National Centre for First Nations Governance.

Umpleby, S.L. (2007). *Crossing the bridge: The educational leadership of First Nations women* [Unpublished doctoral dissertation]. University of Victoria.

United Nations (2007, October 2). *United Nations Declaration on the Rights of Indigenous Peoples: Resolution adopted by the General Assembly*. A/RES/61/295. https://www.refworld.org/docid/471355a82.html

Universities Canada. (n.d.). *Universities Canada principles on Indigenous education*. Retrieved June 14, 2023, from https://www.univcan.ca/wp-content/uploads/2015/11/principles-on-indigenous-education-universities-canada-june-2015.pdf

Universities Canada. (2018). *Advancing reconciliation through higher education: 2017 survey findings*. https://www.univcan.ca/wp-content/uploads/2018/10/Indigenous_survey_findings_2017_factsheet_25Apr_.pdf

University of Lethbridge UNews. (2017, March 6). *Little Bear plays role in bringing bison back to Banff*. https://www.ulethbridge.ca/unews/article/little-bear-plays-role-bringing-bison-back-banff

UofM Indigenous leader resigns, says administration frustrated anti-racism efforts. (2018, December 6). CBC *News*. https://www.cbc.ca/news/canada/manitoba/university-manitoba-indigenous-provost-resignation-1.4936274

Van Maanen, J. (2011). *Tales of the field: On writing ethnography* (2nd ed.). University of Chicago Press.

REFERENCES

Vizenor, G. (1999). *Manifest manners: Narratives on postindian survivance*. University of Nebraska Press.

Voyageur, C. (2008). *Firekeepers of the twenty-first century: First Nations women Chiefs*. McGill-Queen's University Press.

Voyageur, C. (2011). Female First Nations Chiefs and the colonial legacy in Canada. *American Indian Culture and Research Journal*, 35(3), 59–78. https://doi.org/10.17953/aicr.35.3.tx7pth12527049p7

Voyageur, C., Calliou, B., & Brearley, L. (2015). *Restorying Indigenous leadership: Wise practices in community development* (2nd ed.). Banff Centre Press.

Walters, D., White, J., & Maxim, P. (2004). Does postsecondary education benefit Aboriginal Canadians? An examination of earnings and employment outcomes for recent Aboriginal graduates. *Canadian Public Policy*, 30(3), 283–301. https://doi.org/10.2307/3552303

Warner, L.S. (1995). A study of American Indian females in higher education administration. *Initiatives*, 56(4), 11–17.

Warner, L.S., & Grint, K. (2006). American Indian ways of leading and knowing. *Leadership*, 21(2), 225–44.

Waterman, S. (2007). A complex path to Haudenosaunee degree completion. *Journal of American Indian Education*, 46(1), 20–40.

Waterman, S., Lowe, S., & Shotton, H. (2019). *Beyond access: Indigenizing programs for Native American students*. Stylus.

Weaver, J. (2007). More heat than light: The current state of Native American studies. *American Indian Quarterly*, 31(2), 233–55.

White, N. (2010). Indigenous Australian women's leadership: Stayin' strong against the post-colonial tide. *International Journal of Leadership in Education*, 13(1), 7–25. https://doi.org/10.1080/13603120903242907

Wilkes, R., Duong, A., Kesler, L., & Ramos, H. (2017). Canadian university acknowledgement of Indigenous lands, treaties and people. *Canadian Review of Sociology*, 54(1), 89–120.

Wilson, A. (2016, December 6). *Coming in to Indigenous sovereignty: Relationality and resurgence* [Video]. YouTube. https://www.youtube.com/watch?v=XkQo_yr4A_w&t=2352s

Wilson, S. (2001). What is an Indigenous research methodology? *Canadian Journal of Native Education*, 25(2), 175–9.

Wilson, S. (2008). *Research is ceremony: Indigenous research methods*. Fernwood Publishing.

Wolfe, P. (2006). Settler colonialism and the elimination of the Native. *Journal of Genocide Research*, 9(4), 387–409.

Womack, C. (2008). A single decade: Book-length Native literary criticism between 1986–1997. In C. Womack, D. Heath Justice, and C. Teuton (Eds.), *Reasoning together: The Native critics collective* (pp. 3–104). University of Oklahoma Press.

Yahia, L.M.S. (2016). *Voices of racialized and Indigenous leaders in Canadian universities* [Unpublished master's thesis]. University of British Columbia.

NOTES

1   I emphasized quality over quantity in selecting participants, focusing on depth to achieve richness of data (Kim, 2016). To ensure the trustworthiness of the study, I aimed to obtain a broad representation of participants who worked in universities across Canada, including the Western provinces as well as central areas of Ontario and Quebec, until I reached saturation (Merriam, 2009). Saturation on the number of participants was attained after reaching eleven participants because there are few Indigenous women working in senior leadership roles in universities in Canada at the time of my study (2017–19).

As part of my recruitment process, I employed purposeful sampling, which involved isolating and selecting known, information-rich cases (Patton, 1990). Drawing on my own professional networks as well as publicly available information from university websites, I reached out to potential participants via email, introducing myself and inviting them to participate in the study. As an Indigenous administrator myself, I had pre-existing relationships with some of my participants (e.g., we had sat on committees together). Kovach (2010) indicates that pre-existing relationships with Indigenous participants in Indigenous research is common, and supports relational approaches to research.

Nearly all participants in the present study reported being among an influx of Indigenous leaders hired into leadership positions in Canadian universities since the TRC's final report was released in 2015. The types of leadership positions that participants were recruited to were nearly equally distributed across three main categories: (1) academic administrators (e.g., associate vice-provost), (2) staff administrators (e.g., executive director), and in some cases (3) interim administrators (e.g., special advisers). Although academic administrative structures and institutional titles varied across universities and may therefore be difficult to compare, all the participants carried specific and focused roles and responsibilities in the area of Indigenous education. While the majority held permanent administrative appointments that saw them oversee broad academic support across the university (e.g., vice-provost), some participants held temporary roles (e.g., special advisers), and still others held roles focused solely on Indigenous student affairs and Indigenous community engagement. Professionally speaking, these women were not all situated at the same levels and within the same reporting structures in the university.

2. Ethical tensions emerged in this study when I chose to keep participants' names anonymous. At the proposal stage, my supervisor and I had many conversations around this decision since the topic and questions of my study centred on Indigenous women administrators' resistance in their leadership practices. Considering the small and highly visible population with which I was working, it became clear that I needed to protect individual participants' anonymity should controversial themes emerge that could jeopardize their employment. As I moved on in the research process, I began to recognize the challenges my research design placed on me in terms of protecting my own confidentiality as a named participant in my study. Fortunately, I maintained the power to select and de-select certain accounts that might identify me. Nonetheless, I chose to maintain all the participants' anonymity by not naming them in the study, and by fictionalizing narratives for the dramatic scenes. Unsurprisingly, one participant rightfully asked me why I chose to keep participants unnamed, since there is a growing practice of naming sources of Indigenous knowledge in Indigenous research (Canadian Institutes of Health Research et al., 2014, 2018). Considering the sensitivity of my research topic and the potential harm naming could bring to certain individuals, I explained my decision. Thankfully, the participant understood my rationale and agreed to continue with the project. As the research continued on, the dangerous grounds upon which Indigenous women administrators operate became clearer, and I understood more fully the implications of my work and the responsibility I have as the primary researcher to protect individual participants and weigh the risks against the benefits of naming sources of knowledge.

Unsurprisingly, I also experienced ethical tensions in writing the fictionalized dramatic texts. As well, there is a certain level of ethical care needed when taking up Indigenous oral stories and using Weesakechahk as a narrator. Engaging my participants in collaborative re-storying processes, and consulting a cultural adviser and language expert around the ethics of Indigenous oral storytelling and the usage of Cree words, was tremendously helpful to me. Their contributions supported me in clarifying my role and responsibilities and in identifying areas of the writing that I needed to go back to for reflection and/or clarity.

3. Considering the small number of Indigenous women administrators in Canada, and my focus on centring their experiences and stories of resistance, I have been careful to maintain participants' anonymity. To protect participants,

NOTES

including myself, I have used pseudonyms when sharing direct quotes, and created fictionalized characters and universities for the dramatic texts. In both cases, I have taken great care when writing about individuals' experiences to remove identifying information.

In documenting information for this study, I used four open-ended confidential strategies: a codebook, a field log, personal journals, and document data (Merriam, 1998). All research documents (transcribed interviews) were shared with participants via Western University's secure content-management platform. All documents were kept in a personal, locked filing cabinet and within password-protected computer systems. I strived to protect participants' anonymity by giving each a pseudonym in all transcribed interviews, field logs, and field journals. I used a codebook to document these changes. I stored transcripts, field logs, and field journals separately from the codebook to reduce the possibility of anyone finding the materials and reconstructing identities.

4   I completed a first interview with each of the eleven participants in the fall of 2017. I sent all participants interview questions via email prior to meeting with them. Questions were open-ended. I approached the interviews as semi-structured, in-depth conversations (Kovach, 2010). The interviews sometimes went beyond the pre-planned questions. The first in-person interviews allowed me to build and strengthen relationships with participants. These interviews, conducted at a location of each participant's choice, focused on the participant's journey to becoming an administrator and their experiences in the Indigenizing movement in the academy. When participants wished to be interviewed at their office on a university campus, I obtained a confidential ethical approval from their home institution to conduct research at that location. The second interviews focused on participants' use of policy in their leadership work, and on their experiences related to resistance. I completed the second set of interviews with only ten participants. Nine of the ten participants agreed to have this second interview by telephone, and with the tenth participant in person. After several failed attempts at scheduling, I was unable to complete a second interview with the eleventh participant.

During the interviews, I occasionally shared my own stories because Indigenous conversational approaches recognize that sharing supports validity and authority (Kovach, 2010). I encouraged participants to talk about their experiences and feelings through holistic, felt-sense sharing. I also asked each participant questions related to metaphoric knowledge. Chilisa (2012) outlines the value of metaphors in Indigenous research: "In traditional oral societies, some forms of language are proverbs and metaphorical sayings, which uphold and legitimize the value system of a society" (p. 131). In my research, I asked, "If you were to use a metaphor to describe your leadership work in universities, what would it be?" The purpose of this question was to invite participants to share holistic, embodied, and Indigenous knowledge. I audio-recorded all interviews, and hired a professional, confidential transcription company to transcribe all interviews verbatim, including silences and laughter when possible.

5 Congruent with Indigenous storying as a methodological approach (Kovach, 2009; Phillips & Bunda, 2018), I drew on autobiographical elements of my own stories as an Indigenous woman and university administrator. Over the time during which the present study was conducted, I experienced many professional changes, including being appointed special adviser to the provost (Indigenous initiatives) and later acting vice-provost/associate vice-president (Indigenous initiatives). These experiences were relevant to my research, and important for me to reflect on, so, as the twelfth participant in the present study, I answered many of the research questions in my own personal research journals; I then used these as field texts during my analysis of data. Beyond my research journals, I used a field book to document and reflect on some of my interviews and on methodological considerations. Journals provided me with opportunities to reflect on my own interconnected stories, and to think about methodological tensions that I was working through as part of the research process.

6 Recognizing that Indigenous stories come in various shapes and forms, I invited all participants via email, prior to the first interview, to think about and share an object that told a story about their leadership experiences in universities. This request was based on the notion that the collection of field texts in narrative research happens through various forms, including personal journals, letters, interviews, photographs, and even artifacts. My motivation for inviting object data into the interview process was to open up unique modes of storytelling related to Indigenous storying approaches. While most participants did not bring specific objects to their interviews, some talked at length about their chosen objects. One participant, for example, shared her experiences of purchasing a painting from a student; another shared the story of receiving her spirit name and how she carried that gift (while not an object, it was nevertheless a story about a gift) with her in her leadership.

7 Because the present study focused on policies and Indigenous women's experiences in Canadian universities, I also gathered policy documents, news articles, and participants' professional biographies (which were available online) throughout the research process. I did not analyze these documents as primary sources; rather, I used them as secondary sources of data in the triangulation process. In many cases, these secondary sources validated participants' stories, such as their accounts of how certain universities made

NOTES

declarations and portrayed women leaders in troubling, tokenistic ways in their communications.

8 To begin my open coding process, I read my interview transcripts aloud—over five hundred pages of text. This first round of "open coding" (Strauss & Corbin, 1990) required reading each transcript up to three times and making notes in the margins about ideas and topics that surfaced during my reading. At this stage, I noted policy tensions and personal/cultural dissonances, and reflected on consistencies I heard across participants, including shared words, values, and patterns of thinking, feeling, and (re)actions.

After doing several cycles of open coding, I applied a second, phased "axial coding process" (Strauss & Corbin, 1990), which involved organizing texts, including direct quotes and references, under larger categories in a separate document. At this stage, I uncovered some early themes across participants' experiences, themes related to policy messiness, including structural limitations; categories for experience included dangerous work and Indigenous resistance.

After another couple of rounds of axial coding, I applied a third and final phase of coding that involved returning to the academic literature and to key theoretical concepts to discover whether any specific concepts could explain the larger themes that characterized participants' experience. At this point, concepts such as Indigenous refusal and the triple bind came to the fore.

9 Triangulation: The triangulation of various sources of data is commonly used to increase credibility in Indigenous research (Chilisa, 2012). To strengthen the credibility of the present study, I sent all transcribed documents and fictional performance writing to participants to ensure accuracy. Such a step is part of a collaborative re-storying approach (Bishop, 1999).

Member checking: I attempted to conduct member checking for both interviews with all participants. I sent interview transcripts to participants via a secure, password-protected university platform and gave participants up to two weeks to respond. Several participants, because of their busy schedules, reported challenges accessing the site and reviewing the transcripts. As a result, only two participants confirmed member checking of the first set of interviews, and no participants confirmed member checking of the second set of interviews. As secondary forms of member checking in the analysis process, I shared by email a set of four preliminary research findings with participants. Seven of the eleven participants responded quickly with enthusiasm.

Verisimilitude: I checked for verisimilitude by sharing fictionalized performance writing with participants and asking specific questions (listed earlier in this chapter). In narrative approaches, verisimilitude is often used to determine trustworthiness of data (Van Manen, 1988). The quality of verisimilitude involves others having a vicarious experience when reading stories and being able to relate to similar situations themselves.

    Critical self-reflexivity: I engaged in ongoing critical self-reflexivity in my field journals by documenting my feelings, thoughts, concerns, ideas, and problems throughout the research process. According to Chilisa (2012), researchers in Indigenous paradigms must critically reflect on themselves "as knower, redeemer, colonizer and transformative healer" (p. 174), and she argues that critical self-reflexivity plays a key role in the research process. In personal journals, I reflected in various ways: I documented many answers to the research questions and reflected on my inner responses to research-related experiences. Ongoing critical reflexivity was an imperative exercise for me as it helped me separate my own experiences from the experiences of participants, and critically interrogate my own biases, perceptions, and interests. Because I came to this study embodying many complex roles and identities, critical self-reflexivity also allowed me to create distance from my role and challenge myself to think more deeply about participants' stories and my ethical responsibilities for capturing different voices in responsible and respectful ways.

    Admittedly, I initially planned to work with participants in more comprehensive and collaborative ways throughout the analysis process, but I quickly realized that this was an unrealistic expectation—they were all extremely busy professionals living in various places across the country. Furthermore, the COVID-19 pandemic, which began after the study had commenced, further complicated and constrained my initial plans to share interim dramatic texts in person.

INDEX

Absolon, Kathleen E., 105; *Kaandossiwin: How We Come to Know*, 39
academic administrative spaces: Euro-Westernized nature of, 246; male domination of, 159, 160, 168; trickiness of, 93; unsafe nature of, 237
academic freedom, 24, 156, 157
academic governance system, 192, 212
affective economy, 55
Ahenakew, Freda, 34
Ahmed, Sara: *On Being Included*, 98; concept of feminist killjoy, 97; on experience of non-white bodies, 70; on institutional speech acts, 186; literature review of the word "use," 193–94; *Living a Feminist Life*, 95–96; on politics of language, 220, 222; *What's the Use?*, 193; *Willful Subjects*, 98
Almeida, Deirdre, 54, 55
American Indian Movement, 35
Andreotti, V.D.O., 45
Anishnawbe people, xiii, xv–xvi, 240
anti-Indigenous racism, 156, 157–58
Anzaldúa, Gloria, 90

Archibald, Jo-ann (Q'um Q'um Xiiem), 113, 114; *Indigenous Storywork*, 91
Asch, M., 63, 65
assumed assimilation process, 26, 27–31, 34–35
âtalôhkâna nesta tipâcimôwina: Cree Legends and Narratives from the West Coast of James Bay (Ellis), xiv
atalohkan stories, 91
Attawapiskat First Nation, 70–71

Ball, Stephen, 93
Battiste, Marie, 19
beading, 101–2, 104
Bédard, Renée Mazinegiizhigo-kwe, 54
Bell, Derrick, 226
Benham, Maenette K.P., 106, 110, 113, 114
Bill C-31, 127
Bird, Louis (Omushkego Cree storyteller), xiii, xiv
Bishop, Russell, 112
Bishop Horton Residential School, 7
Blackmore, Jill, 68
Black people, 89
Board of Governors, 23
borderland theory, 89–90
Boushie, Colten, 188–89

Brunette, Daisy (née Rueben), 1–2, 7–8
Brunette, Wilfred, 2
Brunette-Debassige, Candace: background of, xiii, xiv, 1–2, 8; Indigenous scholarship of, xiv, 3, 4, 8; leadership of, 6; passion for storytelling, 6–7; sense of Indigeneity, 1, 2–3
buffalo: Indigenous attitude to, 249–50; as metaphor of higher education, 240, 250; restoration of, 250; settler colonists and, 249
"buffalo jump cliff" metaphor, 245
Bunda, T., 110, 178, 180
bush: symbolism of, 104–5

Cajete, Gregory, 83
Calls to Action Accountability: A 2020 Status Update on Reconciliation (report), 62
Campbell, Lori, 61
campus power dynamics, 24
Canadian Association of College and University Student Services (CACUSS), 37
Canadian Association of University Teachers (CAUT), 41
Canadian Journal of Native Education, 40
Canadian Journal of Native Studies, 40
Canadian universities: administrative settings, 10, 166; appropriation of Indigenous names, 33; as business ventures, 24; criticism of, 186–87; curriculum, 200–202, 234; diversity policies, 95; epistemic ignorance in, 196–97; equity projects in, 208; establishment of, 18; European fundamentalism in, 18–19, 157; flags permitted on campuses of, 195; food services policy, 197; free speech policies, 157; gender-related challenges, 167–68; governance of, 23–24, 32; historical roots of, 31–32; land acquisition, 16; legal status of, 23; limits of existing policies, 192; neoliberal paradigm and, 24, 25; organizational change, 47; participation of Indigenous people in, 5, 12, 26, 63–64, 204, 205; policy discussions, 47; public apologies of, 33; regulation of, 24; relationship with church and state, 18, 33; settler colonialism in, 241; smoke-free policy in, 196; types of, 23; workforce data collection, 51
Capper, Colleen, 76
Castellano, Marlene Brant, 34
Chavez, A.F., 78
Chilisa, B., 297n4, 300n9
civilized society, 138–39
Clandinin, D. Jean, 110
Clark, Natalie, 88, 89
Clute Township, 2
Cochrane, Ontario, 1, 2
collaborative storying, 112–13
Collège de Québec, 18
Collins, Patricia Hill, 69
colonial Indian policies, 206
colonialism: education system and, xiii, 4, 5, 9
coloniality, 17
colonial tokenism, 217, 229
"conditional inclusion," 55
Connelly, F. Michael, 110
co-optation. *See* settler co-optation
Corntassel, Jeff, 63, 64, 80

INDEX

corporate approaches to education, 24
Coulthard, Glen, 186
Coyote (Trickster figure), xiii, 91, 92
Cree floral research design, 13, 105
Cree people: beading practices of, 101–2, 103; cosmology of, xiii–xiv, 92; epistemological understanding, 8; identity, 3, 104; storytelling tradition, xiii, xiv–xv, 7, 91
Crenshaw, Kimberlé, 88
critical reflexivity, 300n9

Daigle, Michelle, 62
Debassige, Brent, 98
Dechinta Bush University, 63–64
decolonial-Indigenization, 210
decolonial-Indigenization process, 184, 210–11, 218, 246
decolonization: approaches to, 45–46; conception of, 217–18, 222; criticism of, 58, 59, 220; debates on, 241; definition of, 57–58, 59; as distraction, 220; in education, 58–59, 158; as global movement, 57; Indigenization and, 59, 218; as messy process, 246; metaphorization of, 58, 95; threat for free speech and, 156–57
Dickason, Olive, 34
different worlds: notion of, 79
diversity work, 194, 222
doctrine of discovery, 22, 41
double bind (a.k.a. dual consciousness) concept, 69, 89
Dubois, W.E.B., 89

EagleWoman, Angelique, 244–45
educational leadership: as academic field, 67, 71–72; colonial tropes, 68, 69; decolonial approaches to, 77; Indigeneity and, 78; interpretivist approach to, 77; scholarship on, 72, 79; scientific and instrumentalist approaches to, 76; structural functionalist approach to, 76–77
educational system: colonialism and, xiii, 4, 5, 94; storytelling traditions and, xiii
Elders, xiv, 114, 197, 238
embodied sovereignty, 71
emotional labour, 55, 56
enfranchisement laws, 33–34
Enlightenment, 17
episteme, 20
epistemic ignorance, 174, 196–97
epistemic violence, 21
epistemological unconsciousness, 76–77
equity policies, 208
Eurocentric fundamentalism, 16–17, 19
Euro-Western academy: colonial ideologies, 25, 34; hegemonic nature of, 5; hierarchies of knowledge, 19; history of, 12; Indigenous communities and, 43, 90, 248; male-dominated, 154–55; racism in, 54, 87
exclusion and forced assimilation process, 26, 27–31, 31–34

feasting on university campuses, 197, 247
Federal Contractors Program, 51
Federation for the Humanities and Social Sciences, 41
feminist killjoy, 96, 97
First Nations people: access to education, 33, 34–35, 36, 240

Fitzgerald, Tanya, 69, 72
Flight: Journeying for Change
(play): characters of, 117–18;
enactment of speech act, 190–91;
Indigenous refusal theme in,
223; intersectional Indigeneity
in, 150; playwright notes, 118;
scenes, 13, 118–48; "Weesakechahk
Flies South with the Waveys" as
inspiration for, 8, 118
floral research design, 101–3
Fort Albany First Nation, xv, 1, 2
free speech policy, 156, 157

Gaudry, A., 44, 45, 53, 63
geese: symbolism of, 104–5
gifting tradition, 104
Gift Is in the Making, The (Simpson),
114
"glass cliff" phenomenon, 244–45
global capitalism, 23, 25
global universalizing movement, 17
Glooscap (Trickster figure), xiii, 91
good leadership, 67
Government of Canada: apology to
residential school survivors, 39
Gradual Civilization Act (1857), 33
Grande, Sandy, 25
Grosfoguel, Ramon, 15, 18
Gunter, H., 76

Hart, Michael, 252
hetero-patriarchy, 25, 85–86, 87
higher education: aims and priorities
of, 242; in Canada, pillars of, *16*;
colonialism and, 9; global human
rights in, 47; individualism in, 243;
marketization of, 24; new buffalo
metaphor, 248–49; perceived

benefits of, 241–42; relationship
building in, 82; systems of
thinking, 241–42; Western *vs.*
Indigenous approaches to, 240
Highway, Tomson, 91, 92
Hohepa, Margie, 83, 84
hospitality: Western notion of, 190
Huron College, 33

Idle No More movement, 70
in-between spaces, 242
Indian Act (1876), 2, 22, 33, 68, 141, 151
"Indian problem": in Canadian
universities, 194, 223, 224;
colonial tropes around, 73, 249;
Indigenous women leaders and,
216, 224, 236; roots of, 21–22
Indian Residential Schools Settlement
Agreement (IRSSA), 5, 39
Indigeneity, 78, 206
Indigenization: academic freedom
and, 157; challenges of, 6;
decolonization and, 47, 218;
definition of, 47–48, 59–60,
61, 217; discourses of, 65; as
distraction, 220; free speech and,
156–57; Indigenous leadership and,
25, 59, 239, 245–46; institutional,
48; scholarship on, 25, 48; as
shared labour, 168; symbolic
approaches to, 229–30; theories
of, 60–61
Indigenization-inclusion process, 27–31,
35, 39, 44, 48, 49
Indigenization-reconciliation process,
26, 28–31, 44, 45, 48, 56
Indigenizing policies in Canadian
universities: academic structures
and, 212; approaches to, 185;

INDEX

as assimilation project, 188; budget planning processes and, 187; categories of, 44–45; challenges of, 6, 9, 42, 185, 192; communication practices, 190; contradictory nature of, 192–93; co-optative tendencies, 218, 224–25; as corporate public affairs opportunity, 188; curriculum development and, 200–202; debates over, 9–10; documents on, 41–42, 187–88; evolution of, 194; goal of, 224; Indigenous agency, 247–48; institutional strategies of, 227; limitations of, 186–88, 193, 198, 220; measurement of success of, 10, 202–3; as politics of recognition, 188; research on, 12, 44–47; settler colonialism and, 65, 94, 195–96

Indigenizing policy enactments: challenges of, 6, 185, 190–91; contested nature of, 184, 191–92, 195, 198; criticism of, 189, 206; effects of, 191–92, 246–47; governing limits of, 210–13; institutional speech acts and, 184; limitations of, 13, 213; as messy practice, 195–96, 209–10, 213, 243; non-Indigenous policy actors and, 207, 208, 209; patriarchal white sovereignty and, 184; power dynamics in, 207; research on, 11–12; settler co-optation in, 206–8; trickiness of, 13, 184, 185, 240, 242–43, 248

Indigenous administrators, 52, 210, 211. *See also* Indigenous women administrators

Indigenous adoptees, 206
Indigenous advisory councils, 211
Indigenous axiology, 105
Indigenous communities: collectivism of, 243; colonial relationship and, 88–89; co-optation and, 224–25; corporations and, 229; divisions within, 65, 169; social life in, 172; universities and, 211, 212, 234–35; women status in, 169, 172–73
Indigenous consciousness, 8
Indigenous educational institutes: advocacy for, 241
Indigenous educational leadership: "code-switching," 79; different worlds of, 79–80, 145; essentialist and authenticity discourses in, 83; expectations from, 54–55; Indigeneity in relation to, 84; Indigenous communities and, 79–80, 82; recurring themes in, 77–78; research on, 75–76, 254–55; strengths and barriers, 79
Indigenous educational sovereignty, 5–6, 47, 80–81, 99, 187, 210–11
Indigenous Education Council, 232
Indigenous education in Ontario, 3–4
Indigenous epistemes, 20, 174
Indigenous epistemology, 75, 105, 106
Indigenous ethics, 113, 296n2
Indigenous faculty: authentication of, 204, 205; faculty association policies and, 192; gender gap, 50; recruitment of, 199–200; responsibilities of, 198–99; statistics of, 50; under-representation of, 51, 198–99
Indigenous feminism, 85, 86, 87, 105
Indigenous identity, 203–4

Indigenous initiatives offices, 247, 298n5
Indigenous intellectual sovereignty, 43
Indigenous knowledge:
    marginalization of, 19, 25–26;
    in neo-liberal paradigm, 25;
    promotion of, 193; sources of, 158;
    vs. Western knowledge, 19–20
Indigenous leadership: barriers to, 69, 223–24; as collective political process, 238; colonial tropes of, 68; in community context, 174–75, 182; studies of, 83, 84; support network for, 251–52; training programs, 250–51; Weesakechahk story and principles of, 258
Indigenous nation-building, 47, 63
Indigenous ontology, 105, 106
Indigenous paradigm, 60
Indigenous people: collective values, 172; colonial positioning of, 194; conditional inclusion of, 55; contribution to the academy, 195; disenfranchisement of, 206; enfranchisement of, 33–34, 141; Euro-Western approaches to, 84; impact of higher education on, 9, 19, 25, 26, 49, 54–56, 241–42; indoctrination into Christianity, 4; limits of representation of, 52–53; naming of, 142; negative perception of, 138; new technologies and, 84; Othering of, 20–21, 194; racialization of, 21; relationships with the land and non-humans, 250; sense of "fatigue," 56; stereotypes, 160; Western research on, 20
Indigenous post-secondary education, 36, 38–39; timeline of, 26, 27–31

Indigenous refusal: as acts of resistance, 236–37; boundaries of, 225; conception of, 96–97, 98–99, 215–16; critical self-reflexivity around, 237–38; as decolonial intervention, 220, 236–38; emergence of, 13; enactment of, 11, 99, 235; examples of discreet, 231, 232; generative nature of, 248; investigation of, 216; to non-Indigenous scholars research, 225; opting out of administration as, 233–35, 244–45; to performative approaches, 229–30; to settler co-optation, 225–26; strategical, 231–33; types of, 217, 237; *vs*. willfulness, 98
Indigenous research: analysis process, 300n10; anonymity, 296n2, 296n3; axiology of, 116; braiding approach to, 60; coding process, 110–11, 299n8; critical self-reflexivity, 300n9; documentation of, 297n3, 298n5; ethics of, 113, 115, 296n2, 297n4; gathering methods of, *102*, 103, 109; interviews, 297n4, 298n6; marginalization of, 228; meaning making, *102*, 103, 109; metaphors in, 297–98n4; methodology, 105–6, 113–15, 297n4, 298n5; Mushkego Cree epistemology of, 103–5, *104*; overview of, 9–12; participants of, 107–9, 295n1, 296n2, 296n3, 300n10; primary sources, 109; qualitative paradigm, *102*, 103, 105–6; responsibility in, 106, 116; secondary sources, 298n7; self-location in, 3, *102*, 103, 115; storying approach, 13, *102*, 103, 106–7, 109–10, 111–13, 115; thematic approach,

109, 110–11; theoretical framework of, *102*, 103, 105; triangulation of sources of data, 299n9; Trickster tropes in, 105; verisimilitude checks, 112, 299n9

Indigenous resurgence: academic discourses of, 63–64, 217; advocacy of, 64; colonial structural challenges of, 64; decolonization and, 63; scholarship on, 65

Indigenous scholarship, xiv, 4, 6–7, 8, 35, 39, 40

Indigenous staff members, 51, 53, 200, 203, 212, 245, 247, 254

Indigenous storytelling: as acts of survivance, 7; beading practices and, 101; colonialism and, xiii, xiv; educational system and, 9; ethics of, 113–14; identity sharing, 78; Indigenous knowledge, 91, 125; intellectual sovereignty of, 93; non-Indigenous approach to, 92; relational ontology of, 8; as research methodology, 13, *102*, 103, 106–7, 109–10, 111–13, 114, 115, 257–58, 298n5; seven principles of, 113–14

Indigenous students: activism of, 138, 139–40; admissions policy, 171; ancestry-verification process, 203; assimilation of, 38; classroom experience, 50, 227–28; feeling of ambivalence, 171–72; gender gap among, 50; interruption of studies, 49; Othering of, 37; reconciliation movement and, 227; self-identification, 204–5; services units, 37, 38, 42, 151; statistics of, 49; stigmatizing of, 37–38; university policies toward, 194–95, 202–3

Indigenous studies programs, 40, 42–43

Indigenous theatre, xiv

Indigenous ways of knowing, 193, 196, 197–98, 228, 251, 257

Indigenous women: disenfranchisement of, 69; educational leaders, 69, 70, 72–73, 74, 75, 77; exclusion from communities, 126–27, 132, 151; gender discrimination, 169; lack of agency, 74; learning experience of, 128, 129–30; Othering of, 21; resilience of, 74–75; social and legal status of, 68–69; stereotypes of, 70, 71; in white spaces, 127–28

Indigenous women administrators: academic credentials of, 153; administrative pressure on, 12, 151–52, 155, 203, 225–26; adoptions of university policies, 162–63, 194; anti-Indigenous bias and, 160–61, 163; attempts to neutralize political language of, 221–22, 223; "buffalo jump cliff" workplace of, 245; challenges of, 10, 12, 64–65, 154, 156, 164, 181–82, 211–12, 246; code-switching, 155, 225; colonial power relations and, 8, 11, 12, 150, 195–96, 215–16; communication style of, 156; credibility of, 162, 166, 211; critical self-reflexivity of, 237; criticism of, 178; cultural dissonance, 11; decision-making capacity, 169–70, 212–13; decolonization and, 12, 213;

Indigenous women administrators *(continued)*: educational background of, 109; embodied experiences of, 150, 159, 184; emotional labour of, 170–71, 180, 182; epistemic ignorance of, 174, 196–97; faculty members and, 153–54, 208, 209; feeling of being trapped, 150, 179; free speech policy movements and, 156, 157; gender relations and, 151, 154–55, 167; growing number of, 4, 10; hierarchal authority system and, 175, 238; hyper-visibility of, 159, 165, 166; Indigeneity of, 108, 155, 161, 162, 163; Indigenizing work of, 42, 207–8, 216, 226, 236–38; Indigenous communities and, 152, 168–69, 176, 178, 182, 216, 238; Indigenous refusal of, 97, 225, 228–30, 237; institutional neglect of, 167–68; institutional norms and, 174, 175, 241, 242; interest convergence dilemma of, 226, 227; intermediary role of, 177, 179–80, 221; marginalization of, 11, 159, 163, 164, 165–66, 195, 212; micromanagement of, 163–64; operation on the borderland, 174–75, 177, 178–79, 216–17; Othering of, 98, 159–60, 173, 182; as part of Indian problem, 224, 236; perceptions of, 96, 173, 245; performative approaches and, 229–30; positionalities of, 176; racial battle fatigue of, 180; recruitment of, 152–53, 161–62, 184, 187; relations with media, 229, 230; resignations of, 187, 233–35, 244–45; resistance to colonial tokenism, 229; rewards, 168; scholarship on, 11, 107–8; scrutiny of, 164, 165; sense of ambivalence, 180–81; stereotypes of, 97–98, 161, 163; stories of, 149–50; strategical refusal of, 231–33; subordinate status of, 209–10; triple bind experiences, 166, 180, 181; types of positions, 153, 154, 295n1; under-representation of, 155, 213; university activities and, 228–29; white faculty members and, 158; workload of, 166–67, 213

Indigenous work in the academy, 5, 9–10, 61, 65–66, 81, 98, 226, 245–46

Ininew Friendship Centre, 2, 3

Innes, Robert Alexander, 91

institutional speech acts, 186–87, 188, 189

interest convergence, 226

interpretivism, 77

intersectional Indigeneity, 89, 150

intersectionality, 88

Jewell, Eva, 61

Johnson, W., 75

K-12 education, 36

Kaandossiwin: How We Come to Know (Absolon), 39

Kelley, Robin D.G., 98, 99

Kempf, Arlo: *Troubling Truth and Reconciliation in Canadian Education*, 63

Kirkness, Verna J., 34

knowledge, 19–20, 163. *See also* Indigenous knowledge

INDEX

Kovach, Margaret, 102, 106, 226
Krumm, B., 75
Kuokkanen, Rauna, 20, 173, 190

Lajimodiere, Denise, 73, 75
Lakehead University, 245
language of diversity: critique of, 220
Lavallee, Lynn, 59, 73, 96, 203, 236
leadership: in academic discourses, 75; colonial tropes of, 68; critical decolonial questions, 252–54; Indigenous *vs.* Western conceptions of, 82–83, 174–75, 182, 221; normative approaches to, 251; nuances of, 238; positionality of, 252; praxicality of, 253–54; structuralist and culturalist considerations, 253; transformability of, 254
Liberal government's White Paper of 1969, 35
liberal recognition politics, 186
Li'l Beavers program, 3
Little Bear, Leroy, 249, 250
Littlechild, Wilton, 4
Living a Feminist Life (Ahmed), 95–96
"the look": notion of, 159
Lorenz, D., 44, 45, 53, 63

McIvor, Sharon, 2
meaning-making process, 109, 110
memoranda of understanding (MOUs), 189–90
Mignolo, Walter, 17, 19, 90
Mihesuah, Devon Abbott, 47
modernity, 17, 45
Mohawk College, 33
moon: symbolism of, 104–5
Moose Factory, Ontario, 2

Moran, Ry, 61, 62
Moreton-Robinson, Aileen, 63, 86, 87, 184
Mosby, Ian, 62
Mushkego Cree epistemology, 103–5, *104*
Mushkegowuk Cree Nation, xiii, 1
Mushkegowuk stories, 91, 125–26
Musqueam lands: sale of, 33

Nanabozoo (Trickster figure), xiii, 240
narrative-inquiry methodology, 110
National Aboriginal Student Services Association (NASSA), 37
National Centre for Truth and Reconciliation, 61
National Forum on Reconciliation, 39
National Indian Brotherhood, 35, 36
National Indigenous University Senior Leaders' Association, 251–52
National Inquiry into Missing and Murdered Indigenous Women and Girls (NIMMIWG), 71
Ng, Roxana, 150
Nipissing University, 33
Nishnaabeg First Nation, 114
Nishnaabeg thought, 81
Nokomis (Anishnawbe storyteller), 240

Omushkegowuk stories, xiii
On Being Included (Ahmed), 98
ontology of hierarchy, 67, 175
Ortega, Mariana, 90
Othering: concept of, 20
"Other-within": notion of, 69
Ottmann, Jacqueline, 92, 251

patriarchal white sovereignty, 86–87, 184–85, 186, 197–98, 213
Peace, Thomas, 32

Peawanuk First Nation, xv
Peetabeck (Water in the Bay), 1
performativity, 95
phenomenology of whiteness, 70
Phillips, L., 110
Pichette, Doreen (née Brunette), 1–2
Pichette, Julien, 1
Pidgeon, Michelle, 47
Plains Indigenous societies, 249, 250
"Please Be Careful when You're Getting Smart" (Simpson), 240
policy enactment, 93–94
policy work: as mode of surviving in the academy, 194
politics of declarations, 95
politics of distraction, 99, 209, 225, 251
politics of language, 223
possessive logics of patriarchal white sovereignty, 184–85, 186, 213
post-secondary education, 36, 37
Post-Secondary Student Support Program (PSSSP) funding, 36
Principles on Indigenous Education, 41
Puwar, Nirmal, 159

racial battle fatigue, 180
racialized women, 96
Raven (Trickster figure), xiii, 91
recognition politics, 94
recolonialization, 84
reconciliation: barriers to, 62; in Canadian institutions, 61, 62, 183–84; conceptual ambiguity of, 62, 222; cost of, 132; decolonization and, 219; as distraction, 219–20; Indigenous initiatives, 131, 219; meaning of, 217–18; memoranda of understanding on, 189–90; promises of, 143, 144–45;
scholarship on, 65; settler colonial co-optation and, 206–7, 218; shortcomings of, 62–63, 218–19, 227
red intersectionality, 88, 89
refusal: concept of, 98–99. *See also* Indigenous refusal
relational ontology, 175
residential schools: administration of, 32; architect of, 32; colonialism and, 4, 5; establishment of, 4, 22; universities and, 18
residential school survivors, 4, 5
resurgence, 218
Rigney, Lester-Irabinna, 47
Royal Canadian Mounted Police (RCMP), 4
Royal Commission on Aboriginal Peoples (RCAP), 5, 38, 39, 41
Royal Society of Canada, 32

Sanlo, R., 78
Scott, Duncan Campbell, 32
self-location, 3
settler colonial academy, 22–26, 216
settler colonialism, 16, 18, 22, 25, 94, 210, 245
settler co-optation, 206–8, 218, 224–25, 251
settler laws, 22
shared governance, 192
Simpson, Audra, 70
Simpson, Leanne Betasamosake, 71, 81, 92; *The Gift Is in the Making*, 114; "Please Be Careful when You're Getting Smart," 240
Sinclair, Murray, 4
Sixties Scoop, 206
Smith, Graham Hingangaroa, 81, 99, 226, 248, 252

INDEX

Smith, Linda Tuhiwai, 20, 81, 93, 185, 252
Smith, Malinda S., 52
smudging policies, 193, 196, 197, 247
Social Sciences and Humanities Research Council of Canada, 41
Spence, Theresa, 70–71
"spot the Trickster" movement, 93
Stein, Sharon, 55; *Unsettling the University*, 33
Stonechild, Blair: *The New Buffalo*, 239–40
strategic concessions, 226
strategic essentialism, 60
structural functionalism, 76
students: as consumers, 24
Styres, Sandra: *Troubling Truth and Reconciliation in Canadian Education*, 63
Sutherland, Xavier, xv, xvi, 114, 118

Taylor, S., 93
terra nullius doctrine, 22
The New Buffalo: The Struggle for Aboriginal Post-Secondary Education in Canada (Stonechild), 239–40
Toronto Metropolitan University, 64
trickiness, 93, 185
Trickster figures, xiii, 91–92, 93
Trickster theory, 13, 92
Tri-Council Policy Statement 2, 225
triple bind concept, 69, 150, 154, 159
Troubling Truth and Reconciliation in Canadian Education: Critical Perspectives (Styres and Kempf), 63
Truth and Reconciliation Commission (TRC): 94 Calls to Action, 4, 5, 41, 62, 211; establishment of, 4–5, 39, 61; final report of, 3, 41, 44; impact of, 9, 142–43, 191
Tuck, Eve, 25, 58, 62, 96, 97, 218, 240
Turtle Island: colonization of, 101; storytelling traditions, xiii; Westernized university system in, 18

United Kingdom universities: equity policies in, 95, 98, 194
United Nations Declaration on the Rights of Indigenous Peoples (UNDRIP), 39, 41
Université Laval, 18
University Act, 210
University of British Columbia, 33
University of Manitoba, 33, 187
University of New Brunswick, 18
University of Toronto, 18
Unsettling the University (Stein), 33

Valaskakis, Gail, 34
verisimilitude checks, 112–13

waterways: symbolism of, 104–5
Weesakechahk (mythological figure): enactment of speech act, 190–91; Eurocentric view on, 91–92; Inninewowin meaning of, 92; as pedagogical figure, 8–9, 92, 112, 114, 117–18, 215
"Weesakechahk Flies South with the Waveys" (story), xv, xvi–xviii, 8, 118
Weesakechahk stories: cultural protocols for, 114; ethical and linguistic practices, xv, 113–14; Indigenous research and, xiv, 93, 105; mistranslations of, 92;

Weesakechahk stories *(continued)*: in relation to leadership, 258; style of, 126; as theoretical framework, 91, 257–58; value of, xiii, 243–44; versions of, xv–xvi
Westernized university, 15, 16, 17–18, 19, 22
Western University (London, ON), 32–33
What's the Use? (Ahmed), 193
white liberal feminism, 87

willfulness, 98
Willful Subjects (Ahmed), 98
Wilson, Alex, 91, 92
Wilson, Angela Cavender, 47
Wilson, Marie, 4
Wilson, Shawn, 60, 105–6
workplace feminization, 244

Yahia, L.M.S., 54
Yang, K.W., 58, 62, 96, 97, 218, 240
Yellowhead Institute, 63, 64

Candace Brunette-Debassige is Mushkego Cree of Petabeck First Nation in Treaty 9 with mixed Cree and French lineage, born and raised in Cochrane, Ontario. She is an Assistant Professor in the Faculty of Education at Western University where she has also served in various leadership roles. Candace was the recipient of the 2021 George L. Geis dissertation of the year award by the Canadian Society for Studies in Higher Education and the 2019 Peace Award for Truth and Reconciliation from Atlôhsa Family Services.